ECONOMICS OF
THE KENNEDY YEARS

Seymour E. Harris

ECONOMICS OF THE KENNEDY YEARS

and

a Look Ahead

HARPER & ROW, PUBLISHERS

New York, Evanston, and London

FOR THE LATE PRESIDENT,

JOHN F. KENNEDY

CONTENTS

vii

Preface

This is an analysis of the economics of the New Frontier.

President Kennedy was in office two years, ten months, and two days. But this book covers policies of the years 1961–1964, for it is already clear that most of the policies of 1964 derived from John F. Kennedy. Moreover, the years 1965–1970 will also feel the impact of New Frontier economics.

However, President Johnson will obviously want to put his own stamp on economic policy. Already, his budget and spending pattern have differed from that of the Kennedy administration. Naturally, changing conditions require adjustments in policies. Also, President Johnson seems to be somewhat more conservative than his predecessor. His great appeal to businessmen, already evident in 1964, supports this conclusion. Yet President Johnson cannot abandon the Kennedy policies if he is to win the northern industrial area in the 1964 election.

This book is the result of much reading, innumerable meetings, and discussions of relevant issues with top officials. Reading material is indispensable, but in a period when the telephone is increasingly the medium for policy formulation, there is no substitute for oral communication.

I first met John F. Kennedy informally when he was a young member of Congress from my district in Cambridge. My wife, along with many other Cambridge constituents, wrote to him asking for a new post office. The one built in 1919 in the midst of Harvard Square traffic was inadequate. He replied in a friendly fashion and ultimately the Harvard section had a new post office.

One Saturday late in August 1952, John Kennedy telephoned me at my summer home on Cape Cod. He said he was in Hyannis Port, about twenty miles away, and asked if he could call on me, which he did. The congressman was running for the Senate. I was then working on some economic problems of New England with the New England governors and others, and had published a book on New England economics. We discussed such problems as the migration of industry from New England, unfair competition of the South, relations of Massachusetts with the federal government, and related problems. In these years, 1952–1958, the New England governors had periodic meetings with New England congressmen. They generally invited me to be present as an expert, and Senator Kennedy usually attended. As I shall explain later, the problems confronting Senator Kennedy in Massachusetts were not without influence on his economic policies in 1961–1963.

This first visit at the Cape was a prelude to other visits from the Senator, including calls at my Harvard office and home, and my visits to the Senator's office in Washington. I also helped in a limited way during the 1960 campaign.

In 1960–1961 I served as a member of the President's Task Force on the Economy, as a member of the Public Advisory Board of the Area Redevelopment Administration from 1961 to 1964, and as an occasional adviser of the Council of Economic Advisers and of the Attorney General.

Early in his administration President Kennedy had suggested to Secretary Dillon that I might help to improve the contribution to economics in the Treasury. Hence I served as senior consultant to the Secretary beginning in early 1961. In this capacity, I mobilized more than twenty-five top economists, mostly academic, for periodic discussions of economic problems with the Secretary of the Treasury and other Treasury officials, with the President's Council of Economic Advisers, with the director of the Budget Bureau, and officials of the Labor Department, the State Department, and the Department of Commerce. In these meetings the consultants considered economic prospects, the dollar problem, debt management, monetary policy, and other aspects of economic policy. We gave high officials, including the President, the results of these meetings.

For more than ten years I had the privilege of being an occasional adviser of the President. I observed the evolution of his economics and ideology. In the years before 1960 I frequently counseled him on economic issues. When he was in office, I saw the President less frequently, but we still discussed economic problems and exchanged letters several times a year. In October 1963 he decided to recommend me for appointment to the Federal Reserve Board for a vacancy as of January 1964.

I do not wish to give the impression that I had a great influence on the President. He sought advice from many, and then after careful consideration made up his mind. Yet the trend of his economics was along lines that I approved.

The President had a remarkable memory. He called me in July 1958, when I was at a conference in Long Island, inquiring whether or not he should vote for a tax cut in the midst of the 1958 recession. I urged him to vote yes, and he did. In 1961–1962, when the tax cut was again discussed, he mentioned my 1958 advice to Walter Heller, and he also reminded me of the arguments I had used then.

Perhaps my longest discussion of economics with the President occurred aboard the destroyer U.S.S. "Joseph P. Kennedy, Jr.," on September 22, 1962. (The President and Mrs. Kennedy had invited my wife and me to spend a day in Newport watching the boat race, the America's Cup.) At that time I was greatly impressed by the growth of John F. Kennedy as an economist. His understanding and knowledge showed that he had outstripped his predecessors in his grasp of economic principles.

Here, I have given myself the luxury of omitting footnotes and tables whenever possible. This book is for college students who want to learn about economic policies and trends in a crucial four-year period and for the intelligent laymen with similar needs.

I believe that the results in this period have been very good on the whole, in contrast to the past, because government intervention has played a somewhat larger part. I do not imply that no mistakes were made. Far from it. But the achievements were large.

Naturally, Presidents cannot thrive on economic advice alone. The advice of economists is important but not necessarily decisive. The President who wants to put through important programs has to weigh political and other institutional factors as well as economic ones. The result may not be based on the best economics. All of this President Kennedy realized, as many economists did not.

I am indebted to Miss Marion Wilson for intelligent typing of a a difficult manuscript, to Richard Sylla, a Harvard graduate student, for reading the manuscript with care, and to Andrew Schaffer, then an able and mature Harvard senior, for research. My wife, Ruth B. Harris, also contributed to this volume, and also was the ideal listener.

S.E.H.

La Jolla, California
June 1964

PART I

The Large Issues

I

The Large Issues

INTRODUCTION

When John F. Kennedy assumed the presidency in January 1961, the country had been in the midst of a recession since April 1960. However, in the latter part of 1960, administration leaders had been denying this fact. An examination of the leading indicators of the National Bureau of Economic Research reveals the downward course of the economy. For example, the average workweek was declining; the layoff rate of workers was increasing, as were initial claims for unemployment insurance. Meanwhile, new orders of machinery, construction contracts, nonfarm housing starts, corporate profits, prices in relation to unit costs, profits per dollar of sales—all pointed to unsatisfactory conditions.

Candidate Kennedy stressed the following failures of economic policy:

1. A decline of gross national product (GNP) in 1960, the best over-all index of economic conditions

2. The rise of unemployment—in February 1961 unemployment had risen to a record of 8.1 per cent, and the increase in unemployment of 1.2 million of persons from February 1960 to October 1960 (which in my opinion, had cost Nixon the election)

3. Restrictive monetary policy, which helped account for the slow economic growth, and despite which the Eisenhower administration experienced an almost record peacetime price increase from 1955 to 1958

3

4. The emerging dollar crisis, which Senator Kennedy associated with slow responses by the Eisenhower administration.

The Democratic platform stressed the need to move ahead. But like many other platforms, the promises exceeded probable achievements—not only because of Congressional opposition, but also because the platform moved ahead of the candidate.

Senator Kennedy wanted to increase GNP at a more rapid rate that the 2½–3 per cent that prevailed under Eisenhower. In the almost three years of the Kennedy administration he kept his promise on GNP partly because, unlike President Eisenhower, he achieved an expansionist monetary policy. Adequate supplies of money are a condition for expansion. Obviously extra money enables the businessman to produce more goods and services and to provide more jobs.

The President's policies reflected the views of his advisers. Most of his advisers, unlike Eisenhower's, had been brought up in the modern school of Keynesian economics. This was the background of all five men he appointed to the Council of Economic Advisers; of David Bell, the director of the Budget Bureau; and of the President's unofficial and occasional academic advisers such as J. K. Galbraith, and Paul Samuelson.

These economists all believed that the government must tailor its spending and tax policies to the needs of the economy. When demand and spending in the private economy were deficient, as during excessive unemployment, the government should increase its spending and deficits and reduce its taxes. These men did not believe in the inevitability of economic declines. In one sense they were right. As of June 1964, we had an economic recovery of more than three years, an almost record duration for peacetime, with continued recovery expected. This is in contrast to the other peacetime recoveries in recent years. The difference in 1961–1964 was a greater disposition of the late President, and his successor, President Johnson, to use government intervention.

Above all the Kennedy administration sought more rapid growth and induced adequate fiscal policies that included expenditures on education, health, and research, relative price stability, treatment of the unemployment problem, and an attack on poverty.

I do not mean to suggest that the President easily accepted

modern Keynesian economics. He had to be shown. It was a long struggle. By 1963 he had clearly become a convert. The President was much influenced by the political consequences of Keynes' system. The average American is greatly disturbed by rising deficits. He tends to apply principles of private finance to the public sector. Concerned over his own debts, he tends to compensate by opposing government spending and deficits. In an article I wrote in 1961 for a weekly journal, I implied that the President followed Keynesian lines. After telling me that he liked the article, he said with a grin, "But do you think it is wise to label me as a Keynesian?"

Not only did the President have to abandon the ideas of his early economic training, but he had in his cabinet Secretary Douglas Dillon and Labor Secretary Arthur Goldberg (and later Willard Wirtz) who were not as enthusiastic about Keynesian economics as were the members of the Council of Economic Advisers, the budget director, and some unofficial advisers. The Secretary of the Treasury gradually accepted the tenets of Keynes, though with much less enthusiasm than the council members. Labor secretaries tend to explain unemployment not by deficiencies of demand but rather by imperfections of the market. They stress structural unemployment—that is, unfilled vacancies coincident with unemployment which is due to lack of skill or geographical imbalance.

No economist who had discussed economics with Kennedy would say, as Keynes did after a session with Franklin Roosevelt in the thirties, that the President was an "illiterate in economics." Hugh Sidey wrote: ". . . the economists never had a President so willing to listen to them. Kennedy trusted hard facts, not hunches, and though the science of economics was to a degree based on hunches, it could marshall an impressive array of figures and charts to support the hunches. The politicians could not match that, and so the pragmatic Kennedy naturally turned to the economists."

I often wondered how the President could afford so much time for economics. Once I even asked him if he should give so much time and energy to economic issues, when the security of the nation was the top priority. But the President in commenting envisaged a close relationship of the state of the economy and the security of the nation, and he also knew that jobs, price stability, and standards of living were crucial for winning supporters for his whole program.

ACCOMPLISHMENTS

In the almost three years of his administration, following the first quarter of 1961, the President could boast of an estimated rise of GNP of about $100 billion in current dollars, or an increase close to 20 per cent. In stable dollars, the rise came to 5.5 per cent a year to early 1964. This was a very satisfactory rate of growth, even if measured from a low level of the first quarter of 1961. A good index of the quality of the improvement is to compare the gain of GNP with the accompanying price rise. Improvement in output is likely to be accompanied by a price rise. One is traded against the other. In the three years ending March 1964, the ratio of the percentage of GNP (real) rise to the percentage of price rise was more than 4 to 1 (estimated). This is a very satisfactory ratio. Surely a rise of GNP four times as great as the accompanying price rise indicates a successful economic policy. In the years 1952–1960, the ratio was 3 to 2. Even this advance—25 per cent gain in GNP against 16 per cent price rise—is worthwhile.

On the unemployment front the Kennedy administration's record was less satisfactory than that of the Eisenhower administration, despite the fact that President Kennedy was more disposed to treat economic disease than his predecessor. Unemployment is too high, considering past accomplishments, the records in Western Europe, and the objectives expressed by the President and his party.

In defense of President Kennedy, the following can be said. An increasing trend of unemployment was already apparent in the later Eisenhower years: Unemployment at cyclical peaks was rising. For certain reasons (to be discussed later), the amount of additional GNP required to accompany an increase of X jobs was nearly doubled under Kennedy. In 1961, it seemed possible that an increase of GNP of $75 billion in stable prices would reduce unemployment to 4 per cent or less within three years. It is now clear that the combination of monetary and fiscal policy required to bring unemployment down to 4 per cent by 1964 or 1965 would be very difficult to achieve. As we shall see, there are limits on the contribution of monetary policy, and hence the need of greater recourse to fiscal policy. But an annual needed rise of GNP of $40 or $50 billion would require a cut in taxes plus a rise of federal spending which would not be acceptable to the Congress or their constituents. In the years 1950–1962, the average rise of GNP (1962 prices) was but $18 billion, and only in three years did the rise exceed $30 billion.

Despite the substantial rise of output, President Kennedy succeeded in stabilizing prices. Wholesale prices actually declined, and the cost of living rose little more than 1 per cent per year. For the first time since Grover Cleveland's day, a Democratic President had succeeded in stabilizing the internal value of the dollar. To be fair, one should note that the association of Democrats with inflation, aside from the greenback, silver, and populist movements of the last quarter of the nineteenth century, has been related to their unfortunate incumbency in war times. It is rather unexpected that prices, on the average, should have risen substantially more under Eisenhower than under Kennedy, and especially since the inflation under Democrats was the major economic issue raised by Eisenhower in 1962.

Among the factors responsible for the satisfactory price history under Kennedy were attempts to keep wages and prices from rising in crucial industries, the awareness that costs must be kept down in order to increase exports and reduce imports and thus strengthen the dollar, restraints on excessive increases in the monetary supply, and unusual gains in productivity, at least for 1961–1963. This stable price history prevailed despite the fact that the government and the monetary authority did not allow international deficits of a few billions each year to be reflected in related declines in the supply of money. The orthodox approach demands monetary restraints as reserves decline, the theory being that the resultant decline of money, and hence prices, would increase exports and reduce imports.

Kennedy inherited a serious balance of payments problem. At least thirty important measures were taken to correct the situation. But deficits of $2 to $3 billion continue, though the deficits are less than they were in 1959 and 1960. This problem has been much more intractable than was anticipated in 1961, though in late 1963 and early 1964 the deficit was reduced greatly.

In welfare programs, the gains were not as large as had been promised or anticipated. The President fought for advances in many programs—area redevelopment, manpower training, liberalization of old-age, survivors and disability insurance (OASDI), unemployment compensation, extension of housing programs, Medicare, mental health and retardation, transportation, development of natural resources, and several other programs. As a measure of good intentions, the Democratic administration deserves respect for promoting numbers of programs. Welfare expenditures, though substantially greater than under Eisenhower, were not as high as had been promised. The rise of security and space outlays, the general hostility toward public expenditures in the nation, the shift of emphasis to tax reduction—all of these contributed to a slowing down of the rate of expenditures on welfare. Although the rise of outlays was not insignificant, there was a definite decline in relation to needs.

In agriculture Kennedy pushed for high farm supports and income but tried hard to cut production. Here he had only limited success. The farmers wanted higher incomes, but were not disposed to accept strong controls.

OBSTACLES

Kennedy's accomplishments might have been greater, but several factors worked against him. One was, of course, the close election. A second was the troublesome problem of the balance of payments, which seriously hampered expansionist policies. It was widely believed (and with some justification) that short-term interest rates had to be kept at levels competitive with those offered by foreign lenders, and also (with less justification) that federal deficits had to be kept at minimum figures. Moreover, Western Europe was emerging as a serious competitor to the United States in the production and sale of manufactured goods and in its capacity to impose trade policies harmful to the United States. A fourth item was the crisis of confidence that comes once in a generation and in 1962 brought a serious decline in stock market prices. A fifth development was the emergence of civil rights as a vital issue, and one which reduced the cooperation of southern congressmen in the furtherance of welfare measures. A sixth point was the rising power of the House Rules Committee. A seventh factor was the sluggish economy, punctuated by anemic recoveries, that President Kennedy inherited. By 1960 the backlog of demand for capital and consumption goods following fifteen years of depression and war had been largely used up, as had the liberalization of financing terms that stimulated buying under Eisenhower. Unusual gains of productivity further increased unemployment.

TACTICS

The President's detractors found many weaknesses in his approach: He had, according to some, given us the third Eisenhower administration; his efforts were limited, for he assumed that making speeches was the equivalent of putting a program through; he appeased the Congress instead of fighting it; he accepted Congressional decisions instead of appealing to the people; he compromised with the Congress even as he launched his programs and thus gave away his program even before the contest had begun. These were mainly attacks from the left; from the right the charge was that he offered too many programs, and was an irresponsible spender. Caught between the fire of the left and of the Republican right, the latter bolstered by the Democratic right, the President had little room to maneuver.

How valid are these criticisms? It would surprise most Republicans to discover that Kennedy and Eisenhower agreed on economic policy. Consider but one item: The Republicans do not insist that fiscal policy stimulates the economy, or that increased taxes and reduced spending will cure an overstimulated economy. Rather the reverse. The Republicans approve a tax cut when the economy is exuberant, that is, when taxes should be raised, not lowered.

Those who claim that Kennedy's and Eisenhower's policies were similar should compare the programs offered and those achieved. The difference between the two Presidents was substantial on achievements, but with the current functioning of the Congress, the difference was even greater in programs offered.

Was the President wrong in not appealing to the public, when the Congress thwarted him? I doubt it. Congress largely reflects the views of its constituencies. The American public is no more disposed to modern fiscal theories than is Congress. Congressmen are not asked to use the Keynesian weapons. Instead, the public's complaints are concerned with excessive taxes and spending. Otherwise, the public has a limited understanding of modern theories. Congressmen are honest when they return from a testing period at home and announce no great enthusiasm for a tax cut accompanied by a rising debt.

On at least three occasions, the President appealed to the country directly: on Medicare, on the tax cut, on foreign aid. Moreover, his numerous press conferences were meant to educate the voter. The three direct appeals were effective presentations. But they did not seem to have much effect; and any gains may have been offset by increased resentment by the Congress for his direct appeal to all the people. I suspect that the people lead the Congress on the subject of Medicare. As for tax cuts, the Congress probably reflects the views of their constituencies. I believe that the Congress is more disposed to foreign aid than are the people.

It is not really worth answering the charge of lack of effort. No President of recent times faced as many day-by-day crises, with the possible exception of Franklin Roosevelt, and yet continued to plug for his important programs.

Did the President compromise too much in submitting his programs? There may be differences of opinion here. The President should and did lead the Congress. Disagreements arise on the question of how far he should have. The blocker on the football field who leads his runner by twenty yards is hardly effective. The President's failure in putting over some legislation he proposed suggests that he was far ahead of Congress. Consider, for example, his Medicare program, proposals for permanent changes in unemployment compensation, transportation subsidies, aid to education, and agricultural policy. In each instance the President led Congress by a substantial distance; but in most cases Congress did not move. Would it have helped if the President blocked at forty yards distance from the ball carrier rather than twenty? I think the President would then have been less effective.

Some of the President's supporters argued that he should have submitted an audacious program, and that if he received one that fell below his standards, he should have threatened a veto and, if necessary, vetoed the bill. He then would have won a moral victory. This seemed to me unwise. It would not have been sensible to veto an $11 billion tax cut because the Congress refused the suggested tax reform and because the President wanted a $15 billion tax cut, with no restraints on usual rises in spending. It was better to wait for the tax cut than to win a moral victory and repudiate the program.

RELATIONS WITH THE CONGRESS

With substantial majorities in both the House and the Senate (257 Democratic House members and 178 Republican House members, and 67 and 33, respectively, in the Senate in the Eighty-eighth Congress in November 1963), greater achievements might have been expected. But aside from the handicaps mentioned earlier, there are special reasons for President Kennedy's failure to achieve more. On the whole his gains were, however, substantial in the Eighty-seventh Congress (1961–1962).

Among the factors accounting for the limited cooperation of the Congress were the long delays—for example, the lack of progress in putting through appropriation bills in 1963, with important bills still not acted on as late as November; the emergence of the civil rights issue, which resulted in delays in other legislation plus the growing reluctance of southern congressmen to agree with their party on other issues; and the rising level of discipline among Republican congressmen.

Undoubtedly the executive departments and agencies are hampered by the demands Congress makes upon high officials. In 1963, the Secretary of the Treasury spent most of his time on the Hill. The long-sustained treatment of the tax bill, the debt ceiling, and the interest rate equalization tax required the presence of the Secretary and top aids on the Hill continuously, and when they were not on the Hill they were collecting material for hearings or for the elucidation of the committees writing the bills. Under Secretary Henry Fowler and Assistant Secretary Stanley Surrey had to devote virtually all their time to attempting to get a tax bill through; and yet they had to forego many of the reform provisions on which they had worked for two years.

Democratic defections greatly hampered Kennedy's legislative program. There were relatively few economic programs of the administration that received the support of a majority of the Republicans. In 1963, for example, the only significant administration programs which won the Republicans' support were a mental health bill, the college aid program, and the vocational education bill.

It has sometimes been said that Kennedy suffered from the change of leadership from Senator Johnson to Senator Mansfield in the Senate and Congressman Rayburn to Congressman McCormack in the House. Undoubtedly the inexperience of the new leaders increased the difficulties of obtaining approval for the Kennedy program. There was also a weakening of discipline among the Democrats coincident with new Republican strength. With time and experience, the Democratic leadership should improve. But perhaps more important than lack of leadership was the breakdown of the Congressional process. In the *New York Times* of November 12, 1963, Cabell Phillips noted consternation among congressmen at the achievements of the Eighty-eighth Congress. President Kennedy had received approval of but seven of his twenty-seven major legislative programs. The *Congressional Quarterly* of November 8, 1963, put the box score at eight out of twenty-five.

SOME ECONOMIC ISSUES

Primary objectives of economic policy were increased growth and stability; but the Kennedy administration was also concerned with equity issues. Liberalization of OASDI and of unemployment compensation, the struggle for civil rights, the extension of welfare programs generally—all of these reflected an interest in equity issues. Large outlays for welfare may contribute to equity, growth, and recovery. But under some conditions, for example, in advanced stages of recovery with low unemployment, there may be conflicts between the stability and equity objectives. At such times large outlays for welfare may well contribute to inflation. Even in conditions of unemployment, welfare financed out of taxes, e.g., the social security program, may be costly in incentives and output; but the favorable effects on demand are an offset.

I have already suggested that one has to trade gains in growth against any cost in price inflation. A 10 per cent growth rate and 1 per cent price rise per year are indeed a large achievement, but most would not welcome a 1 per cent growth rate and a 10 per cent rise in inflation. The ratio of growth and price rise, below which growth should be sacrificed in order to assure a greater degree of price stability, is to be determined on both economic and ideological grounds. For example, is the rising ratio of growth to prices, 3 to 1, or 1 to 1, the point at which it becomes desirable to sacrifice growth to price stability? Price instability beyond a certain point injures the economy (economic consideration), and is harmful to those with relatively fixed income (an ideological issue). Slow growth and price stability are costly to the economy and are accompanied by inadequate employment and, hence, mean heavy costs for a small part of the population, the unemployed.

Three major weapons are at the disposal of the economic therapists, namely, money, fiscal policy, and direct attacks on unemployment, e.g., by manpower training. An increased recourse to monetary policy means less need for fiscal policy, that is, for the employment of government tax, spending, and debt policies to treat the economy. One able economist suggested that a reduction of money rates by 1 per cent as a stimulant saves the government $12 billion of spending. The more monetary and fiscal policies are used, the less the need for structural approach.

But substituting money and fiscal policy for structural therapy is limited in its effects. General measures, e.g., more money and more spending, will cut down unemployment in depressed areas. But even with easy money and deficits of $20 billion per year, the textile towns in New England and the coal mine towns of West Virginia would still experience substantial unemployment, above the national level.

General measures to solve the structural problems beyond a certain point can be highly inflationary and wasteful. Here, it is important to encourage new industries, train workers for available jobs, encourage migration to areas where there are unfilled vacancies, and so on. That an additional job can be had at a cost to the government of $1,000–$2,000 against $10,000 or thereabouts through fiscal measures strengthens the case for the structural approach. But much unemployment and limited unfilled vacancies restrict the use of the structural approach.

The recovery in the years 1961–1963 was unique in that it did not bring the rise of money rates of preceding recoveries. Both the Federal Reserve, by controlling member bank reserves and increasing the short-term rates that could be paid on time or savings deposits, and the Treasury, through large issues of short-term securities, managed generally to keep short-term rates competitive with rates abroad. But despite the high short-term rates, long-term rates were remarkably stable.

Hence, it may be said that the recovery profited from expansionist monetary policies. The rise in the supply of money was not spectacular, though it was relatively larger than in the 1950s; but if allowance is made for the very large increase in time deposits or if one concentrates on new financing, the large contribution of increased liquidity is evident.

Fiscal policy was the major weapon of the Kennedy administration. The rise of spending was crucial, though the increase was only partially connected with economic objectives; the major part of the rise stemmed from increased needs to assure maximum security. By 1962, tax cut policy took precedence over spending. Widespread support for the tax cut rather than spending, and the President's conversion to the theory that deficits are helpful in periods of unemployment, account for the acceptance of a policy of tax reduction not only to increase growth but also to extend the recovery and weaken recessionary forces.

In order to achieve a tax cut of substantial proportions, the Kennedy administration had to stress modern fiscal theories. At first they urged a balancing of the budget over the business cycle, not each year. But by 1963 it was clear that they had to take a more advanced position—namely, that deficits must continue into the advanced stages of recovery so long as unemployment was still high at the top of the cycle. They hoped that large induced deficits would raise GNP sufficiently so that within a reasonable time unemployment would fall to 4 per cent or less and the budget would be balanced.

Undoubtedly the country would have been much closer to a full employment economy if the balance of payments had not been so troublesome. But the steady deficits in the balance ruled out highly expansionist monetary policies and even weakened fiscal policies to some extent. In fact, many who favored restrictionist policies and discipline on other grounds favored the adverse balance of payments as a weapon to be used against the expansionists. But there was a persistent loss of reserves. Until July 1963 the administration depended primarily on orthodox measures: raising interest rates, curbing inflationary pressures, diverting aid dollars to American markets, borrowing in foreign markets, orthodox expansion of international reserves. But in July 1963 the government introduced its interest rate equalization tax, a measure aimed at discouraging the excessive tapping of the American capital market by foreign interests. Large improvements followed in 1963–1964.

Finally, there is the intractable unemployment problem. In the midst of a highly prosperous economy, with a GNP of $600 billion, or 20 per cent above the level at the beginning of the Kennedy administration, the country, in late 1963, was still confronted with unemployment of about 4 million, a rate of 5.5 per cent. Because unemployment is concentrated among the young, Negroes, the unskilled, and those living in surplus labor areas, the costs of a given level of unemployment are greatly increased. No one would have anticipated early in 1961 that a *real* rise of GNP of 5.5 per cent a year would fail to bring unemployment down to 4 per cent or even lower by 1963. This was the greatest disappointment for the Kennedy administration. (By May 1964, unemployment had fallen to 5.1 per cent.)

In order to treat the unemployment problem, the President had to press for advanced fiscal policies. With unemployment at about 4 per cent, the government would have been satisfied with smaller deficits. And yet in order to cope successfully with the unemployment problem, the planned deficits would have to be even larger than the President proposed.

One problem is that rising productivity—a welcome development in itself—is a partial cause of unemployment. It is possible that the structure of productivity changes has altered so that transitional unemployment problems have become more serious. If the problem is not solved, one may be sure that labor will insist upon a solution through reduced hours for the same pay. This would be unfortunate, for costs would rise and our competitive position deteriorate.

When confronted with a question on the relation of automation and jobs in his press conference of October 31, 1963, the President said:

. . . So automation does not need to be, we hope, our enemy. What is of concern now is this combination of a rather intensive period of automation, plus the fact that our educational system is not keeping up, so that we are graduating or dropping out of high school so many millions of young men and women who are not able to operate in this new society. . . .

. . . I think machines can make life easier for men, if men do not let machines dominate men. . . .

2

JFK: Economic Background

In his years as a congressman and senator (1946–1960), John F. Kennedy represented a highly industrialized state with many problems. It is important to remember this background in order to understand his economics. Before 1946, Kennedy was probably unsophisticated in his economic thinking. At Harvard he had taken Economics A with a skilled young instructor with leftist tendencies. (At Hyannis Port, in August, 1960, he told several of us of his Ec. A experience and his C grade). But his studies of economics at Harvard and at the London School of Economics (with Harold Laski) did not influence his ideology.

In 1952, Kennedy ran for the Senate, and his interest in economics quickened. At this time (late summer 1952), when he was running for the Senate, he called at my Cape home to discuss some of the campaign issues. We had a long discussion of the problems of Massachusetts. Since 1952, I had an opportunity to learn what problems concerned him and to estimate his economic aptitude. We also frequently attended meetings of New England congressmen.

In the Congressional years 1946–1960, Massachusetts had serious losses of industry, partly because its industrial structure was tied to old and declining industries—such as textiles and shoes—and partly because the Commonwealth had to compete increasingly with the low-wage and emerging-industrial South. Kennedy was naturally under great pressure to do something for Massachusetts. Hence his interest in minimum wage legislation, which could narrow the wage differential between North and South. His other concerns were: sheltering Massachusetts textiles, through trade restrictions, from the "unfair" competition of Japan and other low-wage countries; improving unemployment compensation, area redevelopment, and increased federal spending in Massachusetts—all measures directed to treating the burden of unemployment and migration of industry; opposing the use of tax exemption of state and local securities by southern states as a means of pirating industries from the North; and voting against price-raising agricultural programs. The latter tended to increase the price of food and clothing, thus compounding the costs of government policy for New England workers as well as contributing, through higher prices for raw cotton and wool, to the gains of synthetics and losses in cotton and woolens, the staple stand-bys of New England.

One should not minimize the difficulties confronting a senator who becomes President. The transition was particularly difficult for President Kennedy because, as a senator representing a declining economy, he often had to fight for policies which as the nation's President he could not support.

As senator he courageously voted against a crucial agricultural support bill. At this point, his economics was excellent. Few economists would support agricultural policies on the basis of economic considerations alone. Here a shift was necessary. Kennedy merged economic and political considerations by providing support and higher prices, but on the condition that strong measures were taken to restrict output and bring supply and demand nearer to equilibrium.

To understand Kennedy's legislative program, one must remember his interests as a member of Congress. The area redevelopment program, the temporary Unemployment Compensation (U.C.) Act, the proposals for improvements in the permanent U.C. program; pension reserves; the youth training programs, liberalization of the old-age survivors and disability insurance, the Manpower Training Act, Medicare—these all reflect concern for the surplus labor areas and for industrial societies in general.

Kennedy emphasized these direct approaches for solving the

problems of unemployment and the underprivileged generally more than most economists would, since the latter are apt to stress fiscal and monetary policy, that is, over-all demand. Throughout, the President had to adapt his policies to the requirements of the Presidency. One of his greatest victories (although it was blunted by de Gaulle's affront to the British), was the Trade Expansion Act, one of the most liberal trade programs in all of our history. This was a clash with the restrictionist programs he had to support as senator, and promised a collision with his New England constituency and with the politically powerful southern textile industry. To assure ultimate victory, he had to make concessions to the textile and oil industries.

In short, the President's legislative program reflected his earlier interests both in what he proposed and accomplished, and in what he failed to achieve. It is not surprising that his victories were in legislation that was closely related to his experiences as a congressman.

Many of Kennedy's last days in the Congress were concentrated on labor legislation. He led the fight against the 1960 legislation which attempted to curb labor unions. Yet he showed little interest in rewriting the Taft-Hartley Act or the labor legislation of 1960. Undoubtedly, one reason for inaction was the sluggishness of the trade union movement in the early 1960s, and a growing criticism of trade unions which in several cases irresponsibly shut down vital industries. New labor legislation was more likely to hurt the trade union movement rather than help it.

As President, Kennedy was confronted with many economic issues that did not concern him greatly as a member of the House or Senate. A crucial issue was the balance of payments. But in the preceding fourteen years, his major interest in the balance of payments was in restricting imports of textiles from low-wage countries. He had had little opportunity to study the problems of the balance of payments, of the weakness of the dollar, of the alternative therapeutic measures. At Hyannis Port in the late summer of 1960 as his boat was ready to dock, I went over the issues in an hour's presentation. Later, he had to spend much time on these problems. But I was impressed with his quick comprehension. He then had little interest in such programs as education and resource development. Perhaps he remained relatively uninformed on the most crucial issues of economic policy, money and fiscal policy, though he had received much information and instruction on these issues during the 1960 campaign.

Those early pressures and interests explain President Kennedy's early resistance to modern economics and his greater successes in the "direct" approach, e.g., area redevelopment. Because the Department of Labor had similar views on the relative desirability of direct or indirect (fiscal and monetary policy) measures there was an underutilization of fiscal policy at first. A few years of discussions between the President and the members of the Council of Economic Advisers, especially Heller, also Samuelson and others, were needed to convince the President of the relevance of adequate money, tax cuts, deficits, and the like. He remained unconvinced of the need for substantial increases in public spending for welfare, first because of the heavy burdens of security; second because of a reluctance to support large deficits, a political liability; and third because tax cuts, more generally acceptable than increased spending, brought substantial deficits. In the President's view, greater deficits were not tolerable.

3

The Kennedy Team

In order to understand the economic policies of the Kennedy administration, it is necessary to consider the influence of the Council of Economic Advisers, a three-man board which advised the President, and also the Secretary of the Treasury. The background of the council—which consisted of Walter Heller, chairman, James Tobin, and Kermit Gordon (the latter two were later replaced by Gardner Ackley and John Lewis)—differed greatly from that of the Secretary of the Treasury.

When Secretary Dillon complained early in 1961 to the President about the lack of mature economists in the Treasury—Secretary Humphrey had driven most of them out—the President suggested that the Secretary invite me to serve as an economic adviser to the Secretary. I therefore became the Secretary's economic adviser. I was, hence, in a good position to observe the differences between the council and the Secretary, the main architects of economic policy, and their reconciliation. It was also an embarrassing position, since my views were much closer to the council's than to those of the Treasury, which tended to support orthodox positions. More than once when there was a conflict of views, members of the council and their staff criticized me for repudiation of principles. The council did not seem to realize that the Treasury could not move ahead as rapidly as the council; nor that, as the department primarily responsible for the financing of

21

the government and the preservation of the value of the dollar abroad, the Treasury had to retain some confidence of the financial community. Thus, prior to the acceptance of modern economics, the Treasury had first to educate the financial community.

Secretary Douglas Dillon came to the government from finance. A Republican, he joined the Kennedy administration after a distinguished public career as Ambassador to France and Under Secretary of State. Like most men of finance, Dillon believed in the balanced budget and restrained public spending. He also favored interest rates determined by supply and demand for capital, instead of rates to be depressed by the creation of money.

All five members of the council *believed* in Keynesian economics. They therefore, above all, sought adequacy of demand. That is, when the private economy is foundering because the goods being produced are not being taken off the market at profitable prices and, hence, output falls below the potential—at such times the government should intervene through increased public spending (and) or reduced taxes. The objective of economic policy is a balanced economy, not a balanced budget.

The council also *advanced* Keynesian economics. They especially emphasized the brake on economic recovery of rising tax receipts as the economy advanced and, hence, the anemic recoveries; and they stressed the gulf between actual and potential output. Their therapy was more public spending, reduced taxes, and through monetary creation, lower interest rates which would stimulate investment.

Secretary Dillon was hostile to large and continued deficits. In the formulation of the 1963 budget (released in January 1962), the Treasury and the council disagreed. The council's estimate of gross national product and revenue was excessive, with the result that given the large rise in expenditures, a substantial deficit emerged in the fiscal year 1963. The Treasury was displeased with the resultant deficit; the council would have preferred the high GNP forecast, but nevertheless considered the deficit associated with a disappointing GNP as a necessary contribution to a healthy economy.

Both in spending policies and in the timing and amount of the tax cut, the council was ready to move sooner and more substantially than was the Treasury. But Secretary Dillon, with the important help of Under Secretary Fowler, ultimately accepted and fought vigorously for a tax cut, even one imposed upon an existing deficit. From the beginning, Dillon favored tax policies that would improve incentives and stimulate investments.

Secretary Dillon has been a fine Secretary of the Treasury, even though through his great influence with the President he succeeded in moderating the advance to needed spending and tax policies. Unlike most finance men and virtually all recent secretaries of the Treasury, he did not close his mind to new ideas. In a period of three years he had moved from a position of hostility to the unorthodox, to the acceptance of unbalanced budgets, substantial deficits, tax cuts superimposed on unbalanced budgets, and had even condoned deficits at the top of the cycle so long as unemployment was substantial. Many of his old colleagues in finance repudiated him, although through his conscientious support of the Kennedy policies he converted many of them. Unlike secretaries Morgenthau, Snyder, Humphrey, and Anderson before him, he learned the simple lessons of arithmetic involved in Keynesian economics; and if he had not moved on the basis of these new precepts, President Kennedy would probably not have launched his revolutionary fiscal policies.

I do not intend to minimize the contributions of the council and particularly those of Walter Heller. More than anyone else, the highly articulate and intelligent Heller won the President over to modern views of economics. He accomplished this despite many obstacles, especially since the President in 1960 had not been convinced of the usefulness of budgetary deficits. Because he was confronted with a President who at first seemed allergic to modern economics, Heller deserves all the more credit. His predecessors, Leon Keyserling, Arthur Burns, Raymond Saulnier, had views similar to those of their Presidents, and hence they had none of Heller's problems.

Heller continued to influence President Johnson along similar lines. Of course, he had help, not only from his able colleagues in the council, but also from David Bell of the Bureau of the Budget and such occasional advisers as Paul Samuelson, Kenneth Galbraith, and Carl Kaysen. The distinguished historian Arthur

Schlesinger, Jr., was also interested in economic issues and generally supported the council position.

Other departments and agencies also contributed to the formulation of economic policies. In particular, the Department of Labor under secretaries Goldberg and Wirtz pressed for a solution of the unemployment problem beyond that of the stimulation-of-demand approach. As a result of their views and the President's interest in the direct approach—that is, the treatment of structural unemployment—the government achieved much more through such programs as re-education, vocational guidance, and manpower training than would otherwise have been possible.

The differences between the council and the Treasury were not restricted to the acceptance or rejection of Keynesian economics. From the beginning the council sought increased international reserves or liquidity through unorthodox approaches. They believed that if more reserves were available, the government would not have to respond to deficits in the balance of payments by restricting monetary supplies and containing government deficits excessively, and thus inducing economic declines or moderating the rate of recovery. Under the impact of the brilliant under secretary, Robert Roosa, the Treasury was reluctant to accept the various proposals to create vast international reserves. Instead Roosa sought additional reserves through less extreme measures, such as increased help from the International Monetary Fund, sales of U.S. Treasury issues in foreign markets for needed foreign currencies, swapping of currencies with foreign countries, and so on. Above all, Mr. Roosa feared that excessive supplies of international reserves would preclude taking necessary measures for dealing with international disequilibrium, such as monetary restraints, reduced prices, and improved competitive position. By 1963–1964, the Treasury, whose progress in solving the dollar problem was disappointing to some, had agreed to investigate further various methods of increasing international liquidity.

There were, of course, inevitable conflicts of views. The gifted Theodore Sorenson often helped the responsible officials adjust their differences; and continued disagreement often resulted in discussions with the President.

A new, unique institution was the Secretary of the Treasury's panel of about twenty-five of the top economists of the country, which I mobilized and for which I acted as chairman. In these lively meetings, held several times a year, the Secretary, members of the President's Council of Economic Advisers, the budget director, a member of the Federal Reserve Board, and high officials of other relevant agencies went to school again. But these meetings also served to clarify many problems and helped bring a measure of agreement on such important problems as deficits in the balance of payments, tax policies, management of the national debt, monetary policy, plus the assessment of the economic situation and its treatment.

4

*Eisenhower and Kennedy Economic Policies**

The economy that Kennedy inherited was not an unhealthy one, though there were problems. Indeed, growth had been rather inadequate at 2.5 per cent per year during the Eisenhower years. Price inflation had been modest in the early years, with an average rise of 0.5 to 1 per cent from 1952 to 1956, but substantial thereafter for nonwar years—3 per cent per year in the next four years. Large wage increases had added to the inflationary pressure.

Perhaps the most troublesome problem was the balance of payments. Beginning in 1953, when a loss of $2 billion of reserves occurred (inclusive of increased short-term debts) the Eisenhower administration watched losses of $16 billion, and yet was very slow to take corrective measures.

Let us compare Kennedy's record from 1961 to 1963, and President Eisenhower's from 1952 to 1960.

In consumer prices, Eisenhower's administration experienced an *average* increase of 1.4 per cent; the Kennedy administration, 1.1 per cent; in wholesale prices, a rise of almost 1 per cent per year under Eisenhower, and a decline under Kennedy. Despite the great emphasis on halting inflation, the Republican administration ex-

---

* Parts of this chapter come from Seymour E. Harris, "Kennedy and the Liberals," *New Republic*, June 1, 1963 (with permission).

perienced a rise of prices in excess of that of the Kennedy administration. This is a great achievement for any administration, and especially for a Democratic one; for the Democrats, in contrast to the Republicans, tend to stress objectives such as growth and full employment somewhat more than rigid price stability.

One reason for the better price record of the Kennedy administration was the pressure put upon labor to keep wages in line with productivity gains; and on industry to relate prices to wage increases. Whereas, in the years 1952–1960, average annual wage rates in manufacturing rose by 5 per cent, the estimated rise in 1961–1963 was only 3 per cent.

However, the better record under Kennedy is partly related to the higher level of unemployment. Labor is less aggressive in seeking wage increases when unemployment is large.

The liberals complained of the President's unwillingness to spend and incur adequate deficits. But from fiscal year 1953 to fiscal year 1961, Eisenhower's (estimated) expenditures rose by $7 billion; Kennedy's, in three years, by $17 billion.

At an annual rate Kennedy expenditures rose at six times the Eisenhower rate. The following points are worth remembering. Under Eisenhower, the Congress led the President; under Kennedy, the President led the Congress for enactment of necessary spending programs. Three-quarters of the increase of spending under Kennedy was for military and related programs, and these outlays increase the difficulty of achieving larger advances in the welfare area. The espousal of a tax-cut program meant less reliance on spending programs. Once deficits become uncomfortably large as a result of a tax cut, it becomes more difficult to increase deficits through spending programs. Like some of President Kennedy's critics, I would like to see more expenditures on medicine, education, and housing. But one reason for the almost unanimous support of a tax cut among economists was that the Congress did not seem disposed to support that kind of spending program.

In his campaign and platform, President Kennedy urged a growth of 5 per cent per year. He more than achieved this from the first quarter of 1961 to the end of 1963. This may well continue in 1964; but it will be more difficult to maintain a 5 per cent rate after 1964. The growth record so far has been better than that under Eisenhower; but we should allow for the low (and favorable) base period of the first quarter of 1961.

Moreover, the inflationary cost of each percentage of growth was much less under Kennedy. In 1952–1960, the ratio of percentage rise of growth over percentage rise of prices was 3 to 2; in 1961–1963, 4 + to 1.

In one area the Eisenhower administration functioned better than the Kennedy administration: Unemployment averaged 4.9 per cent under Eisenhower. But note a steady trend upward. Under Truman the average was 4.2 per cent. In the first four years of Eisenhower, unemployment averaged 4.3 per cent; but with an average of 5.5 per cent in the last four years the Eisenhower administration was beginning to experience the sluggishness in the economy. Under Kennedy, the average was 6.7 per cent in 1961 (reflecting the inherited recession), 5.6 per cent in 1962, and 5.7 per cent in 1963. Improvement here has been slow. Yet the Kennedy administration fought for and got a Manpower Training Act that would deal directly with areas of infection.

In monetary policy, there is no comparison in the achievements of the two administrations. The Eisenhower administration and its financial agencies had a complex on inflation, with the result that interest rates were steadily raised, with unfortunate effects on investment. To take an important example: From 1952 to 1960 the yield on corporate Aaa bonds rose from 2.96 to 4.41 per cent, or by almost 50 per cent; from 1960 to 1962, the yield dropped from 4.41 to 4.33, or by 2 per cent. Despite concern over the balance of payments, this rate was still 4.42 late in 1963. It is most unusual for rates to drop consistently in a long recovery period. This did not happen without hard work. The President, Dillon, Heller, and Roosa must have made the needs of adequate supplies of money clear to the Federal Reserve Board, and yet without raising troublesome issues of its independence. This easy money policy, the new depreciation and investment credit policies and the increased likelihood of a tax cut in 1963 began to be reflected in a rising volume of investment.

At least until the early summer of 1964, the record was good. How long rates will continue to be low in the midst of a sustained recovery will depend in part on the developments in the international accounts. In the middle of July 1963, the Federal Reserve announced its first rise in the rediscount rate since 1960, and the justification lay in the large outward movements of short-term capital. Higher rates would, it was hoped, reduce that outflow. The President, in his balance of payments statement of July 18, 1963, expressed a hope that the effects on long-term rates would not be serious. As will be discussed later, the two markets are not exactly segregated ones and, hence, long-term rates may also rise. But in view of the other devices proposed by the President in July 1963 to treat the adverse balance, continued high short-term rates may not be necessary. Moreover, there is some evidence that the availability of credit in 1963 was high, and availability may be more stimulative than a somewhat higher price, for money discourages investment.

Perhaps in no area has the government made as much progress as in fiscal policy. In the midst of the Berlin crisis in 1961, the President at first wanted a tax increase to match the rise of military outlays. He was dissuaded from introducing a fiscal policy that would be associated with presidents Hoover and Eisenhower and secretaries Humphrey and Anderson rather than with Democratic policies. By May 1963, as revealed in his brilliant address to the Committee for Economic Development, the President proved that he had learned the lessons of modern economics.

Finally, what of the troublesome problem of the balance of payments? It is still a threat to expansionist policies. But, at least, strong measures have been taken and a substantial improvement achieved: Whereas, from 1958–1960 the average deficit in the balance of payments was $3.7 billion, in 1961 and 1962 the average was only $2.2 billion; and the excess of exports of goods and services over imports was $2 billion in the earlier period and $5 billion under Kennedy.

To some extent this comparison exaggerates the degree of improvement. Temporary gains, such as prepayments of debts to the United States, contributed to the improvement. If we allow for these factors, the advance over 1958–1960 might be cut by one-half. And it appears that some unorthodox measures may be necessary. The interest rate equalization tax, proposed July 1963, is one such measure. But an unexpectedly large improvement in the year ending June 1964 reduces the likelihood of radical surgery.

By 1963, the President achieved a rise of GNP of about $100 billion in a period of three years, an increase which, though falling short of solving the unemployment problem, was substantial, especially when related to the small rise of prices which had accompanied growth. He also deserved credit for a sustained recovery which greatly exceeded the average period of rise over twenty-two peace time cycles since 1854.

In the welfare area, the disappointments were in Medicare and education. I do not think that the President could be accused of lack of effort on Medicare. In education there was some bungling. But even under the able operations of Commissioner Francis Keppel, it was possible to make only limited, though important, gains. Educational legislation was very difficult to achieve, due to the opposition of those fearful of government spending, of federal control of education, of government use of federal programs to impose segregation. Also, educational interests failed to combine in pressing their demands. Eisenhower's record in education was not very good; but under the pressure of Sputnik, he did put across a $900 billion four-year National Defense Education Act. Though Kennedy tried harder, he accomplished less than had been anticipated: The opposition had hardened. Undoubtedly, under the rising deficit and the tax cut, enthusiasm for spending programs waned to some extent, and that included education. In the light of all these problems, the educational legislation of 1963 is a good omen.

In other welfare areas, the President had some success: housing, area redevelopment, manpower training, liberalization of the social security act, and the Peace Corps. But on the whole the record on welfare was disappointing. In some programs, greater efforts by the Executive might have helped. But the road blocks were primarily elsewhere: Congressional opposition, the restraints on Congressional activity, the choice of tax cuts over welfare spending, and the demands of the national security programs.

PART II

Politics and Business

5

*The Economics and Politics of Public Policy**

When Harry S Truman was President and Edwin Nourse was his chairman of the Council of Economic Advisers, it was said that Nourse annoyed Truman because he gave only "economic" advice and refused to suggest any general course of action to the President. In Nourse's view, the economist's task was restricted to "economic" analysis. I once asked the members of President Kennedy's council whether they restricted their advice to the economics of the issue. Their reply was that they would be thrown out of the President's office if they proposed policy on purely economic considerations.

President Kennedy was attentive to economics; but he was also aware that political and other considerations are relevant. He was prepared to take political risks, for example, in running substantial deficits; but he was not prepared to follow the principle of "balancing the economy rather than the budget" if the result was likely to be deficits of $20 billion per year. This would be political suicide. Neither the Congress nor the public would accept such budgets in peacetime.

One of the main difficulties in dealing with the economic prob-

* This chapter is based largely on my article, "The Gap Between Economists and Politicians," *New York Times Magazine,* April 14, 1963 (with permission).

lems of the United States is the gap in understanding between professional economists and professional politicians. The gap is widening because economists tend to give too much weight to purely economic reasoning in matters of policy and because politicians are too slow in recognizing the importance of new ideas in economics. It is important that this gap be closed. As we shall see, the 1963 tax proposals reflected an unusual accommodation of economic views to political necessities.

There is nothing new, of course, about the time lag between the formulation of an economic idea and its acceptance as public policy. Adam Smith's *Wealth of Nations,* for example, with its plea for free trade, appeared in 1776. England's Prime Minister William Pitt, because he had read the book, arranged a trade treaty with France in 1786. But it was not until seventy years after 1776 that England really achieved free trade, and even then it first required the heroic efforts of two of the most persuasive men of modern times: Richard Cobden, the articulate reasoner, and John Bright, the master of oratory.

In our own century, more than thirty years have passed since Lord Keynes stated that it is the government's responsibility to adapt its contribution to spending to the fluctuations and trends of the private economy. Due to Keynes's skill, this simple maxim and related ideas have been built into an economic system. Yet the doctrine is still far from being accepted in practice by many politicians.

The extent of the gap in understanding between economists and politicians can be shown by four case studies from the Kennedy administration. These cover fiscal policy, the dollar problem, the trade expansion program, and agricultural policy.

First, fiscal policy. In the summer of 1962, our group of twenty-five top economists was unanimous in its view that the economy needed an immediate lift. We felt that an immediate tax cut was the only practical therapy. Yet the President at that time decided against it.

Why? The refusal to press for a tax cut was not due, as Senator Javits suggested, to "agonized indecisiveness." The main reason was that the President, after a careful polling of leaders of Congress, became convinced that he could not count on their cooperation, since they had already taken eighteen months to consider a relatively modest tax bill. There was also considerable doubt that Congress would accept the principle: A $10 billion tax cut might spur a rise of $30 billion in the gross national product and produce $5 billion in additional tax receipts, but the total deficit for the fiscal year of 1964 could still reach $12 billion (inclusive of the likely pretax-cut deficit). Congress seems to have felt that a deficit of these proportions would be a political liability, and the President perhaps shared that view. At any rate, he was not disposed to accept a gratuitous rebuff from Congress. A President will fight for a program only when there is a reasonable chance of victory.

By late 1962 and early 1963, the situation had changed: A substantial reduction of taxes and a resultant increase of gross national product of two to four times the tax cut and many times as large as the increase in the deficit associated with the tax cut—on these a consensus had emerged. The President, labor, business, and economists were in agreement. Economic wisdom had miraculously become politically palatable.

A similar conflict between economic theory and political expediency exists over the dollar problem. Many of America's best economists would suggest a devaluation of the dollar vis-à-vis foreign currencies, or a rise in the price of gold, or at least flexible exchanges.

But this would deal only with the purely economic issues. When a country has difficulties in paying its bills abroad, the economist tends to seek the simplest way out, and devaluation improves the competitive position in the quickest, surest way. Dollars become cheaper in other currencies while retaining, at least temporarily, their original purchasing power at home. Hence, it becomes cheaper for other nations to buy goods in the United States (which means more exports) and more expensive for Americans to buy abroad (which means fewer imports). Yet neither in New York nor in Washington is there any serious talk of devaluation or a rise in the price of gold. I am not at all convinced of the merits of the economic case for devaluation for a reserve currency, particularly in a period when inflation is still a possibility.

The President expressed his opposition to devaluation several times. Washington prefers to improve our competitive position by containing wage and price inflation, by raising productivity, by stimulating the marketing of goods and services, by encouraging foreign tourists, by transferring some of the burden of military expenditure and foreign aid to its allies, by discouraging excessive exports of capital, and by increased procurement at home for economic and military aid abroad.

This approach is favored in Washington although it is the hard way out. It imposes discipline on the managers and operators of the American economy, keeping money supplies and debts down; it protects America's prestige abroad, which might be hurt by devaluation, and it assures the United States position as a reserve center.

Thus, to a considerable extent for noneconomic reasons, the government (and practical men of finance) are again at odds with the economists. Devaluation or a rise in the price of gold will receive consideration only if the formidable arsenal of weapons mobilized—and others still to be exploited—fails to bring the dollar market into reasonable balance. And improvements since 1960 have been large, though not adequate.

Over the third major issue—trade expansion—there was little disagreement. But the passage of the trade expansion bill, allowing the President greater freedom to negotiate with the European Common Market, was mostly due to his political genius. As one who for years watched Congressional attitudes on trade matters for the New England governors, I was convinced that such an extreme move toward trade liberalization could not be accomplished. Increasingly, since the war, Congress has shown itself to be more and more protectionist. Yet President Kennedy saw the political as well as the economic possibilities and achieved a great victory. He capitalized on the fact that the Ways and Means Committee, which was allergic to spending programs, was nonetheless amenable to other legislative steps—such as trade expansion—that might raise income without raising taxes.

Under Secretary Ball's contributions were important, but had not the President appeased, with tariff concessions, the textile, glass, and other interests first—and thus assured the support of a dozen key senators—it is extremely doubtful that he could have put his bill across.

Finally, there is the vexed issue of agricultural policy. Few economists of the last generation have any respect for it. Artificially high support prices and great advances in productivity have contributed to larger and larger surpluses and costs to the taxpayer. The obvious solution, for economists, is to reduce support prices and thus encourage a curtailment of output. This was the theory behind the program of Secretary Ezra Taft Benson under Eisenhower. It was also implicit in the Committee for Economic Development program of 1962, and in a similar plan by the distinguished Professor H. S. Houthakker. Both tried to soften the impact of withdrawing supports by suggesting temporary subsidies and other measures.

What happened? Benson, of course, failed and the CED spokesmen before the House Agricultural Committee did not even get to first base—although, among others, a top businessman and economist, Theodore Yntema, a vice president of Ford represented them, and although four able economists had worked on the program. Why did they receive such a cold reception? They had largely disregarded the political issues involved.

In farm policy, the Kennedy administration was more politically adept than either Benson or the CED. The President compromised with the farm interests; in return for adequate income, the farmer had to pay in production controls. But though he almost achieved victory in 1962, he was rebuffed by the farmers in 1963. The farmers wanted higher incomes; but they were unwilling to accept serious controls of output. Here President Kennedy underestimated the political difficulties of imposing severe controls.

Over each of these disputed issues the advice of professional economists had been either rejected or substantially modified by politicians with executive or legislative responsibility. The underlying reason was the economists' neglect of the powerful noneconomic factors involved in the making of public policy.

The remedy is probably the responsibility of the economists. If they do have the specialized knowledge required to solve the nation's economic problems, they must first demonstrate it to the politicians. They will succeed only by broadening their studies into the wider realm of political economy—as distinct from theoretical economics; by demonstrating their awareness and understanding of the other relevant social and political factors at work, and by taking such practical limitations into account.

In return they are entitled to expect a greater willingness from politicians to listen to new ideas, and a new readiness to reject outworn economic dogma in favor of a more pragmatic approach to contemporary problems.

The precise nature of the contributions made by economists naturally depends on whether they work inside or outside the government. On the outside, in the academic world, their primary task is to advance the frontiers of economic knowledge, while on the inside they are mainly required to perform as economic technicians.

Major gains in pure economics, and ultimately in economic engineering (public policy), come from academic economists. These are the men who form the theories of income formation, production, growth, economic incentives, money, prices, wages, distribution, interest rates, consumption, investment taxation, spending, fiscal management, the balance of payments, and so on, and their views are ultimately reflected in official policy.

However, in the last generation, the trend of economics has been slowed in one respect, and the contribution of academic economists has diminished. This has resulted from the invasion of economics by mathematicians. Academic economists are becoming increasingly intrigued by mathematics but, unfortunately, its excessive use diverts our best brains to comparatively minor problems.

Economists should remember that Lord Keynes once said:

Mathematical economics often exercise an excessive fascination and influence over students who approach the subject without much previous training in technical mathematics. They are so easy as to be within the grasp of almost anyone, yet do introduce the student, on a small scale, to the delights of perceiving constructions of pure form and place toy bricks in his hands that he can manipulate himself, which gives a new thrill to those who have had no glimpse of the skyscraping architecture and minutely embellished monuments of modern mathematics.

For those economists who feel that politicians do not pay sufficient attention to their ideas, Lord Keynes also wrote:

The ideas of economists and political philosophers, both when they are right and when they are wrong, are more powerful than is commonly understood. Indeed the world is ruled by little else. Practical men, who believe themselves to be quite exempt from intellectual influences, are usually the slaves of some defunct economist. Madmen in authority, who hear voices in the air, are distilling their frenzy from some academic scribbler of a few years back. I am sure that the power of vested interests is vastly exaggerated compared with the gradual encroachment of ideas.

6

Relations with Business

In a capitalist society, the confidence of businessmen is obviously important. If businessmen sense that the government is hostile to their interests, the result is apt to be less enterprise and less investment. Even Keynes, who did not value businessmen highly, nevertheless warned President Franklin Roosevelt, in a letter dated November 2, 1938, that the recovery would be jeopardized if the President persecuted businessmen. After urging the President to improve confidence and thus stimulate investment, Lord Keynes wrote:

Businessmen have a different set of delusions from politicians; and need, therefore, different handling. They are, however, much milder than politicians, at the same time allured and terrified by the glare of publicity, easily persuaded to be "patriots," perplexed, bemused, indeed terrified, yet only too anxious to take a cheerful view, vain perhaps but very unsure of themselves, pathetically responsive to a kind word. . . . If you work them into the surly, obstinate, terrified mood, of which domestic animals, wrongly handled, are so capable, the nation's burdens will not get carried to market; and in the end public opinion will veer their way.*

On September 26, 1962, President Kennedy told the business editors:

* Sir Richard Kahn, Lord Keynes' favorite student and coworker, kindly put this letter at my disposal and gave me permission to quote it.

I would like to say one word about the competitive market system because I think there seems to be, on occasion, some questions among businessmen as to the views of those of us in Washington on this matter. *Our experience during the present expansion has also demonstrated our ability to achieve impressive economic gains without shrinking the area of market freedom.* I regard the preservation and strengthening of the free market as a cardinal objective of this or any Administration's policies.

It is well to remind ourselves from time to time of the benefits we derive from the maintenance of a free market system. The system rests on freedom of consumer choice, the profit motive, and vigorous competition for the buyer's dollar. By relying on these spontaneous economic forces, we secure these benefits. . . .

. . . .

The free market is a decentralized regulator of our economic system. *The free market is not only a more efficient decision maker than even the wisest central planning body, but even more important, the free market keeps economic power widely dispersed. It thus is a vital underpinning of our democratic system.*

Earlier, at a press conference of April 18, 1962, following the serious differences with the steel industry, the President said, "We were not then and are not now unmindful of the steel industry's needs for profits, modernization and investment capital."

Unlike Franklin Roosevelt, Kennedy was not disposed to abuse businessmen. But there were times when he had to speak frankly to them. The steel episode is one example. Boeing's refusal to accept the open shop, with the result that operations in the aerospace industry were curtailed, elicited a severe criticism of a strong business organization. Against such criticisms, the President also could rebuke labor men when he considered them unreasonable and remiss in not fulfilling their responsibilities—as when he criticized the labor leaders in the New York newspaper strike. Again at a White House Economic Conference of May 21, 1962, the President rebuked "a number of New York bankers who had been present in Vienna [and] had spoken in very alarming terms about the . . . federal deficit . . . and prophesized that it would bring inflation . . ." This talk, of course, would weaken the dollar.

Again, in his famous Yale speech of June 11, 1962, the President undoubtedly irritated many businessmen. His general theme was that businessmen tended to swallow myths.

Mythology distracts us everywhere—in government as in business, in politics as in economics, in foreign affairs as in domestic policy. But today I want to particularly consider the myth and reality in our national economy. In recent months many have come to feel, as I do, that the dialogue between the parties—between business and government—is clogged by illusion and platitude and fails to reflect the true realities of contemporary American society.

There are three great areas of our domestic affairs in which, today, there is a danger that illusion may prevent effective action. They are, first, the question of public fiscal policy . . . third, the matter of confidence, business confidence or public confidence, or simply confidence in America. I want to talk about all three, and I want to talk about them carefully and dispassionately—and I emphasize that I am concerned here not with political debate but with finding ways to separate false problems from real ones.

If a contest in angry argument were forced upon it, no Administration could shrink from response, and history does not suggest that American Presidents are totally without resources in an engagement forced upon them because of hostility in one sector of society. But in the wider national interest, we need not partisan wrangling, but common concentration on common problems. I come this morning to ask you to join in this great task.

At the very beginning of his administration, Kennedy ran afoul of businessmen. For years a Businessmen's Advisory Council (BAC) had been more or less attached to the Department of Commerce. Members of this group had access, prematurely, to government plans and thus achieved advantages over their rivals. Even under Eisenhower they had experienced some conflicts with Congressional leaders. Under Kennedy, a head-on clash occurred between the leaders of business thought and the Kennedy administration. Hence, even before the steel episode there was trouble. The BAC had been a primary source for recruiting businessmen for the Eisenhower administration.

BUSINESSMEN AND FISCAL POLICY

In some aspects of its tax programs, the Kennedy administration invited the antagonism of the business interest. In the 1961 tax program, the Treasury was especially anxious to remove a tax inequity, not only on the grounds of equity, but even more to improve the balance of payments. The Treasury's position was that large exportations of capital were contributing to the weakness of the dollar; and these exports were the result partly of the non-taxation of profits reinvested abroad by affiliates of American corporations. Domestic corporations were not allowed this privilege. But American corporations operating abroad protested vigorously on the grounds that the government was changing the rules of the game after business, assured of this tax favoritism, had invested abroad. Corporations with foreign affiliates are generally large and well represented. They publicized the view that the government was now trying to determine the allocations of resources through a new tax policy. A similar barrage of criticism was evoked when, in July 1963, the administration proposed an interest equalization tax as a means of discouraging capital exports. In its own defense, the government could say that there is never a guarantee that the tax structure will not change. But the administration lost this battle on the whole—not only was the legislation on taxing foreign affiliates defeated but the administration's attempt to secure the change earned it the hostility of certain strong business interests.

In some respects it is difficult to understand the hostility of businessmen to the Kennedy administration unless it is because businessmen often oppose the government and especially Democratic regimes. The Kennedy administration offered businessmen an investment credit program, and a liberalization of depreciation allowances at an annual cost of $2.5 billion, a program to which the reaction of businessmen was surprisingly cold.

In another area, the government also attempted to oppose business; but here again the major results were inadequate legislation and administrative rulings and hostility of business. The issue was travel and entertainment expenses allowable as deductions against income in the determination of tax liabilities. Abuses are numerous. Businessmen force the government to share the costs of luxurious living through the large deductions allowable under entertainment and travel for businessmen. The view was expressed that the Kentucky Derby would be liquidated under the new legislation since it was largely supported by expenditures allowed as business expenses under the income tax law—and similar outlays were allowable as expenses under the income tax law. Even before any serious changes became applicable, a mammoth campaign by hotels, restaurants, and other interested parties forced the administration to modify the proposed regulations. This attempt to correct serious abuses in the administration of the income tax again yielded small results and earned the administration business hostility. It had been known for years that in various ways high-income groups, though subject to maximum marginal rates of 91 per cent and average rates of 80 per cent seldom paid more than 50 per cent, with similar reductions for other high-income groups. Excessive allowances for entertainment and travel are relevant here.

Another controversy with businessmen originated when the administration proposed that interest and dividends be taxed at the source. In one campaign of deceit, some of the financial community flooded the Congress with mail, protesting what a large proportion of the writers assumed to be a new tax. Such amounts of mail had not been received since Lend-Lease.

This operation elicited responses from the President on several occasions. Thus, at a May 9, 1962, news conference, he said:

> The paid advertisements and circulars financed by the savings and loan associations, who have made great profits in recent years and paid very little in taxes—I think something like $5½ billion, while paying $70 million in taxes—by banks and others, have led many people to believe (1) that this is a new tax or a tax increase; (2) that it will take money unjustly from honest taxpayers. . . .
>
> Not a single one of these charges is true. . . . This is not a new tax. It has been on the books for years.
>
> That is tax evasion, tax evasion of $800 million a year, which must be made up by other taxpayers who pay their taxes. And it should be remembered that about 80 per cent of dividend income goes to fewer than 7 per cent of the taxpayers, whose income exceeds $10,000 a year. . . .

In the great debate over a substantial cut, in 1962–1963, many businessmen supported the administration. They wanted reduced taxes as a weapon for increasing incentives and profits. Whereas they would have objected strenuously to a stimulation of the economy by an additional $11 billion spending program, they were receptive to an $11 billion tax cut. With help from Under Secretary of the Treasury Henry Fowler, a large group of leading business-men organized to support the tax cut. Though they asked for cautious spending, they did not set the condition that they would support the tax cut only if substantial cuts were made in spending.

Of course, there was not complete agreement between the government and business on the tax cut. Some businessmen wanted large cuts in expenditures; others held that business received an inadequate share of the reduction in taxes; and others saw in the resultant deficit a threat to price stability. One important source of conflict revolved around the issue of tax reform. Originally the hope was that tax cuts would be accompanied by tax reform, with a resultant elimination of loopholes and a broadening of the tax base. But business interests wanted a tax cut without the reform. They won their point, partly because consideration of reform would greatly delay the passage of the tax bill.

PERSUASION ON THE WAGE-PRICE FRONT

President Kennedy's attempt to keep wages and prices from rising excessively was most irritating to businessmen. The administration had pressured the steel workers to keep their wage demands at a level that could be financed without a price rise. But immediately the head of U.S. Steel announced a $6 a ton price increase. Upset by this breach of faith, the President mobilized all his resources to force the steel companies to rescind the price increase. The President succeeded. But the interference with the pricing policies of the U.S. Steel and other companies, and the aggressive manner of correcting the situation, aroused great fears among businessmen that the new administration was out to control the whole economy.

Obviously, the business community would not be pleased with the President's comments in his April 11, 1962, news conference:*

Simultaneous and identical actions of United States Steel and other leading steel corporations increasing steel prices by some $6 a ton constitute a wholly unjustifiable and irresponsible defiance of the public interest. In this serious hour in our Nation's history, when we

* Cf. Chapter 13.

are confronted with grave crises in Berlin and Southeast Asia, when we are devoting our energies to economic recovery and stability, when we are asking reservists to leave their homes and families for months on end and servicemen to risk their lives . . . and asking Union members to hold down their wage requests at a time when restraint and sacrifice are being asked of every citizen, the American people will find it hard, as I do, to accept a situation in which a tiny handful of steel executives, whose pursuit of private power and profit exceeds their sense of public responsibility, can show such utter contempt for the interests of 185 million Americans.

THE PRESIDENT AND THE STOCK MARKET DECLINE

In the spring of 1962, the stock market suffered a serious decline. Looking for a scapegoat, the business community blamed the President. Had he not reduced the prospects of business profits and threatened the free enterprise system through his interference with the steel industry? Had he not, during and after the campaign, threatened the stability of the system through the acceptance of large public spending deficits? Was not the unfavorable balance of payments a symptom of irresponsible fiscal and monetary policies—as evident in the outflow of short-term capital—and, as a result of these policies, had not the country experienced a loss of competitive position related to inflationary fiscal and monetary policies?

I do not think that the stock market decline could be blamed on the President. Such collapses, crises of confidence, seem to occur about once in a generation: 1873, 1893, 1907, 1929, 1962. The unusual prosperity induced by the aftermath of two wars and improved governmental policies postponed the collapse until 1962.

Why did it come at this time? In one sense John Kennedy could be blamed. He had made it clear that inflation was not inevitable: His wage policy was one facet of his anti-inevitability-of-inflation policy. But if he was guilty on this account he could well expect even greater appreciation for his contribution to stabilizing the currency. This was not generally expected from a Democratic President. The relevance of the prospects of inflation for stock market values lay largely in the point that the continued increase in stock market prices was related to inflationary prospects. As inflation proceeds, equity prices rise and even more than commodity prices, for profits tend to rise more than prices, and equity prices depend largely on expected profits.

But aside from revised views on the future of inflation, what else might account for the rather abrupt decline in stock market prices? The explanation is relatively simple. A general consensus had emerged that stock market prices had risen too much.

The rise had been sensational in the years 1942–1962 and 1952–1962:

	1942– March 1962[a]	1952– March 1962[a]
Common stocks[a]	601%	173%
Corporate profits after taxes	169	81

SOURCE: Calculated from President's economic report, 1963.

[a] Peak before 1962 collapse.

By August 1963, the SEC index of stock prices had risen above its previous low.

Prices of equities rise in response to general inflation, to the special gains accruing to owners of equities because the corporation is managed on behalf of the stockholders, and generally to improved prospects for profits. But these prices do not go up forever. At some point, the views of the bears, i.e., those viewing the market as being too high, become the dominant ones, and the price of equities tumbles. This happened in 1962. By early 1962, prices had risen three to four times as much as corporate profits after taxes, an indication of inflationary expectations, now being disappointed.

A relevant factor was the large reduction in the relative return on equities vis-à-vis bonds in 1962 as compared with returns in 1952. The rise of yields on Aaa corporate bonds from 1952 to March 1962 was 2.20 per cent; in the same period, yields on Moody's common stocks, declined by 2.5 per cent. The annual yield had moved 4.7 per cent per year in favor of bonds. Obviously a relative rise of returns for bonds of 4.7 per cent was bound to affect the relative investments in equities unfavorably. Improved business prospects abroad vis-à-vis the United States were also a factor of some importance.

The steel episode did not play a large part, though it probably contributed to a rising consensus that inflation was not inevitable and, hence, that the public had misjudged inflation potentials.

Other factors contributing to a decline of the market were: the increased competitive position of Europe and Japan; a profit squeeze related to excess capacity; sluggish growth (a 10 per cent real rise of GNP from 1957 to 1961); some anticipations of a recession (the market frequently anticipates recessions); and, finally, many irrational factors.

One of the peculiarities of the stock market is its irrational behavior. Professionals are presumed to correct the mistakes of the market. When prices are too low relative to rational expectations, the professionals are supposed to buy and correct the mistakes; and when they are too high, to sell.

Keynes *General Theory* explains why the professionals do not correct errors of the market.

They are concerned, not with what an investment is really worth to a man who buys it "for keeps," but with what the market will value it at, under the influence of mass psychology, three months or a year hence. . . .

Or, to change the metaphor slightly, professional investment may be likened to those newspaper competitions in which the competitors have to pick out the six prettiest faces from a hundred photographs, the prize being awarded to the competitor whose choice most nearly corresponds to the average preferences of the competitors as a whole; so that each competitor has to pick, not those faces which he himself finds prettiest, but those which he thinks likeliest to catch the fancy of the other competitors, all of whom are looking at the problem from the same point of view. It is not a case of choosing those which, to the best of one's judgment, are really the prettiest, nor even those which average opinion genuinely thinks the prettiest. We have reached the third degree where we devote our intelligences to anticipating what average opinion expects the average opinion to be. And there are some, I believe, who practise the fourth, fifth and higher degrees.

On numerous occasions the President was asked about the decline in the stock market. On May 17, 1962, the President said he "would not attempt to figure its ups and downs." But he noted declines in the past had preceded prosperous years. At a White House conference of May 21, 1962, he belittled the effect of lack of confidence in him. Under Eisenhower, business had confidence in the government, and yet there were declines in business and security prices. The President pointed out that "there have been many, at least four, occasions since the end of the second War when the stock market has dropped at the time the economy was rising." On June 7, 1962, the President volunteered the information that the market was overpriced. "Price-earning ratios which averaged on Dow Jones 23 to 1 could not be justified unless there was heavy inflation in prospect. And we have been working to prevent inflation. . . ." Admitting that businessmen preferred a Republican President, the President nevertheless refused to believe that businessmen were using the market decline to force concessions out of him. Clearly the President had received much undeserved blame for the collapse of the market. But as he observed on more than one occasion, he received no credit for the ensuing rise.

RECONCILIATION WITH BUSINESS

Despite the conflicts with businessmen, arising from issues of fiscal policy, tax reform, and wage and price policy, the administration's relations with business greatly improved in 1963. The President was anxious that there should be no persecution of businessmen. He probably realized that businessmen would never be friendly with government. (Even under the friendly administration of Eisenhower, they were not content.) But the President also sensed the relation between business confidence and the state of the economy. He was concerned with the disappointing level of investment in 1961 and 1962, and he could not be certain that administration policies and statements had not contributed to the low level of investment. He also knew that business would have to accept inevitable public programs inclusive of deficits. But wherever possible he would appease business without imposing blocks on important legislation. His investment credit program, the liberalization of depreciation allowances, his taking the businessmen into his confidence on such issues as the balance of payments, tax programs, the foreign aid program, his partial abandonment of a policy of price-wage persuasion, his containment of new spending programs, his reappointment of William Martin, the favored central banker of the financial world, to the chairmanship of the Federal Reserve Board—all of these made the businessmen less hostile to the government than in 1962.

From the start, a grievance against Kennedy was that he had not recruited businessmen in adequate numbers or at high posts as Eisenhower did. I wrote in *The Economics of the Political Parties* that on the first 200 major appointments, business, finance, and insurance had provided only 6 per cent of Kennedy's high level appointments, whereas under Eisenhower their contribution had been 36 per cent of 188 appointments. In the later appointments Kennedy selected more businessmen. But clearly, government and the academic world were much more important origins of high level appointments under Kennedy than under Eisenhower. In *Harper's* (November 1963) Joseph Kraft estimated that a majority of Kennedy's top appointments came from the academic world.

By 1962, the President, undoubtedly in response to criticism, made special efforts to find outstanding businessmen to serve the administration. But he was not very successful, although the scouting for businessmen to administer the foreign aid program was intense. A businessman-lawyer selected to head the Foreign Aid Administration proved to be a failure despite his penchant for administrators who had met a payroll. Corporation leaders are not disposed to allow their better executives to serve the government. Vice presidents who have proved to be liabilities are more likely to be encouraged to migrate to Washington. From the academic world of government, higher levels of talent are available than from the business world.

In an able address at the University of Michigan, on November 15, 1962, Professor James Tobin, a former member of the President's Council of Economic Advisers, attempted to resolve the differences between government and business. He could find little for businessmen to criticize. The government was not seeking nationalization. Expenditures on *civilian* activities, relative to income, had scarcely changed since 1929. The rise of government's relative contribution to the GNP was largely a reflection of increased *security* outlays. Nor was the government trying to swing the balance of power: "I do not see on the national agenda any serious proposal to alter in favor of labor organizations the balance of industrial power. . . ."

On the wage issue Tobin said, "The only course open to the President is to try to throw his own moral weight and that of public opinion on the side of restraint in strategic wage negotiations and related price decisions."

On the issue of use of resources, Tobin implied that too many concessions may have been made to business: "We should not assume that public uses of resources are per se wasteful and burdensome, or . . . that private uses reflecting consumer choice are per se frivolous and valueless." He added that a rise of security outlays should not then necessarily bring a decline of nonsecurity outlays.

In a speech in Florida on November 19, 1963, a few days before his death, the President sought to assure the business community of the friendliness of his administration to business. He offered the following points as evidence: a rise of corporate profits of 43 per cent in three years, the sale of public assets to private interests, the special tax measures on behalf of business, the private operation of the satellite communication system, the small increase of federal spending, and the unwillingness of the government to expand its activities unless the case for federal intervention was indisputable. The President was clearly troubled by business hostility. But whatever he said or did he knew that business would not embrace the government, and especially a Democratic government.

PART III

Specific Problems

7

Fiscal Policy: The President's Weapon

MODERN FISCAL THEORY

Fiscal policy was the new instrument for achieving stability, full employment, and adequate growth. These were the main objectives of the Kennedy administration. Professor Alvin Hansen, writing in the *New Republic* (October 20, 1962) adds, "Lifting the standards of the submerged tenth" and correcting the imbalance between the general private affluence of the great majority of Americans and the poverty of the public sector. . ." is imperative. Where demand is inadequate, the government, through spending programs (and) or tax cuts raises total demand and thus counters inadequate purchases with a rise of the government contribution.

J. M. Keynes relied primarily on adjustments in public spending as a weapon to bring about full employment. He was prepared to stimulate demand even if the public expenditures were otherwise sterile.

"If the Treasury were to fill old bottles with bank-notes, bury them at suitable depths in disused coal mines which are then filled up to the surface with town rubbish, and leave it to private enterprise on well tried principles of *laissez-faire* to dig the notes up again . . . there need to be no more unemployment. . . . The real income of the community, and its capital wealth also would probably become a good deal greater . . ."

President Kennedy's ultimate acceptance of modern economics probably contributed more to the advance of this kind of thinking than did its dissemination by economists, for he had access to the minds of the influential businessmen and politicians who were most obtuse in accepting modern advances. No public official, certainly no President, has matched President Kennedy in his vigorous support and dissemination of modern economics. And he moved ahead even though he was aware that large public spending and deficits were probably not political assets. This required great courage. Indeed he had to weigh the liability of unemployment against the asset of respectable monetary and fiscal policy. But I believe that since a large proportion of our 180 million population fears public deficits and only 1 to 2 million families suffer from excess unemployment, the political liabilities exceed the assets of modern fiscal policy.

EARLY CRITICISM OF THE PRESIDENT'S FISCAL POLICIES

Initially, there was much criticism of the President's views on fiscal policy and, also, of his failure to persuade the American people to accept modern fiscal theories. As early as March 30, 1961, Walter Lippmann criticized the President for accepting the view "that for the present he must follow the Eisenhower economic ideology which was the fiscal orthodoxy of the age before the Great Depression." Lippmann believed that the President should explain to the country that the budget is a great fiscal engine, which "has to be managed in such a way as to promote a stabilized growth of the economy."

Criticisms came especially from those who wanted to introduce a massive spending program. One of the most vocal critics was Oscar Gass, a former adviser of former Secretary Morgenthau. Writing in *Commentary* he referred to the President's early disposition to increase federal spending in the second year of the recession as even less than under Eisenhower. But Gass paid little attention to the political aspects of the problem, as did Robert Lekachman, an able economist writing in the *New Leader*. Moreover, though Lekachman seemed to want a more vigorous fiscal policy and seemed to support a spending program, he was not certain that the problem would be solved by fiscal policies alone. In his view the unemployment problem may be intractable, and may require more fundamental adjustments.

In the second half of 1962, the President became the target of particularly severe criticism, which came especially from economists of liberal persuasion—and perhaps from economists in general. Paul Samuelson, that brilliant economist and friend of the administration, wrote in the *London Financial Times* in July 1962: "The time has come for a sizeable across-the-board reduction in tax rates on persons and corporations. This can be expected to add thousands of millions of dollars to the spending stream, dollars that are sorely needed if recession and stagnation are to be averted." He warned that "a President hated by business who is successful— in the Roosevelt and Truman pattern—is one thing. A President who is hated by business because of policies he feels necessary in the modern age and who can be associated with failure is another. . . ."

FORECASTING

Proper fiscal policy depends on adequate forecasting. If, early in 1962, the President had been assured that the economy, on the basis of current policies, would yield a gross national product, say, of $570 billion plus or minus $5 billion, then he would have had the facts on which to mobilize fiscal and monetary weapons. But the forecast, upon which the 1963 budget was based, was a GNP of $570 billion for the calendar year 1962; the actual GNP was only $553.6 billion—$16.4 billion, or 3 per cent, below the forecast. This may not seem to be a serious error in relation to the total GNP, but it was a rise of $35 billion from 1961 as compared with an anticipated gain of $51 billion. The government's forecast was more accurate for 1963.

How are serious errors incurred? In January 1962, the President wanted a balanced budget for fiscal year 1963. Such a balance could have been achieved only with an optimistic forecast, that is, a high income would yield adequate revenue to balance the budget. It was generally known that the forecast was optimistic. Henry Wallich, the able ex-member of the Council of Economic Advisers, said as much in an article for the *Journal of Commerce* (January 23, 1962). Some presidential advisers realized that if the anticipated income were not achieved a deficit would emerge; and under those conditions a deficit would be necessary. The failure to achieve the anticipated GNP resulted in part from the slow improvement in the balance of payments and the stock market collapse of May 1962, factors contributing to the slow growth of investment. It is indeed unfortunate that forecasts have to be made for periods of six to eighteen months ahead. They are reasonably reliable for six months, and much less so for eighteen months. At the end of 1961, most economists basing themselves on the 1961 improvement were optimistic for 1962. Paul Samuelson wrote in the *Wall Street Journal* from Japan, late in 1961: ". . . if the Kennedy team's luck holds up, the largest of the Free World's nations should help show in 1962 that a 'mixed economy' can develop improved standards of living, widely shared throughout the population."

The Treasury and other departments have been working hard to improve forecasting techniques and thus to increase the contribution of fiscal policy. In this area, the National Bureau of Economic Research has contributed much. One can learn a great deal from their work, especially from the numerous leading indicators that, on the basis of past experience, anticipate economic trends. But it is important to realize that these relationships rest on past policies, which on the whole rule out intervention on the part of government. Where the government is more likely to intervene, or when new and unexpected forces emerge, the results may not conform to expectation. An econometric technique, used by Daniel Suits at Michigan University, provided forecasts which proved reliable on the whole.

THE PRESIDENT'S BACKGROUND AND FISCAL POLICY

The President's whole background was rather unfavorable for the acceptance of the fiscal policy approach. The sons of affluent businessmen are not likely to be enamored with increased government intervention. Moreover, as a congressman, the crucial issue confronting the President was structural unemployment in Massachusetts. Here the cure was unlikely to be rising public outlays to treat general inadequacy of demand but, rather, restrictions on imports to reduce textile competition, minimum wages low enough to impair Southern advantages, and increased defense contracts to reduce unemployment.

THE EARLY POSITION ON FISCAL POLICY

President Kennedy's Task Force on the Economy (Paul Samuelson, chairman) which included exclusively Keynesian economists (such as Heller, Tobin, and myself) reported to the President on January 6, 1961. The report nevertheless was not strongly Keynesian. On public expenditures, the verdict was to go slowly. There was no recommendation of tax cuts, unless the economy improved very little in 1961. But the report raised two issues which were to become dominant ones in the next four years. First, the economy was sluggish, and improvement was imperative. Second, as much as we would like to provide the economy with plenty of credit and low interest rates, the precarious state of the balance of payments precluded a cheap money policy; and, therefore, a larger burden would have to be put on fiscal policy. The President seldom discussed the economy in the next three years without emphasizing its sluggishness (and high unemployment) and the heavy burden which fiscal policy must bear.

In his special message on recovery and growth of February 2, 1961, the President emphasized the need of reversing the downward trend in our economy to narrow the gap of unused potential, "to abate the waste and misery of unemployment." Hence the measures to alleviate distress and stimulate growth. His awareness of modern economics was evident: "An unbalanced economy does produce a balanced budget. The Treasury's pocketbook suffers when the economy performs poorly."

Even as early as March 24, 1961, when the President sent a special message to the Congress on the budget and fiscal policy, he presented a far from stodgy view: "We can afford to do what must be done. . . ." Year-by-year balancing was not necessary. A cyclical balance was adequate, with deficits in recession periods. Federal expenditures and revenue should contribute to "growth and maximum employment within a setting of reasonable price stability:

". . . We will not waste our resources on inefficient or undesirable expenditures simply because the economy is slack—nor, in order to run a surplus, will we deny our people essential services. . . ."

In the President's view the budget should be "made an instrument of prosperity and stability, and not a deterrent to recovery." Yet he still was greatly disturbed by the growing deficit, and he would have hoped later for surpluses to offset deficits.

It could scarcely be said that the President had become a convert by the end of 1961. In the midst of the Berlin crisis in 1961 the President realized that he might well ask for a tax rise because of the increase of defense expenditures of $6 billion since January 1961. In his July 25, 1961, message to the American people on the Berlin crisis, the President seemed to want a substantial tax increase. ". . . Nevertheless, should an increase in taxes be needed—because of events in the next few months—to achieve that balance, or because of subsequent defense rises, those increased taxes will be requested in January." His advisers finally persuaded him that a tax rise at the beginning of a revival would abort the recovery.

His budget review in the latter part of 1961 revealed that the President was still concerned over the budgetary deficit. In view of the demands of the military, he would watch expenditures carefully. Large deficits would bring inflation; but he went so far as to agree that a surplus would depress the economy.

In his 1963 budget, presented in January 1962, the President proposed a balanced budget. But a balancing of this budget required a spirited economic advance throughout the year, which was not forthcoming. Disappointing revenues and some increases of expenditures brought a large deficit which did not please the President. Yet on the whole the situation would have been worse had not the deficit emerged.

A More Advanced Position

By the middle of 1962, prospects looked dim, and in the third quarter of 1962 GNP in stable dollars rose only by $1.5 billion, a rise consistent with a substantial increase of unemployment. Unhappy economic developments in 1962, with advances not nearly as favorable as in 1961; the stock market collapse of May 1962; the steel episode; and the related clashes with businessmen all seemed to drive the President into a more advanced fiscal position.

At Yale University, on June 11, 1962, the President presented the most advanced views on fiscal policy ever made by a President, perhaps the most brilliant address on economic issues ever delivered by a President of the United States. By May 1962 there was beginning to be serious talk of a large tax cut to stimulate the economy. I presided over a meeting of the Treasury consultants at this time which was rather gloomy about prospects and eager for a large tax cut as the most effective way out. The President, according to Joseph Alsop, had heard about this meeting and it had influenced him to move towards a tax cut. Alsop claimed (*Washington Post,* April 26, 1963) that wrong forecasts by these economists had led the President to support a tax cut. But my reply to the *Washington Post* was that whether the forecasts were right or wrong the net result was good; for a tax cut was needed.

In the Yale speech, the President proclaimed: "For the great enemy of the truth is very often not the lie-deliberate, contrived and dishonest—but the myth-persistent, persuasive and unrealistic. Too often we hold fast to the cliches of our forbears. . . ."

On the issue of the size of government the President stated that federal government expenditures and debt were smaller in relation to the economy than fifteen years ago, and that government expenditures for nondefense purposes have grown less since World War II than spending of industry, education, commerce, and agriculture.

On the budget the President showed the absurdity of concentrating on the administrative budget, which excludes trust funds and does not distinguish between long-term investments and operating expenditures and loans from straight expenditures. He also commented on the myth that federal deficits bring inflation. In the early postwar years, he said, sizable surpluses did not prevent inflation, and persistent deficits did not upset the basic price stability.

On the myths of dangerously rising public debt, the President pointed out that debts are declining in relation to GNP, and that whereas private debt rose by 305 per cent since the war, and state and local debts by 378 per cent, the federal debt increased only by 8 per cent.

The objectives of economic policy are clear. But their attainment is difficult. How to regulate money so that expansion is had at home and stability of the dollar abroad? What price and wage policies are to be supported? How can we profit from automation without greatly increasing unemployment? How can we provide adequate demand for our output. . . ?

The President reminded us that Senator Proxmire counseled low money rates and austere fiscal policy; but the Bank for International Settlements urged high money rates and large deficits. Who is right, asked the President?

If there is any current trend toward meeting present problems with old cliches, this is the moment to stop it—before it lands us all in a bog of sterile acrimony.

The stereotypes I have been discussing distract out attention and divide our effort. . . .

THE PRESIDENT AND THE TAX CUT

By mid-1962 the pressure for a tax cut had attracted much support. The President was moving in this direction but was still uncertain about the economic trends and fearful of Congressional intransigence. Therefore, he was disposed to wait until 1963 for any decisive move. For this procrastination he received much criticism.

On January 24, 1963, the President sent his special message on tax reduction and reform to the Congress. Here he presented in much detail the philosophy behind the tax bill. He defended, as he later did in his Committee for Economic Development address of May 9, the tax cut. The objective was not merely to deal with a possible recession, but rather to contend with the long-run problems of inadequate growth and unemployment. A deficit resulting from the tax cut would be much smaller than that associated with a recession. At times he wavered between objectives. Yet he was essentially right in emphasizing the contribution of a tax cut both to increased growth and, also, to the prevention of a recession or the dilution of its strength.

In the middle of his fight for a reduced tax burden, the President warned his staff not to bring in new spending programs for fiscal year 1965. In the Ways and Means Committee, the administration had squeezed through on crucial issues by votes of 11–10; and any further spending programs might well kill the tax bill. This, in a sense, was the President's reply to the liberals who criticised him for not urging larger outlays.

In his tax message he made a substantial concession to the conservative and Republican viewpoint. Indeed he often pointed out the folly of stimulating the economy with a tax cut and then de-flating it with a corresponding reduction of expenditures. But he chose private spending over the public spending route.

The Convert to Modern Economics

In his support and drive for the tax cut, President Kennedy missed very few of the arguments used by economists in recent years. Among the points made were: Our tax system had evolved since the early 1940s as an anti-inflation weapon; but with a slug-gish economy a different tax burden and structure is required. Even as early as 1961, he referred to the $8 billion surplus that would have been available with full employment. But in 1963, he saw in the automatic rise of taxes in response to recovery a deterrent to further advance. In his tax message he said:

. . . But it has become increasing clear . . . that the largest single barrier to full employment of our manpower and resources and to a higher rate of economic growth is the unrealistically heavy drag of Federal income taxes on private purchasing power, initiative and in-centive. Our economy is checkreined today by a war-born tax system at a time when it is far more in need of the spur than the bit.

Undoubtedly the high tax rates in vogue in 1963 contributed to the tax-cut approval. Had they been as high when Keynes urged the expenditure approach, Keynes undoubtedly would have pressed for tax cuts also.

Again the case for the tax cut rested partly on the multiple rise of GNP in relation to the tax cut. Thus in his April 24, 1963, press conference, he said the "tax cut would put $10 billion directly in an 18 month period, into the hands of our people, which under the multiplier, will mean $30 billion, and I think can make a very im-portant difference in reducing our unemployment. . . ."

In an address to the National Conference of the Business Com-mittee for Tax Reduction, on September 10, 1963, the President again stressed the gains to be associated with the tax cut: "Tax re-duction was essential to balance our international accounts, our budget and above all, to balance our economy at levels of full employment."

The resultant rise of investment would improve our competitive position abroad; the gains of consumption and investment would provide more jobs; by "removing a restrictive brake on national growth and income, it [the tax cut would] . . . work against the recurrent forces of recession," and, finally, it would, through raising income and federal revenues, bring the country nearer to a balanced budget.

Again, the President stressed his determination to economize on expenditures. He pointed out that if federal civilian employment had increased in the last year as much as population, the rise would have been eight times the actual increase.

President Kennedy, disturbed over Republican mobilization to kill the tax bill, on September 18 went over the heads of Congress and appealed to the American public to support the tax bill. In this presentation the President was eloquent about the effects of the tax cut on unemployment. Above all, it was necessary to create more jobs, and a tax cut was the way to do it. The tax cut was not the only weapon, but it was "the keystone of the arch." On budget balancing the President insisted that prosperity is the road to a balanced budget. And he agreed with a view of Chairman Wilbur Mills, of September 16, in which the major emphasis was put on the tax bill as a decision to assure that the economy would grow, and that an increased share of output would be subject to the decisions of the private economy. Thus, the tax cut was intended as an affirmation of the appeal of tax cuts against increased public expenditures.

A tax cut on top of a deficit is certainly an advanced fiscal policy approach. The President had to defend this against the antispending school. He told the Committee for Economic Development, on May 9, 1963, that irresponsible finance depends on conditions. With full employment and capacity fully utilized, it would be "dangerous for the Federal Government to raise its expenditures without raising taxes, or to cut taxes without an equal cut in expenditures." The President even approved five deficits and a rise of $23 billion in the national debt under Eisenhower as fiscally responsible programs. ". . . We, too, are adding to the debt at the same time that our gross national product is moving ahead much faster."

Following modern fiscal theory, the President also saw little danger of inflation from the increase of deficits: "Today's large volume of unused resources indicates that the effects of increased demand can be met through expanded production and employment, and that prices and costs need not rise. . . ."

The President was aware that inflation might come from rising demand, in turn related to private as well as public demand. In order to increase demand, it was necessary to stimulate consumers as well as producers to spend more. "When consumers purchase more goods," he told the New York Economic Club on December 14, 1962, "men are hired instead of laid off, investment increases and profits are high."

No President before Kennedy had dared to introduce a tax cut on top of a deficit or ask for deficits not only in periods of recession but even after an extended recovery, so long as demand remained substantially deficient. The President distinguished between deficits in boom times and in periods of large unemployment; he related the deficit to the size of the economy and was not impressed by absolute rises; he saw the need of correcting the drag on the economy when revenues rise more than expenditures. The President could contrast the contribution of the Kennedy administration with an excess of expenditures over receipts in 1961 and 1962 of $5.5 billion as against the negative contribution of Eisenhower, with an excess of revenue receipts over expenditures of $6.5 billion in a similar period.

Massive increases in expenditures were not on the Kennedy agenda. But he did not repeat Eisenhower's mistake of increasing revenues more than expenditures—especially with a sluggish economy.

Many liberals were disappointed that the President did not depend more on a spending program, partly because taxpayers are the affluent group as against those who profit from spending programs, and partly because they believed that public spending was inadequate. They did not agree with an able economist, John Lintner, who told the Joint Economic Committee on February 5, 1963, that the value of additional private spending in the next few years is clearly greater than further increases in federal expenditures. But the spending approach was not available to the President.

8

The Tax Cut and Some Relevant Aspects of Fiscal Policy

MONETARY VS. FISCAL POLICY

In recent years the trend has been from dependence on monetary policy to greater recourse to fiscal policy. Substantial over-all deficits in the balance of payments stemming partly from exports of short-term capital in response to higher short-term interest rates abroad have further strengthened the attraction of fiscal policy. With higher short-term rates the contribution of monetary policy to expansion is reduced, and hence with given objectives, fiscal policy must contribute more.

But the view of the need of greater dependence on fiscal policy was not a universal one. George Terborgh and Beryl Sprinkel (*New Republic,* October 20, 1962 and *Congressional Record,* July 13, 1963, p. 12393) contended that the association of income with monetary supplies is much higher than with government deficits. Hence they would depend primarily on monetary expansion to raise spending. One of the arguments for easy money is that it does not cost the Treasury deficits. (Any inflationary effects and, hence, higher costs are of course an offset.)

In the discussion of tax cuts, the relation of monetary and fiscal policy received much attention. Obviously a rise in the deficit would mean increased issues of Treasury securities. Who would buy them? One can argue that the rise of deficits would bring an increase of income two to four times as great; and with rising incomes, savings would respond and would be the source of increased purchases. Hence there would not follow a rise in the rate of interest. Another approach is to finance the deficit out of created money and thereby to contribute to higher prices of securities and prevent a rise of interest rates. But if savings respond to the rise of income sufficiently there would be no need for creating money to finance the deficit. However, if they do not, and a $10 billion tax cut induces a rise of GNP of $30 billion, then the tax cut may not make a large contribution, a likely outcome should the Federal Reserve System not provide the money needed to validate the $30 billion gain of income.

In his testimony before the Joint Economic Committee, on February 1, 1963, Mr. Martin, chairman of the Federal Reserve Board, seemed to feel that the deficit would not be financed out of increased money.

But the statement of Mr. Martin suggests only that the "Fed" has responsibilities to the nation as well as to the Treasury and that every issue of debt should not require a corresponding expansion of money. In fact his statement admits that the Federal Reserve should match growth with additional money. Perhaps he was implying some doubts on whether a tax cut would yield much additional income. But he was prepared to finance any added income forthcoming.

REPERCUSSIONS OF THE TAX CUT ON INCOME AND EMPLOYMENT

One good reason for a tax cut is that a cut of about $10 billion will bring an annual rise of gross national product, after a few years, of at least $30 billion, and this would be a permanent increase. Most of the additional income left to the taxpayer following a tax cut will be spent, though a substantial part will be siphoned off in tax receipts, repayment of debt, and the like. The rise of consumption will also induce more investment in plant, inventories, and residential construction; and reductions of individual and corporate taxes will further increase incentives to invest.

In its 1963 report, the Council of Economic Advisers estimated that the consumption multiplier, that is, the rise of consumption associated with a $10 billion tax cut, would yield a rise of GNP of $16 billion. Here they allowed for the 45 per cent leakage resulting from additional taxes. They also commented on additional gains related to increased investment. They wisely refrained from supporting staff papers in government which forecast an increase of more than $80 billion on the assumption of no tax cut (3 per cent growth) and $58 billion additional (a total multiplier of 6) on the assumption of the tax cut. Such gains in a few years were possible but most unlikely.

The more the GNP rises the more unemployment will fall and employment rise. Hence in supporting the tax cut, proponents tend to be rather optimistic on the favorable effects on GNP. Keynes, who with Richard Kahn developed the multiplier theory, generally assumed a multiplier of 2 to 3; though for Great Britain, which has large imports, the appropriate figure may be 2. To achieve full employment by 1966, however, a large rise of GNP vis-à-vis the tax cut is required.

One may start with an assumption of a 3 per cent rise of GNP per year under a model without a tax cut. This would yield a rise of GNP of $54 billion in three years. (A 3 per cent rise for three years without a tax cut and following a gain of about $100 billion in the years 1961–1963, may be too favorable an assumption.) How much additional rise is required to assure full employment, that is, 4 per cent unemployment? Here is one approach: To begin with, excess unemployment was 1 million in 1963. Additional members of the labor market in three years = 4 million. (I allow for a rise related to favorable economic conditions.)

In estimating the required rise in GNP, one aspect of the tax cut should not go unnoticed. One objective has been to reduce the take of the tax collector as incomes rise, for the increased taxes tend to abort a recovery. Thus, Lintner, in his February 5, 1963, paper to the Joint Economic Committee, estimated that the increase in federal and state and local government tax receipts (inclusive of corporate taxes on an accrual basis) was 43.7 per cent of the rise of income. Such leakages might take the momentum out of an economic recovery. The council has pointed out that large marginal changes occur in periods of rapid movements of GNP, though note the inconsistencies below (dollar values are in billions).

	Change in GNP	Change in Administrative Receipts (Federal)	Marginal Rate
Fiscal 1956 to 1959	+$47.0	No significant changes	0
Fiscal 1959 to 1960	+$38.2	+$9.9	26%

On a gradually rising GNP, no peak or trough, and with no change in the gap between actual and potential output, 18 to 20 per cent is a good rule of thumb for a rising marginal tax rate; for state and local government, 10 per cent additional. On a *cash* basis, I found that federal receipts rose by 16, 42, 29, 40, and 33 per cent of the gain of GNP in the years 1946 to 1948, 1950 to 1953, 1954 to 1957, 1958 to 1960, and 1960 to 1962 respectively. On the administrative budget the results are not nearly so startling. For 1950–1953, the relative rise of receipts was 33 per cent; for 1954–1957, 14 per cent; for 1958–1960, 19 per cent; and 1960–1962, 10 per cent. Since there were some changes in tax structure during these years, these figures should not be interpreted as reflecting automatic responses of *taxes* to rising income *at a given tax structure*.

THE TAX CUT AND THE DEFICIT

An argument used against the tax cut is that it will increase the deficit. Undoubtedly an $11 billion tax cut will leave a legacy of a larger debt. But the net effect on the budgetary situation depends not only on the tax rate but also on the tax base. If, for example, GNP were to rise by $40 billion then at that time (say by 1966), the additional tax yield would be about $8 billion, or a net cost in taxes for that year of $2 billion. The costs would probably be higher in 1964 and 1965, for incomes would not have risen as much.

A valuable exercise is to estimate how large a rise of GNP will be needed to provide the 5 million additional jobs in the years 1964–1966 required to bring unemployment down to 4 per cent.

In studying this problem, I considered three periods of recovery:

1949–1953, 1954–1957, and 1960–1962. I also studied a council estimate (*1963 Report,* p. 26) covering a longer period ("postwar"): ". . . if GNP were 3 per cent higher than now, the unemployment rate would be approximately 1 per cent lower."

One does not get identical results over four periods. For example, a study of the 1960–1962 period indicates that large increases of GNP are required to assure 1 million additional jobs. This may be explained by large gains of productivity, slow adjustments of manpower to changing conditions in the labor market, and adaption to the recession and then to rising demand by economizing on new jobs.

On the basis of four periods studied, provision of 5 million additional jobs over the four years 1963–1966 would require an annual percentage rise of GNP in stable dollars over 1962 GNP of 7.7, 7.2, 5.1, and 7.2 per cent, or an average of 6.8 per cent. This is more than is likely to be achieved over a period of three years following a gain of $83 billion ($64 billion in stable dollars) in the three years 1961–1963. This table therefore indicates a need even beyond the 1963–1964 proposed tax cuts.

INCREASE OF GNP (IN STABLE DOLLARS)
REQUIRED TO BRING UNEMPLOYMENT DOWN TO 4 PER CENT BY 1966[a]

Years	Rise in GNP per 1 million Added Jobs	Projected Rise in GNP, 1963–1966, per 5 Million Added Jobs	Percentage Rise in GNP, 1963–1966, per 5 Million Added Jobs	
			Total 1963–1966	Per Year
	(billions of stable dollars)			
1960–1962	$27	$135	25%	7.7%
1949–1953	26	130	23	7.2
1954–1957	18	90	16	5.1
Postwar[b]	26	130	23	7.2

SOURCE: My calculations from *Economic Reports of the President.*
[a] Includes Civilian Employment and Armed Forces.
[b] Estimate of Council of Economic Advisers.

In a later chapter on unemployment, I will discuss the relation of additional GNP and additional jobs. What is impressive there is the much larger rise of GNP consistent with X additional jobs in the current recovery than in earlier recoveries, a relationship not as clearly revealed here. In the later study, instead of comparing years, I compare recovery periods from the month of the beginning and the end of recovery (the last one until July 1963).

Professsor Arthur Burns, in a statement to the Joint Economic Committee (February 4, 1963) which attracted much attention, emphasized the unfortunate effects of the tax cut and rising spending on the budget. On the favorable assumption of a 6 per cent increase in GNP per year (current dollars) and a $5 billion rise of expenditures per year, Burns concluded that the budget would still be in deficit in 1972 and from fiscal year 1963 to 1972, $75 billion of debt would have been added. (Using Burns' model parameters I find a smaller rise of deficit than he does.)

One may raise the question whether even the results envisaged by Burns would be disastrous.

1. GNP would rise by about two-thirds, to about $980 billion.

2. Additional federal revenue in such a period of advance, should revenue rise equal at least to 20–22 per cent of the rise of GNP, would be $88 billion. Burns' estimate seems low. By 1972, this would exceed the increase of expenditures of $45 billion, and more than offset the current deficit. Hence there would be a surplus of about $33 billion by 1972. This is the difference between (a) additional revenue of $88 billion and (b) the sum of $45 billion additional expenditures at the end of nine years and the $10 billion (estimated) current deficit.

3. One difficulty with Burns' model is that he has underestimated the tax cut (and) or rise of expenditures required to prevent a deflationary situation from developing.

4. On Burns' assumptions, against an increase of debt of $75 billion and cost of debt financing of about $2 billion, the economy would have gained about $400 billion.

5. The ratio of debt to GNP would have fallen from 53 to 31 per cent and interest payments from 1.69 to 1.31 per cent of GNP.

6. It may even be held that the $75 billion of added federal outlays (or more if the momentum is not to be lost) yield some benefits to the nation, not only in additional net demand but in services needed by the nation.

TAX CUT AND INFLATION

President Kennedy, the Secretary of the Treasury, and the chairman of the Council of Economic Advisers stressed the point that with large amounts of unemployment, inflation is not a genuine threat. The Federal Reserve, with responsibilities for stability, is not quite so certain of this position. But any projection to 1966 with a rise of say 5 per cent or more in real GNP per year is another matter. Here the rise may cause bottlenecks and pressure for rising wage rates beyond the level dictated by increasing productivity. One should not expect an increase of GNP of about $140 billion in three years without some inflationary pressures.

In three earlier periods of substantial rise (1946–1948, 1949–1951, 1954–1957) the rise of GNP was 23, 27, and 22 per cent; of prices (GNP deflator), 19, 9, and 8 per cent; or increases of prices relative to GNP of 83, 33, and 36 per cent. (The first period was abnormal because of the lifting of controls.) But even if we assume a rise of 35 per cent in prices relative to that for GNP, a substantial price rise in 1964–1966 may follow, a rise which might be costly in its inflationary impact or in its containing of the expansion as policy is directed to controlling the price rise. Even an increase of only 20 per cent in current GNP by 1966 on top of that of 1960–1963 may well bring a 7 per cent increase of prices in three years. The government will have to watch this, though a 2 per cent a year rise is not a high price to pay for a gain of about $130 billion for GNP in three years.

CONTROVERSIAL ASPECTS

Many who were rather old-fashioned in their economics were not enthusiastic over a tax cut. They associate economic ups and downs and trends with other factors, for example, investment booms or loss of competitive position. In a paper published by the *Congressional Record,* May 9, 1963, Dr. Raymond Saulnier, former chairman of the Council of Economic Advisers, put strongly the non-fiscal aspects of the rise of 1953–1957 and the decline that followed, a position that he invoked in criticism of the President's emphasis on the unwisdom of a cut of public expenditures. It is interesting to consider President Kennedy's address on the state of the nation (August 13, 1962), when he pointed to a rise of federal expenditures of $7 billion and an increase of revenue of $12 billions, as well as a $7–$8 billion surplus that would emerge with full employment, as developments bringing unsatisfactory economic conditions. Moreover, Saulnier envisaged small effects on employment from tax cuts and rises in federal expenditures. But Saulnier's views were not typical of most economists. There were other critics, including editors of the *New York Times,* who held that the administration was overselling the tax program: It could not raise GNP sufficiently to bring full employment within a few years.

A crucial issue was tax cut versus tax reform. At the beginning much emphasis was put on both the tax cut and reform. The Treasury had worked for two years on a tax reform program which would remove inequities, increase incentives, and increase the tax base. Moreover, a strong case could be made for tax reform, both because this was a way of recapturing some of the costs of the tax cut, and also because reform was needed in order to eliminate the abuses, e.g., oil depletion allowances and taxation at unjustifiably low capital gains rates, which had developed with the high income tax rates. It was appropriate, as rates were cut, to remove the inequities. This was the opportunity to get rid of abuses, when compensation could be offered in reduced rates. Many economists as well as businessmen, were inclined to oppose tax reform at this time as a delaying tactic. Economists were fearful that the tax cut would be too long delayed if tax reform were on the agenda; businessmen, such as the Committee for Economic Development, were against reform, possibly because tax reform might especially hurt business interests. They wanted a tax cut without reform. The President vacillated to some extent. His political position was difficult. Above all he sought a substantial tax cut to stimulate the economy; but with Congressman Mills, chairman of the powerful Ways and Means Committee, determined to have reform as well as cuts, the President had to agree. Despite about eight months of consideration, the ultimate bill released by the committee included relatively little reform.

Tax concessions to consumers or to businessmen? Some, like

Burns in his 1963 statement to the Joint Economic Committee, argued that since what was needed was more investment, the major cuts should favor business. The actual proposal of the Ways and Means Committee was $8.7 billion of tax cuts for individuals and $2.3 billion for corporations. But corporations also had received $2.5 billion from the investment credit and liberalized depreciation provisions. With corporate profits about one-ninth of national income and about one-third of corporate and income taxes, about 35 per cent of the gains going to corporations seemed more than adequate. It is extremely doubtful that a distribution, say, of $6.5 billion for corporations and $7 billion for individuals instead of $8.7 and $4.8 billion would have been acceptable to the Congress. On the whole the division of the gains did not arouse as much unhappiness as might have been expected.

On the stretch out of the tax cut over three years, there was much criticism (e.g., Nelson Rockefeller in the *Washington Post,* March 2, 1963). Here the President was influenced by the fear of heavy deficits in 1963–1964 and also by a desire to avoid large concentrated rises in GNP that might be inflationary. Like most economists, I would have preferred a $5 billion cut for 1963 and $5 billion for 1964, especially in view of the rise of payroll taxes in 1963, the expected increase of state and local taxes, and the doubts about the economy that prevailed late in 1962 and in January 1963. But the unexpected lift of the economy beginning in early 1963 made the President's proposals more acceptable than had seemed likely in January of that year.

THE TAX CUT AND EXPENDITURES

Elsewhere I have discussed the relative advantages of tax cuts and rising expenditures as routes to more growth and less unemployment. But since opposition to the tax cut arose from the fear of rising expenditures and deficits, further comments are needed.

In the fall of 1963, the Republican assault on the tax program was tied to a demand that the administration should virtually promise no further rises in expenditures. The conservative sources of information supported this approach. Thus the monthly *Economic Letter of the National City Bank* (June 1963), warning its readers that in the seven years 1956 to 1963 expenditures had averaged about $5 billion higher than budgetary estimates, stated:

. . . in today's setting, private consumers, employers and investors should be given a full opportunity first (not a massive spending program). And *Fortune* is so distrustful of spending that it concludes (March 1963) that the Kennedy tax program provides an "expanding program of expenditures utterly inconsistent with a tax cut . . .

. . . taxes are collected to pay for defense and other federal functions; neither the collections nor the expenditures should be used as instruments for managing the economy." Fiscal policy is apparently out for *Fortune*.

What can be said in reply to Congressman John Byrnes, the leader of the tax-cut-cum-reduced-spending school? One answer might be that federal administrative expenditures increased roughly only as much as GNP from 1954 to 1963 and nonsecurity outlays had greatly declined in relation to GNP; that with rising population and improved economic status much greater need for government help emerges—e.g., recreational areas; that the increase of prices and wages is necessarily reflected in rising federal outlays; that the government has sought economies and cost reduction; that services related to defense and growth, such as education, health, research, and housing need more help from the federal government; that they have expanded their needed services in some areas by cutting back elsewhere instead of by proposed indiscriminate cuts; that the nondefense and related outlays are not rising in fiscal year 1964 despite factors contributing to larger outlays; and that even in the 1965 budget, close to $2 billion stems from commitments already made—e.g., rise of federal pay.

President Kennedy and his budget director also exploited devices for keeping budgetary expenses down which had been widely used by the Eisenhower administration. This practice was used to such an extent under Eisenhower that the Kennedy administration was unable to improve the "looks" of its budget as much as the Eisenhower administration had.*

By summer 1963, it was clear that President Kennedy had

* See especially the President's remarks before the American Bankers Association, February 25, 1963, and Budget Director Kermit Gordon's paper before the House Ways and Means Committee on February 18, 1963 on the tax programs; also see Chapter 9 of this book.

clearly moved from an early dependence on spending to a concentration on tax cuts, implemented by pressure for strict economies. Whatever his attitude towards public spending the widespread fear of rising public expenditures and deficits forced the President towards economical management as the price of a tax cut, higher growth, and less unemployment. He was not in a position to accept Leon Keyserling's advice: "So when the Administration commits itself to a freeze on domestic public spending for several years ahead as a quid pro quid for a questionable compound of tax reduction . . . it turns its back on what is essential if our basic needs are to be met. . . ." (*Washington Post,* March 12, 1963).

On a number of occasions the President commented on the surplus at full employment, which was likely to abort a recovery. The way to deal with the full employment surplus was to reduce taxes (and) or increase expenditures. The President was now forced to depend primarily on a tax cut. At different levels of GNP, revenues would vary. As GNP rises from time to time, and expenditures are kept down, then the revenue surplus at full employment will rise, and corrective measures will be necessary. The President distinguished between a passive deficit that prevailed when revenues were low because of inadequate GNP, and the active deficit which was introduced in order to increase GNP and to keep the rising full employment surplus from threatening the economy.

Republican critics of the Kennedy spending policies were not always consistent. The Republican leaders wanted defense spending trimmed sharply but as the *London Economist* (April 6, 1963) noted, they insist on "giving the Administration unwanted spending authority to develop the costly RS-70, a proposed supersonic reconnaissance bomber which may well be incapable of flight. . . . Mr. Halleck, the Republican leader in the House of Representatives and a leading economiser, advocates spending authority of some $24 million—not provided by Mr. Kennedy's budget—to build a deep water port on the Southern shore of Lake Michigan in his State of Indiana. . . ."

Dependence on a tax cut to stimulate the economy, to reduce unemployment, to make American industry more competitive, to prevent a recession, and even to give the private economy a larger relative stake in spending was bound to put pressure on the administration to reduce federal disbursements. For this reason many liberal supporters of the President were unhappy over the course of development, although a vast majority favored a tax cut as the only practical way of treating unemployment and inadequate growth. The restraints on the use of monetary policy associated with the deficit in the balance of payments requires greater recourse to fiscal policy. Despite the magnitude of the tax cut, the net result may not reduce unemployment below 4 per cent by 1965; but the tax cut should prevent further rises in unemployment. It should make the balanced budget more possible, and the ratio of debt and the costs of financing debt in relation to GNP should substantially decline. But I anticipate some pressure on prices before 1966 as GNP rises even as much as is required to keep unemployment from increasing. But even a 2 per cent rise of prices per year may not be an excessive cost to pay for an annual increase of GNP (current dollar) of 5 to 6 per cent. The elimination of unemployment in excess of 4 per cent is likely to require an increase of GNP that will not be attained by an $11 billion tax cut, and if it were, the inflationary pressures would have to be watched.

9

The Budget

Before he retired from office, Maurice Stans, President Eisenhower's last budget director, projected federal expenditures for the next ten years, intending to warn the country against an impending rise of expenditures. The expenditures, on three different alternative bases, high, medium, and low, all revealed steady rises over the period 1960–1970. In one of his early statements, Budget Director David Bell (Address to the National Association of State Budget Officers, August 21, 1961) acclaimed the need of planning ahead, and was disposed to project the budget for the next five years.

In 1958, Otto Eckstein had prepared a projection of expenditures for a ten-year period for the Committee for Economic Development. By 1964 it was clear that expenditures were running rather higher than anticipated by the Eckstein study, with the space program being the major factor in accounting for the excess. Eckstein had also underestimated the rise of trust fund expenditures. But his projection of revenue so far has been remarkably close to estimates. The excess for the outlays in the administrative budget for fiscal year 1964 over projections of 1958 was about $11 billion; for the cash budget, $16 billion. New legislation largely accounts for the excess. Although one cannot put too much faith in these projections, partly because one cannot anticipate such developments as the changing international situation, dollar saturation, and the sluggish economy, nevertheless these projections

78

are useful. They can be corrected from year to year and any trends related to price changes can be treated by estimating in stable dollars.

RISING EMPHASIS ON CASH AND NATIONAL INCOME BUDGET

Attempts to project ahead are decidedly useful. But perhaps the greatest advance under President Kennedy was the increasing emphasis on the cash and national income (NI) budget as against the administrative budget which receives the major attention now. From the very beginning the Kennedy administration attempted to shift attention from the administrative to the other two types of budget. The major reason for this attitude is that the cash and NI budgets have a greater impact on the economy; but there are other reasons given also: first, that the administrative budget in one sense overestimates expenditures because it does not distinguish capital from current items and, second, that the administrative budget tends to show large deficits in the early periods of recovery and hence to discourage deficit financing just when it is especially needed.

Charles Schultze (in the *Review of Economics and Statistics,* February 1962) showed that the administrative budget reveals larger deficits than budgets based on national income accounts. He stressed the wisdom of an accrual budget. With an accrual budget, for example, the President would not have been excessively disturbed by the budgetary situation and would not have sought a balancing of the 1963 budget, which on an accrual basis would indeed reveal a substantial surplus.

. . . an attempt to balance the fiscal 1963 budget, at the levels of GNP then prevailing, would imply an administrative budget surplus (accrual basis) of $5 to $6 billion at *full employment levels of income,* and a national income accounts surplus of $8–$9 billion. This is precisely the kind of fiscal policy which resulted in a premature stopping of the 1959 recovery.

Obviously the administration had to move slowly in its attempt to deflate the administrative budget, not only because it was essential in relation to the appropriation process, but also because they would be accused of trying to give an impression of expenditures or at least deficits lower than that supported by the administrative budget. This charge of underestimating of outlays could not be made against the cash budget, which showed $24 billion in excess of the expenditures under the administrative budget in fiscal year 1964. Conservative interests are supporting the cash budget because it shows the largest outlays. Their support is, however, tempered by a realization that in sluggish periods, this budget may reveal relatively small deficits.

For many years there has been agitation, supported strongly by Senator Morse, for a capital budget, that is, a budget which differentiates between current and capital expenditures. Though economists were at first sympathetic, they seem to be much less disposed to support it, one reason being a fear that many worthwhile outlays, such as education, would be neglected in favor of capital items, which would not count as expenditures in the usual sense.

Supporting himself by a report of accountants, Maurice Stans (*Washington Post,* July 22, 1962) criticized the capital budget. He admitted its appeal in that "present operating deficits would appear to be turned into surpluses." But his main objections were that *all* expenditures should be put on an accrual basis and that, besides, with proper accounting, the financing costs of all capital expenditures, past and present, should be put against the savings on outlays for capital items.

As early as October 30, 1961, Budget Director Bell told the American Institute of Certified Accountants that the cash budget and the NI budget had certain advantages over the administrative budget. The cash budget included trust fund receipts and payments, as the administrative budget did not, and the NI budget had the great advantage of being largely on an accrual basis and, therefore, both budgets measured the economic impact much better than the administrative budget. But the NI budget had one weakness: It excluded credit items which are of some significance for the operations of the economy.

In January 1962 President Kennedy spoke out for the NI budget.

It showed a surplus of $4.4 billion for fiscal year 1963 and measured "the direct impact of Federal expenditures and receipts on the flow of total spending."

In his famous June 12, 1962, speech at Yale, President Kennedy said:

We persist in measuring our federal fiscal integrity today by the conventional, or administrative budget, with results which would be regarded as absurd in any business firm, in any country of Europe.

The Administrative budget has sound administrative uses. But for wider purposes it is less helpful. It omits our special trust funds and the effect they have on our economy. It neglects changes in assets or inventories. It cannot tell a loan from a straight expenditure. And worst of all, it cannot distinguish between operating expenditures and long-term investments.

This budget in relation to the great problems of Federal fiscal policy, which are basic to our country in 1962, is not simply irrelevant; it can be actively misleading. . . .

Because of the rising interest in budgetary accounting I arranged, late in 1962, for a meeting at the Treasury of about twenty of the leading experts on budgets, with a majority composed of the panel of Treasury consultants. The May 1963 *Review of Economics and Statistics* published nine papers presented at this meeting by twelve economists. These papers were republished by the Joint Economic Committee in its useful *Hearings on the Federal Budget as an Economic Document* (April 1963). The introduction to this symposium, with some excisions, follows:

In 1962 we invited a number of experts to participate in a day-long symposium to discuss the Federal budget. Evidence of dissatisfaction with our budgetary accounting had been cumulating for years. From time to time Senator Morse would introduce a bill for a capital budget, and many experts considered with approval the British above-the-line and below-the-line budget accounting. With the size of the budget and of deficits, and the use of budgets to influence economic activity becoming major political issues, politicians and scholars increasingly examine the accounting practices. Since the early 1950's the Government has become increasingly interested in balancing its accounts rather than the budget. Policy was increasingly being determined not by the merits of the case, but rather by whether the expenditures were reflected in the . . . budget. Guarantees became increasingly important, in part because they were not reflected in an increase in the budget. In three recent fiscal years, Federal loans rose by $20 billion; but guarantees by $54 billion, and sales of mortgages and CCC paper to private interests which improved the looks of the budget, increasingly appealed to the government. The budget was thus relieved; but the effects on the economy might be adverse if governmental sales of assets absorbed credit that otherwise might have been available to the private economy. When in the mid-1950s President Eisenhower proposed a $100 billion road program to be financed out of a trust fund and thus escape the scrutiny of the budget director, Senator Byrd really exploded.

In the 9 papers contributed by 12 economists to this symposium, we have the most important analyses of United States budgetary accounting and policies made available in recent years. These authors do not agree on all points by any means. But they are in unanimous agreement that the current policies and accounting practices are not all that they ought to be; and that the Administrative Budget, which is the Budget for the Executive, the Congress, and the public, is far from satisfactory and is becoming increasingly inadequate as a measure of the government's contribution to economic activity. Much credit goes to the Council of Economic Advisers and to the Budget Director for raising questions concerning the shortcomings of current budgetary practice.

What conclusions are we to draw from this symposium? Perhaps the most important is that no one budget is adequate for all purposes. Thus Colm and Wagner ask for a program budget, a budget for financial analysis (cash receipts and payments), and an economic analysis budget (the Federal Sector in the National Economic Accounts or National Economic Budget). But some experts do not favor the last, the argument being that credit items, which are excluded, are relevant in assessing the effects on the economy (Cf. Taylor, Wendel and Brill and Goode). Jaszi, however, offers supplementary material, which would provide a national income budget of adequate comprehensiveness. (He finds a home for the unrecorded transactions of corporate taxes and government loans.) Shoup would limit the items to be included in a Fiscal Policy Budget to those that can be adapted to changing economic conditions—e.g. exclude trust funds because income and outgo should not be varied in response to changing economic conditions.

Perhaps the Cash Budget receives the largest support in this symposium. Its strength lies in its comprehensiveness, in its tie-in with operating statistics, and its relevance for revealing economic effects of the budget. Its inclusiveness is supported by the following statistics: the rise of expenditures in the Administrative Budget from FY [Fiscal year] 1946 to 1964 was $39 billion; in cash payments $58 billion or $19 billion more.

One aspect of the budgetary problem should be mentioned here. Many observers have been impressed by the greater willingness of European nations to follow Keynesian lines, that is, to accept deficit financing to bolster the economy. Thus Edwin Dale, Jr., writing from Europe in the *New York Times* (May 13, 1962) informed American readers that by every generally accepted test of economic performance but one, Western Europe has done better than the United States since 1956.

The rule in Europe has been never to restrict demand by budget surpluses or tight money unless the economy reached the stage of being badly over heated, with a serious labor shortage. . . .
In the United States, partly because of a certain mythology about balanced budgets and partly for more plausible reasons, the rule has been to restrict demand. . . .

Again in a widely read study (which even influenced the President) Andrew Gantt showed that on similar accounting bases, deficits in the United States in the 1950s were smaller than for her major European allies (*Review of Economics and Statistics,* February 1963).

A Comparison of the Three Budgets

The *U.S. 1962 Budget Review* contains the following (page 32):

Federal expenditures and receipts are included in the national income and product statistics of the Department of Commerce on a basis that differs in coverage and in timing from both the conventional budget accounts and the statement of cash receipts from and payments to the public. Like the latter, Federal transactions on income and product account encompass receipts and payments of trust funds. However, they exclude all capital, land, and credit transactions, or, more generally, transactions which consist of exchanges or transfers of claims and of previously existing assets.
With respect to timing, Federal Receipts on income and product account are recorded largely on an accrual—rather than a cash—basis. Similarly, Federal purchases are recorded primarily when goods are delivered and services performed, rather than when the check is issued or the cash paid. Thus, the timing reflected in these accounts generally

corresponds with economic impacts more closely than the regular budget and consolidated cash statement.

For the fiscal year 1962 as a whole, the Federal budget on income and product account is estimated to be almost in balance, showing a deficit of $0.2 billion. This compares with the estimated deficit of $6.9 billion in the regular budget accounts. The difference reflects in large part the more prompt recording of the accrual of taxes related to the rising incomes being generated by the current economic recovery. In contrast, in the regular budget accounts, tax collections, mainly from corporations, lag substantially behind changes in the economic situation.

A very lucid statement on the various types of budgets is to be found in the 1962 *Report of the Council of Economic Advisers*, pages 77–78.

The effects of Federal receipts and expenditures on the income stream are most accurately represented when the budget is viewed in the framework of the national income accounts. These accounts present a consistent record and classification of the major flows of output and income for the entire economy, including the transactions of the Federal Government. There are three major differences between the Federal budget as it is conventionally presented (the so-called "administrative budget") and the accounts of the Federal sector as they appear in the national income. . . .

First, the national income accounts budget, like the consolidated cash budget, includes the transactions of the trust funds, which amount currently to about $25 billion per year and have a significant impact on the economy. Highway grants-in-aid, unemployment compensation payments, and social security benefits are examples of trust fund

TABLE

Major Differences Among Three Concepts of the Federal Budget

Item	Administrative	Budget concept Consolidated cash	National Income accounts
Timing of receipts	Collections	Collections	Accruals
Treatment of net loans and other credit transactions	Included	Included	Excluded
Treatment of trust fund transactions	Excluded	Included	Included

transactions. Because the traditional budget—or administrative budget—is primarily an instrument of management and control of those Federal activities which operate through regular congressional appropriations, it excludes the trust funds, which have their own legal sources of revenue.

Second, transactions between government and business are, so far as possible, recorded in the national income accounts budget when liabilities are incurred rather than when cash changes hands. This adjustment in timing affects both government purchases and taxes, shifting them to the point in time at which they are likely to have their principal impact on private spending decisions. The choice of an accrual, rather than a cash, basis for timing is particularly important for the highly volatile corporate income tax. . . .

Finally, unlike the administrative budget, the national income accounts budget omits government transactions in financial assets and already existing assets. The largest omission is the volume of loans extended by the Federal Government. This volume is estimated at $4 billion net of repayments in fiscal year 1962. While these loans have important effects on economic activity, they are properly viewed as an aspect, not of fiscal policy, but of monetary and credit policy. . . . Borrowers from the Federal Government, like borrowers from private financial institutions, acquire cash by incurring debts. They add thereby to their liquidity, but not directly to their incomes.

Foreign Treatment of Capital Budgets*

The experiences of the United Kingdom, Sweden, the Netherlands, and Canada are especially interesting. In general the origin of the capital budget lies in the realization that inclusion of capital items with current items gives a distorted view of the budgetary situation. Another reason for the capital budget is the help such accounting gives for an understanding of the Treasury's contribution to the savings-investment relationship. When the capital budget is used, the stress is put upon the acceptability of deficits on capital account as against a reluctance to incur deficits in the current account. But this does not mean that the government ignores the total deficit.

Distinctions are often made between unproductive capital in-

* Based especially on Goode and Birnbaum, Government Capital Budgets, IMF, 1956 and JEC, *The Federal Budget As An Economic Document,* 1962, pp. 146–179.

vestments and productive ones, that is, those that do not yield income and those that do. Thus, in Sweden, "expenditures for non-revenue producing capital items are not distinguished from current items. . . ."

To some extent the use of the capital budget and its significance are exaggerated. For example, in the British budget the above-the-line (current receipts and expenditures) and below-the-line (presumably capital items) figures are mistakenly assumed to suggest current and capital budgets. Actually, many items above the line are capital items (e.g., surplus stores and sundry loans) and some items below the line should be above. Moreover, some expenditures above the line (e.g., loans to allies) should be below. Similar remarks for items wrongly included and excluded below the line apply. Thus surplus stores should be transferred from receipts above the line to below; and from above the line, loans to allies should be transferred to payments below the line.

One gets a definite impression that even when the distinctions between current and capital budget are made in the formal accounting system, the effects on policy are not great, though undoubtedly this segregation makes it easier to spend for investment, and with this burden lifted from the current budget, to spend more on current operations. The interest still is largely concentrated on the total expenditures, the total deficit, the use to be made of the excess of receipts. In England, the attempt to publish an alternative accounting giving a genuine current and capital budget was abandoned, with the task transferred to the annual income account, which now presents the national income and expenditures data in such a way as to show the national investment account and the means of finance.

A significant statement was made by the South African government, in reply to a charge that the government taxes the people in order to finance loan programs:

. . . The tendency all over the world has been to finance an increasing proportion of the states expenditures on capital works from current revenue in accordance with the stage of development reached by the economy of the country in question. In the case of highly industrialized countries such as the United Kingdom and the United States, the tendency has culminated in the complete elimination of the distinction between expenditures in capital and revenue accounts. For the purpose of budgeting, their expenditure on both capital and revenue services is met from current revenue. . . .

The budget is increasingly becoming a weapon for treating the economy. This is evident in the increased willingness of governments to spend and to cut taxes in order to stimulate and stabilize the economy. But a view widely held abroad is that this country is still behind Europe, because of its excessive fear of budgetary deficits; and there is some evidence that Western Europe's greater economic gains in the last seven years is associated to some extent with less restrictive and more expansive fiscal and monetary policies.

This chapter is primarily concerned with another problem, namely, the difference made by accounting methods used in presenting the budget, which, after all, is a plan for the public sector of the economy, with emphasis on its impact on the private economy. It has become increasingly clear that the true state of the budget and its repercussions on the economy will be greatly influenced by the accounting system used. The consensus among economists is in favor of the cash budget, with strong support also for the NI budget. In last place is the administrative budget, which because of its exclusions is the least useful as an instrument of fiscal policy. The capital budget, the first serious rival to the administrative budget, is losing ground.

I O

Federal Expenditures

MAGNITUDES

So far we have dwelt primarily with the tax cut and its effect on the economy. But government can also direct the economy through adjustments in spending. In President Kennedy's three administrative budgets, 1962, 1963, 1964, expenditures were $87.8, $94.3, and $98.8 billion—estimated increases respectively of $6, $7, and $4 billion over the preceding year. (Kennedy could take only limited responsibility for the 1962 budget.) Expenditures were clearly rising more under Kennedy than under Eisenhower. From 1954 to 1962, the years for which President Eisenhower can be held responsible, the rise of administrative expenditures was only $20 billion, or an average of $2.5 billion yearly as against an average of $5.5 billion in the years 1963 and 1964 (estimated), for which Kennedy was primarily responsible. The excess under President Kennedy might be even greater if, as so frequently happens, expenditures should exceed budgeted expenditures. But should we compare expenditures other than on defense and related areas in recent years, there is very little difference. The Kennedy rise of expenditures has been primarily in the defense category.

A great deal has been said about the large reduction of federal expenditures in re GNP, a decline from about 19 to 17 per cent of GNP from fiscal years 1952 to 1962. But the results are less impressive if state and local government outlays are included. Thus all governmental expenditures in relation to the national income accounts rose from calendar 1952 to 1962 from 27 to 29 per cent. It is well to remember that on a national income basis state and local expenditures from 1952 to 1962 rose from $25.4 billion to $58.8 billion, a rise relatively 2.5 times as great as for the federal government.

The emphasis in the past has been on the administrative budget; but if we include trust funds, that is, social security funds and the road fund, the rise of expenditures is much greater than under the administrative budget, an increase from 1952 to 1962 of 30 per cent for expenditures under the administrative budget, and 53 per cent under the cash budget.

THE PRESIDENT ON SPENDING

In a preceding chapter, I commented on President Kennedy's increased reluctance to embark on large spending programs. Having embarked on a tax reduction program in an economy likely to experience a substantial deficit even without a tax cut, the administration's chance of achieving new spending programs other than for national security was greatly reduced. Even as early as January 1962, the President's concern about public expenditures rose. The budget of 1963, introduced in January 1962 with moderate rises of expenditures and an attempt to achieve balance, reflected those fears. But in 1961 greater spending had been on the agenda.

The President listed numerous spending programs—temporary unemployment compensation, area redevelopment, housing and construction, development of our natural resources—in his first annual message to Congress on the state of the union (January 30, 1961). In his special message to Congress of February 2, 1961, on *economic recovery and growth,* the President proclaimed the need of a cyclically balanced, not a yearly balanced, budget. He urged a number of spending programs "designed to fulfill our responsibility to alleviate distress and speed recovery. . . . They will sustain consumer spending and increase aggregate demand now when the economy is slack. Many of these expenditures will automatically cease when high employment and production are restored."

In the first year of his administration, the President's therapy was primarily through increasing expenditures. In a special message to the Congress on the budget and fiscal policy, on March 24, 1961, the President, after commenting on increased burdens to be put on fiscal policy, then assumed the need of rising expenditures: "Each expenditure proposed will be evaluated, in terms of our national needs and priorities, consistent with the limitations and objectives described above and compared with the urgency of other budgetary requirements."

By February 1962, the President, concerned with the problem of proper timing of expenditures, asked the Congress for stand-by authority to accelerate expenditures for public works wherever unemployment rose sharply and the standard indicators of economic distress revealed that extraordinary action was required to reverse a serious economic decline.

But by the fall of 1962, the President began to have some doubts. He was concerned over the large defense outlays. In view of these outlays, the President in his budget review in the latter part of 1962 said "it will be necessary to defer or limit increases in many programs which, in more normal times, would be thoroughly desirable." But the President also commented on the high productivity of recent increases both for our security and for treating the recession.

Whereas expenditures had risen by $7.6 billion in fiscal year 1962, the budget for 1963 called for rises of only $3.4 billion in fiscal year 1963. The balanced budget was to be attained by a rise of revenue of almost $11 billion. The government was to be greatly disappointed in revenue received, but did remarkably well in adhering to its budgeted expenditures. But the doubts about rising expenditures were clearly stated in this budget: "The prospects are favorable for further rises in the coming year in private expenditures. . . . To plan a deficit under such circumstances would increase the risk of inflationary pressures, damaging alike to our domestic economy and to our international balance of payments. . . . To plan a larger surplus would risk choking off economic recovery and contributing to premature downturn."

Rising defense expenditures accounted for about three-quarters of the increase in outlays for fiscal year 1963, and exclusive of these increases and interest on the debt, expenditures were virtually stable between 1962 and 1963.

A large budgetary deficit in fiscal 1963 resulted from the failure to achieve an anticipated 2 per cent per quarter rise of GNP (2.5 per cent per quarter from the spring of 1961 to the end of the year had been experienced). With the actual rise less than 1 per cent per quarter, revenues fell substantially below the anticipated amounts.

Contending that the budget supported the activities nurturing the nation's social and economic growth, the President concluded that "this budget meets our national needs within a responsible fiscal framework. . . ."

By the latter part of 1962, the shift of emphasis from spending to tax cut was clear. In an earlier chapter I quoted the President on the shift and the reasons for it. But in October 1962, in numerous visits to states with unemployment problems, e.g., Pennsylvania, West Virginia, Michigan, the President boasted of his welfare expenditures and the restraints put upon the President by Republican opposition. Thus, in a speech at Harrisburg, Pennsylvania, of September 20, 1962, the President exulted at the most comprehensive housing bill in the history of this country, the temporary unemployment compensation payments, the manpower development and training program, a $900 million public works program. Time and again he dwelt on these programs as well as on the heavy military commitments which to some extent slowed down the advances in welfare programs.

LESS ENTHUSIASM FOR SPENDING

By the latter part of 1962, the President had clearly adopted the tax cut line to the virtual exclusion of new spending programs, unless offset by economies elsewhere. To the Economic Club of New York on December 14, 1962, the President said the way to treat the sluggish economy was a tax cut, and the more so since monetary therapy was restricted by the deficit of the balance of payments. We might also have depended on public spending but "such a course would soon demoralize both the Government and our economy. . . ." We must not spend more than our national needs justify. He now could boast of stable civilian expenditures for fiscal 1964 vis-à-vis 1963, a remarkable achievement since, in the last nine years, the average rise for these categories had been

7.5 per cent. In view of the rising population, prices, and wages, he considered this a matter for congratulations.

In his 1964 budget message, the President first pointed out that the budget "is an agenda of our purposes and priorities in the form of a plan for the conduct and financing of the public business . . . [and] the most powerful single tool the nation possesses for linking the private and public sectors of our economy. . . . This budget presents a financial plan for the efficient and frugal conduct of the public business. . . ." With the initial effect of a tax cut increasing the deficit, the President "felt obliged to limit severely [his] 1964 expenditure proposals." The 1964 administrative budget called for an $11.9 billion deficit, which greatly concerned the President. Admitting that some expenditures would continue to rise, he added that "we shall continue and indeed intensify our effort to include in our fiscal program only those expenditures which meet strict criteria of fulfilling important national needs." The President also assured the country that the government was doing its utmost to improve the efficiency of operation and to exclude inflation despite the large deficit, though a substantial inflation is an unlikely development with current levels of unemployment and excess capacity.

In an attempt to assure conservative business interests the President spoke to the American Bankers Association on February 25, 1963. Civilian expenditures, which had declined in only four out of the last fifteen years, were again to decline. The rise of civilian federal personnel had been much less than the increase in population, the President reminded his critics. To the American Society of Newspaper Editors (April 19, 1963), the President pointed out that there is an association of the size of the nation and the budget; and yet nondefense expenditures in relation to GNP had fallen by 7 per cent in twenty-five years. Even at this time, however, the President warned the editors of the calamitous effects of reducing federal expenditures and he could point to the experiences in the last Eisenhower recession. Replying to demands for a cut in the budget to match the tax cut, the President said that "unless there is a good deal more bounce in the economy than we have now . . . a cut of $5 billion to $10 billion from the proposed budget would harm the nation. . . . The right way to a balanced budget is to seek first a balanced economy. . . ." In his special message on tax reduction and reform (January 24, 1963) the President had anticipated the attack on spending policies and had clearly noted the deflationary effects of cuts of spending which would offset the stimulative effects of a tax cut.

By early 1963, it was certainly clear that the administration was not prepared to support numerous new programs. This was the price that had to be paid for saving the tax bill. In attempts to appease the "economizers" the President and his budget director assured the country of their determination to economize, of their hopes that military spending had reached a plateau, of their policy of encouraging rises in outlays in such areas as education, research, urban resource development, but which would be offset by economies elsewhere.

Budget Director Kermit Gordon, in a statement before the Ways and Means Committee on February 18, 1963, dwelt on these points. He also itemized the increases anticipated for fiscal 1964 and the net for outlays other than for defense, space, and interest. The major increases were $1.5 billion on past commitments (e.g., manpower training). Among the declines, the savings on farm price supports were to be $900 million; other built-in decreases (e.g., veterans' readjustment benefits, $800 million); substitution of private for public credit, $1 billion. The net result was to be reduction of $300 million.

Improved Budget Appearances

Both the President and his budget director stressed the savings to be had from substituting private credit for public. This was a weapon for improving the "looks" of the budget, not a genuine improvement. Often the decision to spend or not to spend was determined on the basis of its impact on the appearance of the budget. This is reminiscent of price control during the war when some price administrators tended to allow price rises on items not included in the Consumer Price Index. Transfer of assets held by the government to private interests is one way of improving the appearance of the budget. There were many other "placebo" approaches to improving the appearance of the budget that were used by the Eisenhower administration, such as not transferring earned sums to the Civil Service Relievement Fund. The Eisenhower administration, with its strong antigovernment bias, could justify a policy of getting the government out of markets, e.g., by selling mortgages. At any rate, the Eisenhower administration had largely used up these devices for improving budgetary appearances rather than improving the genuine condition of the budget.

On January 18, 1963, the *Wall Street Journal* had some interesting comments on what it called "shenanigans" in the budget. The author admitted these abuses were common both to Eisenhower and Kennedy. Among the points made were the practice of underestimating expenditures by offsetting receipts against expenditures, e.g., in public enterprises such as the Rural Electrification Administration, the sale of assets to the public—an anticipated $1 billion in fiscal 1963–1964; and the rise in rates on postal services, with a resultant rise of receipts and a masking of increases of expenditures.

SPENDING CRITICS

President Kennedy, pressed by the left to spend more and incur larger deficits and by the right to spend less and cut deficits, was able to satisfy only the less vocal nonpolarized center. On the left the most vocal critic was Leon Keyserling, the able ex-chairman of the Council of Economic Advisers. Writing in the April 1963 *Progressive,* Keyserling attacked the Keynesian "disciples" today "attempting to fight the ill-defined enemy on the wrong front with inadequate weapons." (It is my impression that Keyserling was 100 per cent Keynesian in fighting for massive public expenditures, and some of Keynes' disciples were considering the relevance of some institutional factors that Keynes was well aware of but had failed to discuss adequately.) For Keyserling "the proposed tax program is only a pygmy, but it is faced with a giant's job." His conclusion was that the GNP would be short of need by about $35 billion in 1963, about $65 billion in 1964, and about $87 billion in 1965. He envisaged unemployment of 8.5 million by 1965. His cure would be much larger public spending programs.

A good example of the extreme views on spending was given by

Senator Byrd in the *Tax Review* of April 1963. He advised cutting the authorizations asked for fiscal 1964 by $12 billion from the $107.9 billion requested, and new spending authorizations by $7.1 billion from the budget figure of $98.8 billion. But he did not really explain how this is to be done. All that he offered was a criticism of thirty new projects, and he proposed reductions in expenditures in numerous departments—for example, $1,819 million in defense, $905 million for Health, Education and Welfare, $604 million for other categories. But the budget director would have to know where the almost $2 billion of cuts in defense were to be made. In an earlier release of September 13, 1961, Senator Byrd itemized all the increases in expenditures involved in the President's messages, estimated cash expenditures in fiscal 1965 conservatively at $135 billion, and warned of the failure to balance the budget even over the cycle and of the inflationary threat. His 1965 estimates seem rather high.

The proposed reductions in expenditures were too much for some members of the Republican party. Senators Thruston Morton and Jacob Javits (*Washington Post,* April 1, 1963) could see little chance of reductions of $10–$13 billion as proposed by President Eisenhower. Their targets seemed to be about $3.5 billion. Senator Willis Robertson, conservative Democrat, would cut expenditures by $6 billion. It is not likely that when the year is over, expenditures will be less than the $99 billion budgeted for fiscal 1964. The Congress will refuse to support some programs provided for in the budget; but even the members generally in favor of over-all economy do not practice such economy when the issues are outlays benefiting their states or districts.

Speaking for the Republican party on September 18, 1963, Congressman John W. Byrnes demanded a control of spending as the price for Republican support of the tax cut. In four years, spending would be up by $20 billion and the debt by $35 billion. The congressman could envisage a galloping inflation as the outcome. Whereas the two previous tax cuts, of 1948 and 1954, had been accompanied by reductions of spending, under Kennedy the outcome was to be both a tax cut and a rise of spending. (Byrnes did not mention the recessions that followed these periods of economy and that of 1958–1959.) "It is certainly no news to you that you can't spend more, take in less, and pay off your bills and mortgages—all at the same time. It is no different in Government. If we don't recognize that simple truth, the whole nation is in for financial disaster."

It is not easy to reduce expenditures, in part because the administration had at its disposal balances of $87.2 billion for 1963–1964 from previous authorizations. Hence, to control expenditures the Congress would have to limit expenditures from past authorizations as well as the new authorizations. It is difficult to do this, for the current outlays from past authorizations are likely to be outlays for programs that have to be planned years ahead—e.g., the Colorado River development. Proposals to deal with this problem under postwar legislative reorganization never proved feasible.

In the last few years the Congress has tried to increase its control over expenditures by resisting backdoor financing, a system under which the Executive can plan ahead and obtain necessary funds from the Treasury. This kind of financing would be especially helpful for such programs as foreign aid, assuring a systematic program over the years.

Frustrated because of its failure to keep spending from rising, the Congress in the last few years has especially exploited the debt ceiling. The theory behind this is that when the debt ceiling comes uncomfortably close, the government will cut its outlays in order to stay within the debt limit. But this is an approach difficult to support and only serves to increase the respectability of congressmen in the eyes of those who fear large expenditures. The net result of the ceiling is interference with necessary operations, nonpayment of bills, recourse to selling obligations at higher rates not subject to the debt ceiling, and an unwarranted harrassment of the Executive. The way to control expenditures is for the Congress not to vote them, rather than to try to stop them after they are voted.

Secretary Dillon well told the Ways and Means Committee, on May 23, 1963, that the objective of keeping expenditures under firm control "cannot be attained, however, by exerting controls at the tag end of the expenditure process, when the bills which must be paid are coming in. The debt limit is not, and cannot be made, a substitute for control of expenditures at the decisive stage of the expenditure process—in the decisions on appropriations. . . ."

Spending was the early approach of the Kennedy administration to improved economic conditions. But the growing demands of security and the rising deficit associated partly with a proposed tax cut forced the administration to forego welfare programs as the price of getting adequate support for the tax cut. Required spending programs were concentrated in 1961; 1962 was a transitional year with increasing emphasis on a balanced budget and the need of a tax cut; 1963 marked the ultimate victory of tax cutting over spending and the acceptance of deficit financing in a sluggish economy. If the President could not see his way to supporting concomitantly tax cuts and large spending programs, he did not yield to those who wanted to neutralize the gains of the tax cut by severe control of spending.

The National Debt

MAGNITUDES

The rising national debt has been a matter of great concern. This greatly troubled President Eisenhower who remarked how happy we would all be if there were no national debt. In 1929, the gross federal debt was only $16.3 billion; by August 1963, it had reached $307 billion. Such increases are frightening to many. Yet if this rise is calamitous, one may ask why GNP has risen from $104 billion in 1929 to about $580 billion in 1963, or from $212 billion in 1962 dollars to about $580 billion in 1963. Even per capita disposable income (after taxes) is up by more than two-thirds. One can even argue, as Professor Alvin Hansen has, that the country may be worse off with no debt. For one thing, the availability of debt has made possible an expansion of bank deposits needed for a growing economy that otherwise would not have been achieved.

Moreover, if debt is bad, why is this not also true, for example, for a rise of private debt of more than three times since the end of the war, as compared to several percentage points for the federal government? John Lintner, testifying before the Joint Economic Committee, on February 5, 1963, asked why the vast increases in debt by American Telephone and Telegraph should be helpful and those of the federal government harmful. From 1939 to 1961, AT&T debt rose by 6.5 times, and it has more than doubled since 1948. This rise was necessary to purchase capital goods. Yet AT&T has had a phenomenal record: "It has retained its prime rating among investors because of its solid position in the American economy and the strength and progressiveness of the company. . . ."

The American public would be much less concerned over the size of the debt if they would think in relative rather than absolute terms. On June 11, 1962, President Kennedy reminded his Yale audience that "the debt per person and the debt as a proportion of our gross national product have declined sharply since the end of the second World War. . . ."

TIMING OF DEBT ISSUES

Capable debt management contributes to a sound economy. If the Treasury is too concerned over the cost of the debt financing it may well hurt the economy. Obviously the correct approach is to weigh costs to the Treasury against benefits or losses to the economy. In the decline of July 1957 to April 1958 and the early recovery following, the Treasury made the mistake of issuing excessive amounts of long-term securities, partly to take advantage of the low money rates at this time. But such policies would probably be too costly to the economy, for the new issues absorb cash that should go to the private economy. Obviously some compromise is necessary, or no long-term issues could be made. To some extent these sales will have to be made when rates are high, and thus the debt management will contribute to cooling off the economy; and some issues will have to be made when rates are low, and money is being created for the use of the private economy, thus with unfavorable effect on the private economy.

In an able paper, Julian B. Baird, Under Secretary of the Treasury under Eisenhower, before the Wisconsin School of Banking (August 18, 1960), said: ". . . the Treasury attempts to follow a middle course on reconciling the various objectives. We do attempt to minimize reliance on short-term financing during periods of expansion. We do attempt to handle our financing in a recession in a manner that will contribute to economic recovery. We do borrow as cheaply as possible, consistent with our other objectives. . . ."

Under Eisenhower, there was a tendency to concentrate on

private needs and neglect the problems of the public sector. Thus, Under Secretary Burgess, in 1958, testifying before the Senate Finance Committee (*Investigations of the Financial Condition of the United States, 1957 to 1959*) defended a policy of not issuing long-term securities in the midst of a boom on the grounds that "with an unprecedented heavy demand for funds in the private area we were convinced quite early in our studies that there was no substantial demand for long-term Government securities." Yet a case could be made for such issues at this time even if cash was diverted from private markets and interest rates rose. The long-term issues would have contributed to stability, and later issues of long-term securities in recession and early recovery would have retarded recovery.

In a paper before the Second Duke Assembly (March 1959) Henry Wallich, another member of the administration, presented a much more sophisticated view of the problem. He was not against debt management as an anticyclical weapon. But he took great pains to argue that "in a boom, the managers of the public debt may encounter serious difficulties under present conditions and with present techniques, in the long-term refunding that they are supposed to do." Yet Wallich realized that the Treasury should not issue only short-term issues. To avert the inflationary pressures associated with concentration on short-term issues, Wallich supported the issue of long-term securities in the 1958 recession. I find it difficult to accept this position. The Kennedy administration in 1961 did not repeat the mistakes of 1958. Perhaps the need of higher short-term rates and hence more short-term issues and the use of advanced refunding helped. It will be interesting to see whether in the anticipated boom of 1964 and 1965 the administration issues long-term securities.*

On the whole, the Treasury has been more successful since 1960 in adapting debt management to the needs of the economy than during the Eisenhower administration. The Treasury avoided large long-term public issues in the recovery period; these would raise interest rates at the very time when the objective was low

* I have discussed this issue in my report to the Senate Finance Committee, in *Investigations of the Financial Condition of the United States,* 1959, pp. 2170–2172.

long-term interest rates as one road to more investment. This policy was all the more necessary since the government tended to keep short-term rates high in order to discourage exports of short-term capital.

MATURITY OF DEBT AND ADVANCED REFUNDING

Despite great interest in lengthening the maturity of the debt, the Eisenhower administration failed in its attempts at increasing the average length. But Under Secretary Roosa announced, on September 18, 1963, that advance refunding had had the effect of increasing the length of the debt by more than four months and that with an average length of five years, three months, the Treasury had achieved the longest average maturity since July 1956.

Why is the government interested in lengthening the maturity of the debt, and especially since rates on short-term issues may be lower than those on long-term issues? One reason is that continued issues of short-term securities would raise the rate to or above the long-term rate. Second, short-term issues are a near substitute for cash, and hence excessive short-term issues may mean an economy which may be too liquid and therefore inflationary. Third, too much short-term debt may require frequent interferences with the money market and cause embarrassment to both the Federal Reserve Board and the Treasury. Yet the appropriate amount depends largely on what the market can absorb. Conditions have changed greatly since Keynes, in the middle twenties, announced to the Colwyn Committee that the market could absorb much larger amounts of short-term issues than was generally assumed.

Following a lead given by the Eisenhower administration, the Kennedy administration relied heavily on advanced refunding. With the passage of time, securities with distant maturities gradually become short-term securities. Hence, if the debt is not to become excessively short-term it becomes necessary to issue long-term securities. But the Kennedy administration was not disposed to issue long-term Treasury securities to the market for cash, but relied instead on the advanced refunding technique. The advantage of this approach is that the average length can be increased without serious adverse effects on the private economy during recession or recovery periods. Those holding long-term securities, which are gradually approaching shorter maturities, are encouraged to exchange their issues for the new issues. What is involved is an exchange of issues rather than sales of long-term issues.

Secretary Dillon reported to the Joint Economic Committee, on January 30, 1962, that "advanced refunding involves the exchange of outstanding issues for longer maturities, with a minimum impact on market conditions and flows of funds into productive investment."

Thus in September 1963 the Treasury offered some new securities to investors in $23 billion of securities, maturing from 1964 to 1967, with rates varying from 3¼ to 4¾ per cent. The investors accepted $1,591 million of 1968 3⅞ per cent bonds, $3,869 million of 1973 4 per cent bonds, and $1,260 million of 4⅛ per cent 1989–1994 bonds, or $6,720 million in all, or 28.3 per cent of the total eligible for exchange. Obviously such exchange would greatly facilitate the refinancing in the years 1964 and 1966–1967.

However, advance refunding has not escaped criticism. For example, long-term issues due in ten years may have a coupon rate of 2.5 per cent. In order to encourage the investor to exchange these (say) ten-years-to-maturity issues for issues maturing in forty years, the Treasury offers a 3.25 per cent issue. Then for ten years the Treasury pays 0.75 per cent more than it would have had to pay for the next ten years. But the Treasury is counting on a saving for the remaining thirty years of life of these securities, when long-term money might have to be enticed with (say) a 4.25 per cent rate. The Treasury assumes these gains exceed the losses in the first ten years. Should the tendency of long-term rates to rise be reversed and rates begin to decline, then the advanced refunding might result in large additional costs for the Treasury.

INTEREST RATES

As has been noted, the government was not disposed to allow interest rates on short-term Treasury issues to fall. Rather, the policy was higher rates. Thus, from early 1961 to early 1962, the rate on ninety-day bills rose by 48 basis points (48/100 of 1 per cent), and in the next year by 19 basis points. In the first of these years, rates on issues with longer maturities rose 41, 39, 31, 26, and 21 basis points for one-year, three-year, five-year, ten-year and twenty-year issues. But in the next year, these rises were almost wholly offset by reductions.

Short-term rates rose in the first year, as might be expected with an increase of issues of $8.2 billion. This total reflects new issues as well as effects of passage of time. The rise in rates would have been greater had not commercial banks in 1961 purchased $5.5 billion. In 1962 the net increase was but $1.1 billion, with commercial banks disposing of $135 million. By selling short-term ($944 million) and purchasing $4.44 billion of intermediate- and long-term issues in 1961 and 1962 the Federal Reserve contributed to higher rates in the short-term market and lower rates in the long-term market.

In general, debt management by the Treasury with cooperation from the "Fed" resulted in rising short-term rates on Treasury issues and relatively (net) stable rates on long-term issues. The net effect of a rising total debt would tend to be higher rates. But rates respond to many other factors—the level of free reserves related to open market operations, changes in reserve requirements, the demand for credit, and expectations on inflation.* Undoubtedly, the relative stability of commodity prices in the last few years has contributed to lower rates, for the threat of inflation results in demands on the part of lenders for compensation in higher rates.

Another relevant factor in assessing the net effect of debt management is the relation of public and private rates. It is clear that the net effects of policy were to isolate to some extent short-term from long-term rates. This was done not only by selling short-term issues and avoiding sales of longer maturities to the market, but also by increasing the availability of credit. Even in the short-term market, increased availability offset higher rates. This explains why private short-term rates rose less than public short-term rates. Again by special measures—e.g., reducing the mortgage rates on

---

* More free reserves for banks mean greater demands for securities, and hence higher prices and hence lower rates of interest.

Federal Housing Authority guaranteed loans—private long-term rates could be isolated to some extent from public long-term rates.

That the policy has been successful is suggested by the trends in rates after thirty-one months of recovery. As the table below shows, short-term public rates are higher, and private short-term rates almost stable, but long-term rates, and especially in private markets, are lower. It remains to be seen whether with large Treasury deficits and continued large deficits in the balance of payments, satisfactory rates will continue.

CHANGE IN RATES, 1960 TO SEPTEMBER 1963

90 day Treasury bills	+14%
3- to 5-year Treasury bonds	−3
Taxable bonds	+1
High-grade municiple bonds	−13
Corporate bonds Aaa	−2
Prime commercial paper, 4–6 months	+1
FHA new-home mortgage yield	−12

SOURCE: *Economic Indicators,* September 1963.

Debt management is not facilitated by the fact that numerous federal agencies and departments have the privilege of selling securities to cover their needs. Often the time of issue and conditions of issue conflict with the needs of the Treasury. Alerted by these problems the President appointed a Committee on the Federal Credit Programs which reported on February 11, 1963. These Federal credit programs are introduced "to remove or reduce credit gaps arising from imperfections in private markets, to influence the allocation of economic resources . . ." The committee recommended that when private lenders are unable to assume responsibilities the priority of government aid should be (1) guarantees or insurance of private loans, (2) government aid to new types of private institutions, (3) a government secondary market, and (4) direct loans. The committee also proposed periodic reviews of existing programs. The committee also had some interesting things to say about organization and coordination of the federal credit programs, their limited use for economic stability and growth, and the rates of interest to be charged in relation to costs of money and private charges.

On the whole, at least in the years 1961–1963, the Kennedy administration managed its debt well. Despite the large and extended economic recovery, and despite the need of keeping short-term rates up in order to protect the balance of payments, the trend of public rates, other than short-term, was neither up nor down; private short-term rates were kept relatively stable; and long-term rates tended down. In the light of the large public deficits, the net results are all the more striking. On the whole, the record in 1961–1963 has been more impressive than that of 1957–1959, when debt management was not used effectively to stabilize the economy.*

It is also useful to note that the national debt is not a threat to our economy. Its contribution to economic stability and adequate demand is an additional argument for a national debt, though, of course, this does not suggest the more debt the better.

* Cf. next chapter, on monetary policy, where upward movements in rates in the second half of 1963 are revealed.

1 2

Monetary Policy

POLICY UNDER EISENHOWER

Under President Eisenhower, monetary policy tended to be restrictive, with an annual rise of GNP in current dollars averaging four times that of the increase of money. Entering on a platform of anti-inflation the Eisenhower administration, ably backed and sometimes led by the Federal Reserve, tended to favor slow responses of money to rising output. To some extent this deficiency was made up by larger rises in substitutes for money—e.g., time deposits.

There clearly was an accord between the President and the Federal Reserve. At a news conference on October 5, 1956, President Eisenhower said: "The Federal Reserve is not under my control, and I think that it is proper that Congress did set it up as an independent agency." In view of the willingness of the Federal Reserve to restrict monetary supplies in accordance with Republican views on monetary policy, and even to the extent of inducing unemployment when it refused to validate inflationary wage and price policies through corresponding creation of money, there was no reason for the President to protest at the independence of the Federal Reserve.

When confronted (in the *Review of Economics and Statistics,* August 1960) with the charge of restrictionism, experts of the Federal Reserve could point to an unfortunate inflation in 1955–1958, to the uncertainty of the relation of more federal credit

106

to monetary expansion, and of the latter to spending, and also to large additions of *total* credit during the Eisenhower years (not merely demand deposits). Hence the need for caution. According to a report of the Joint Economic Committee (*Official Views on Monetary Policy,* April 1956), the President, reaffirming the independence of the Federal Reserve, "acknowledged that the policy of credit stringency now (Spring, 1956) being pursued by the Federal Reserve was one that raised grave doubts on the part of his own advisors. . . ."

In its May 1961 report on the 1961 *Economic Report of the President,* the committee, persistently critical of monetary policy, presented an interesting chart which showed that from 1950 to 1960 the following had occurred:

PERCENTAGE RISE

GNP = In excess of 75
Money supply = slighty in excess of 20
Annual rate of turnover of deposits = 50
Bond yield, Long Term = almost 70

This is indeed strong evidence of restrictive monetary policy, with the rise of the supply of money equaling only about one-quarter that of GNP, and with the long-term rate of interest rising almost 70 per cent in ten years.

POLICY UNDER KENNEDY

In its 1962 report, the Joint Economic Committee revealed a substantial reduction in the ratio of money supply and of liquid assets to GNP. Even in its 1963 report the committee, disagreeing with the Council of Economic Advisers, held that even in 1961 and 1962 monetary policy had been inadequate.

. . . Monetary policy must help fiscal policies to do the stimulation job which unfortunately the monetary authorities have not done. . . .

We recommend that the monetary authorities follow a policy of assuring that the money supply expands in line with the rising needs of an expanding economy. . . .

An examination of the ratio of money supply to GNP—a decline from 28 per cent in 1960 to 26.4 per cent in 1962—supports the committee's position. But the rise of the percentage of liquid assets from 79.0 to 80.9 per cent of GNP as well as the unusual net stability of long-term rates during a recovery of thirty-three months (1961–1963) point to the conclusion that the JEC may be expecting too much from monetary policy—and especially in view of the demands of the dollar problem. In testimony before the JEC, on February 1, 1963, Chairman Martin of the Federal Reserve Board emphasized the ease of monetary conditions: Financing for the year had attained a record figure of $58 billion, loans and investments of commercial banks alone increased $19 billion, and the small rise of demand deposits could be explained by very large gains in savings deposits as returns on these greatly increased. But the case for monetary expansion becomes stronger with the unusual rise of velocity, further increases necessarily taper off.

In contrast to the views of the Joint Economic Committee, Daniel Brill, an economist with the Federal Reserve Board, writing in the June 1963 *Federal Reserve Bulletin,* strongly supported the view that the Federal Reserve was expansionist. The creation of credit need not have resulted in such large expansion of liquid assets. That it did is associated with the high returns on liquid assets, e.g., savings deposits. In the absence of the expansionist policies, a serious rise of long-term interest rates would have emerged, in Brill's view, with unfortunate effects on the economy.

Monetary policy was relatively easy. Whereas in earlier recoveries, the Federal Reserve had introduced restrictive policies, in the latest recovery the Federal Reserve did not. Perhaps the explanation was a new administration with different views on the contribution of money; or perhaps excessive demand was no longer a concern of monetary authorities. Indeed in the middle of 1962, the Federal Reserve showed some concern lest liquidity was becoming excessive, and similarly in the last quarter of 1962. Perhaps the greatest doubts held by those fearful of Federal Reserve restrictionist policies emerged in early 1963, when the chairman of the Federal Reserve Board told a Congressional committee that he would not finance the new deficit out of created money but rather out of savings. He was, however, willing to finance any resultant expansion of output with additional supplies of money.

On February 1, 1963, Martin told the Joint Economic Committee:

. . . The Open Market Committee of the Federal Reserve System would be derelict in its responsibilities were it—in the light of a large deficit—to add to bank reserves and to bring about substantial credit expansion solely to facilitate the financing of the deficit. It would be improper to risk unsettling the balance of payments or to tempt banks to make imprudent investments through a sudden expansion of liquidity. Above all, it would be ill-advised to generate the danger of inflation, either long or short, by creating redundant dollars, in order to make easier the financing of the deficit.

. . . The Treasury obviously would not expect the Federal Reserve to inflate the money supply, thereby putting the entire economy into jeopardy, merely so that the Treasury could get money at an artificially low rate. . . .

. . . But this does not mean that bank credit should be expanded automatically by the amount of each Treasury issue that goes to market.

. . . I have never said that there should be no monetary expansion in a year in which the Federal Government is incurring a deficit. . . .

What we should do, and will try to do, is to maintain conditions of reserve availablity in the banking system which will help to match the rate of total bank credit and monetary growth to the needs of the total economy. . . .

On the basis of rate movements and the level of free reserves, and in view of the international monetary situation, I believe that the Federal Reserve pursued a policy of ease during most of this period. Indeed, as Dr. Edward Bernstein has often said, the low long-term rates must also be associated with the large savings that could not be wholly absorbed by investment. But the Federal Reserve, through its monetary policy, even in that kind of relationship, could induce higher rates.

Of course, there were differences within the administration and within the Federal Reserve. The council, especially concerned over the general economic situation, would of course seek more money and lower rates. In a brilliant speech, on November 14, 1962, to the President's Advisory Committee on Labor and Management, Walter Heller made it clear that in his view "the question is not whether bonds are sold to the public or to the commercial banks, but whether—if they are sold to the banks—the Fed. provides additional reserves to accommodate the purchases." He clearly wanted more credit and enough to preclude a rise in rates. The Treasury generally was not as expansionist as the council but more disposed to have additional credit than the Federal Reserve. William Martin, Jr., chairman of the Federal Reserve Board, in a December 1962 speech to the American Economic Association (reprinted in the *Federal Reserve Bank of New York Monthly Review,* January 1963) made clear his reluctance to expand credit further (as he did on several other occasions in 1963). Yet he clearly was more expansionist in 1961 through 1963 than in the 1950s, as is evidenced by large free reserves through two and one-half years of recovery, purchases of long-term securities in 1961 and 1962, and his statement to the JEC in 1963 quoted elsewhere in this chapter. But here is what he said in December 1962:

Indeed, my present feeling is that domestic liquidity of our banks and our economy in general is now so high that still further monetary stimulus would be little, if any good—and might do actual harm—even if we did not have to consider our payments situation at all. This means that if any additional governmental action is needed in the financial field in order to give fresh expansive impulse to the economy, it would probably have to come from the fiscal side. The part played by monetary policy . . . would then have to be mainly supplementary and defensive.

It is clear that Martin, greatly concerned over possible effects of monetary expansion on prices and the international situation, had to be cautious and had to be pressed toward an easy money policy. In the 1963 Joint Economic Committee hearings, George Mitchell of the board urged an active monetary policy directed to depressing rates rather than the current passive policy. In the second half of 1963, moreover, in response to the balance of payments deficits, we have experienced a rise of short-term rates and a substantial reduction of free reserves. Yet with all of that, I conclude that the board provided the country with a reasonably easy money policy.

But as I suggested earlier, rates rose in the second half of 1963, partly because of action taken by the Federal Reserve. In December 1963, Chairman Martin, before the Senate Finance Committee said, " . . . As the economy expands in response to tax cuts, there will be a tendency for credit demands to grow. Treasury will be bidding with private borrowers for funds and rates will rise. . . ."

Examining the supply and demand situation for funds in 1964, *Business Week* (December 28, 1963) concluded that the rate trend would be up in 1964. The upward rise of savings will taper off, and demand for funds by corporations and the Treasury will help push rates up. Hence 1964 seemed likely to be the crucial year. Intervention by the Federal Reserve might send rates up, a development more likely if serious inflationary symptoms emerged (cf. discussion in last chapter).

THE PRESIDENT'S VIEWS

President Kennedy was at first inclined to be critical of Federal Reserve policy. But the increasing concern over the threat to the dollar made him more sympathetic. In his message of February 2, 1961, on programs for economic recovery and growth, the President reiterated the need of low long-term interest rates but warned against a reduction in short-term rates with the dollar in trouble: "The Treasury and the Federal Reserve System already are working together to further the complementary effectiveness of debt management and monetary policy."

And in his message on budget and fiscal policy of March 24, 1961, he first made a point that was repeated later: " . . . Because of the limits which our balance of payments deficit currently places upon the use of monetary policy . . . our budget and tax policies must assume a heavier share of the responsibility."

But on October 13, 1961, Walter Heller, in an able paper to the American Life Convention, emphasized the point that general demand was not at a level which might bring inflation. Nor did he see any emerging bottlenecks that would jeopardize the stability of the currency. A wage inflation was possible. But he cited figures to show that wage rises had been most reasonable and in fact at a rate relative to foreign increases which was having the effect of improving our competitive position.

In his January 11, 1962, state of the union message the President took a similar line: "Our first line of defense against inflation is the good sense and public spirit of business and labor—keeping their total increases in wages and profits in step with productivity. . . ."

The President's *Economic Report of January, 1962* dwelt on the monetary ease of the Federal Reserve, and on supplementary policies directed to reducing long-term interest rates. Business had responded to rising demand by producing more, not by raising prices. But in a later passage where he commented on the increasing part played by fiscal policy in restraining inflation, he added that "with monetary and related policies relieved of a substantial part of this burden, they can more effectively be used to assure a flow of investment funds which will transform the economy's present capacity to save into future capacity to produce." (This might have been a hint that the Federal Reserve was not adequately expansionist.)

On April 19, 1963, the President, in a meeting with the newspaper editors, was confident that it was deflation, not inflation, that threatened the economy. So long as large amounts of unemployment and unused capacity prevailed, he was not concerned over the inflationary threat. Even the wage-price push would not be sustaining under competitive conditions. He told the Committee for Economic Development, on May 9, 1963, in a similar vein that inflation was not on the agenda. Production will respond to rising demand; and with improved conditions, unit costs will decline. Moreover, in response to rising income, employers will seek new markets, automation will be stimulated, and featherbedding discouraged. But he now expressed some concern over the possibilities of a wage inflation.

By July 1963, undoubtedly concerned over the slow improvement in the balance of payments, the President, when confronted with the platform promise of cheap money, at a press conference (July 17) replied:

You will realize that we are talking about [an increase] in short-term rates, and that under this Administration, mortgage rates and other rates which affect business have dropped since this Administration took office . . . and it is our hope . . . they [the Federal Reserve] will also make an effort to maintain the stability of long-term rates. This is the policy of the Government, that is the effort of the Federal Reserve. . . .

In his balance of payments message of July 18, 1963, the President again stressed the need of high short-term and low long-term rates and complimented the Federal Reserve and the Treasury for their cooperation and success.

. . . Experience in the recovery under way over the past 2½ years provides a solid basis for expecting that a determined effort can succeed in keeping long-term investments and mortgage money plentiful and cheap while boosting short-term interest rates. From February 1, 1961 through July 12, 1963, the rate on newly issued 3-month Treasury bills rose 76 basis points, while the rise in long-term Treasury bond yields was held to only 22 basis points and the yield on high-grade corporate bonds and mortgages actually declined.

. . . I have been assured by both the Treasury and Federal Reserve officers that they intend to do everything possible through debt management policy and open market operations to avoid any reduction in domestic credit availability and any upward pressure on long-term interest rates while the economy operates below capacity without inflation. . . .

Under Eisenhower, Chairman Martin of the Federal Reserve, basing himself on the theory of an independent Federal Reserve, generally supported and even led the policy of restrictionism.

I have grave doubts about the whole theory of independence. Monetary policy must be related to general economic policy. I am convinced that Martin's apparent independence stemmed from the fact that President Eisenhower would not intervene, since the Federal Reserve policy agreed with his ideological and economic position. Under Kennedy, the government pressed the Federal Reserve to be less restrictive and even expansionist. The chairman of the board went along. His policies reflected the wishes of the President. Indeed, different views on the nature of the presidency may also have contributed to some extent to the varying degrees of control of the board.

In the early Kennedy period, Martin tended to use his influence against expansion. In fact when confronted, in 1961, by a member of Congress with a statement that the President wanted easy money and low interest rates, Mr. Martin replied he would be glad to give consideration to any statement made by the President. This was not the kind of response that was likely to please any President.

It was generally expected that Kennedy would be a strong President, and hence would not be willing to accept the theory of an independent Federal Reserve. At least some of his advisers in 1960 both raised the issue of independence and also pointed out that, in view of the dollar problem, it would not be easy to strike any frontal blows at the board's posture of independence. In the campaign he was largely silent on the issues. But on a few occasions he clearly expressed disappointment at Federal Reserve policies. In a talk to businessmen he said:

. . . each successive valley in the economy has ended with higher and higher rates—with the result that paradoxically high rates accompanied heavy unemployment, low production and a slack economy.

. . . Without rejecting monetary stringency as a potential method for curbing extravagant booms we would make use of other tools.

At a meet-the-press session on October 16, 1960, the then Senator pointed out that high rates had induced recession but had not stopped inflation. The Kennedy Task Force on the Economy (with Paul Samuelson as chairman) warned against interfering with growth through restrictive monetary policies. If necessary, new tools may be needed to contend with inflation.

But despite these early avowals of presidential interest in monetary policy, the President moved cautiously. On April 17, 1962, he had asked the Congress for a "revision of the terms of the Chairman . . . so that a new President will be able to nominate a Chairman of his own choice at the beginning of his term. . . .

". . . The principal officer of the system must have the confidence of the President. . . ."

But the Republican party interpreted this as an attack on the independence of the Federal Reserve (as to some extent it undoubtedly was), and little has been heard of this since. Indeed at a press conference of June 14, 1962, the President replied to the Republican attack: "We (the President and the Chairman of the Federal Reserve Board), after all, are very closely associated in our responsibilities, though the Federal Reserve is independent and reports to the Congress. . . ."

Undoubtedly the weakness of the dollar and perhaps also an unwillingness to irritate financial and business leaders during a period of rapproachment following the steel crisis of 1962 contributed to the President's unwillingness to raise fundamental issues here with the Federal Reserve.

At a meeting with the New York Economic Club (December 14, 1962) he made his fullest statement, when he was asked whether the deficit would be financed out of savings or created money. The President virtually said that the responsibility for this policy was with Martin. But he was careful also to state that as the Europeans had suggested, we would do better to depend less on monetary policy for expansion (in view of the dollar situation) and more on fiscal policy.

I would hope, however, and I am sure that he [Martin] will agree, that he will—any deficit which has to be financed will be financed in a way which will do the maximum degree possible to stimulate the economy without increasing the prospect of another inflationary or speculative spiral. So it is a fine adjustment which Mr. Martin will make, but I am sure he will be as concerned as all of us to get the benefit such as it may be out of the deficit, and also at the same time keep and use our monetary tools wisely enough to keep matters in control. His judgment will be, because of the Federal Reserve law, final.

POLICY, *1961–1963*

Undoubtedly Secretary Dillon, Chairman Heller of the Council of Economic Advisers, and Under Secretary Roosa urged the Federal Reserve to move in the direction of ease. That they were, on the whole, successful is attested by the trends in interest rates: after thirty-three months of recovery, long-term private interest rates had actually fallen—a unique development after a protracted recovery.

This decline occurred despite the need of keeping short-term interest rates up in order to discourage exports of short-term capital to markets with high short-term rates. It is not easy to depress long-term rates if short-term rates have to be kept high.

With high short-term rates, borrowers tend to shift to the long-term market, where rates are lower, thus tending to raise those rates; and lenders shift to short-term markets, again with the result that long-term rates tend to rise. In response to inflated short-term rates, supplies of funds are smaller in the long-term market and demand greater; and, hence, the need to keep short-term rates up interferes with a cheap long-term money policy, the objective of which is to stimulate investment as costs of money decline relative to expected returns.

That short-term rates were kept up because of the need of controlling net losses of short-term capital is revealed by the high short-term rates as compared with earlier periods of recovery, and the recent decline of long-term rates. The decline in the long-term rate since December 1960 in the face of rising short-term rates does point to the conclusion that the high short-term rates did not greatly affect the long-term market.

In this connection, John Gurley has pointed out that whereas before the late 1950s, a rise of x percent in short-term rates was accompanied by an increase of $0.4x$ in long-term rates, more recently the response of the long-term rate has been only $0.15x$. In other words, the long-term rate is more isolated from the effects of movements in the short-term rates than in the past. The table below suggests this general position.

	Yield on 3–Month Treasury Bills	Yield on Aaa Corporate Bonds
1954	0.953%	2.90%
1958	1.839	3.79
1960 (December)	2.272	4.35
1963 (October 19)	3.458	4.31

It should not be assumed that the Federal Reserve and Chairman Martin yielded on monetary policy without a struggle. Most financial men are fearful of cheap money. To some extent this may be explained by the fact that bankers think they prosper when the price (rate of interest) of their commodity (money) is high. But this is only part of the problem. They are also fearful of inflation, which is a constant threat to the system. And this country has had substantial inflation, particularly during periods of war which, unfortunately for the Democrats, were years of Democratic incumbency. But the large amount of excess capacity and unemployment in the early 1960s made it easier to pressure the Federal Reserve into supporting policies of adequate supplies of money. With large amounts of unemployment, additional supplies of money were likely to be reflected in increased demand and greater output, rather than in rising prices*

Yet the Federal Reserve was probably reluctant to follow the wishes of the administration. When the President first announced his 1963 tax reduction program, the chairman of the Federal Reserve responded by warning that the deficit would have to be financed out of savings. By this the chairman meant that he would not provide the additional money to purchase the new federal securities as deficits grew. Hence, their prices would fall, that is, the rate of interest would rise, until in response to higher rates, additional savings would be had to purchase the additional issues related to the tax cuts and rising deficits.

To this original statement of Chairman Martin, Congressman Wright Patman, a persistent critic of the Federal Reserve, replied that Martin had no right to veto the tax cut. The chairman soon revised his earlier statement. An appropriate position, it seems to me, is that when the deficit appears, the policy of the Federal Reserve should be to cooperate, that is, to make additional money available for the purchase of securities, if substantial inflation does not prevail or threaten, but it should follow a policy of restrictionism, yielding higher rates, if inflation is a real threat.

All of this does not mean that the Federal Reserve is independent. There are degrees of independence. The chairman goes along with the Executive; a modus vivendi prevails. But the Federal Reserve is one of the major agencies contributing to the formulation of policy; and in expressing fears of an expansionist policy, it contributes to this formulation. But once policy is determined by the Executive the Federal Reserve is likely to cooperate. Besides, to satisfy the demand for an independent board, on the part of financial men in particular, it is important for the Federal Reserve to give an impression of a degree of independence that does not

* See Chapter 16.

in fact prevail. Chairman Martin is an able and intelligent central banker, and knows only too well how much discretion the FRB in fact has, and the extent to which it can deviate from providing monetary policy consistent with the growth, employment, and stability goals of the administration.

Confusion on the issue of independence stems in part from ignorance concerning the meaning of the term. In the famous accord between the Treasury and the Federal Reserve in 1951, inspired by Senator Paul Douglas, the Federal Reserve was no longer to peg the price of government securities. This was a decision that in pursuing its policies, the Federal Reserve was not to jeopardize our economy by weighting the interest of the Treasury excessively and bringing about continued inflation. To that extent the board was to be independent. But the Accord did not say that the Federal Reserve was to be independent in the sense that it could operate independently of the goals set by the Executive, in turn tied to some extent to legislation. Thus we can explain Senator Douglas's authorship of the Accord, and his strong criticism of failure of the Federal Reserve to provide adequate supplies of money. Moreover, in his February 1, 1963, statement to the Joint Economic Committee, Martin did not exactly say that the FRB was independent. He merely reiterated the terms of the 1951 accord which had provided that the Federal Reserve was not required to finance a federal deficit in a manner to impose inflation on the economy. And though the President often affirmed the independence of the Federal Reserve, it is quite clear from statements already quoted that he nevertheless made his wishes clear to the board.

Keeping interest rates down and raising investment levels are not merely a matter of the increase in the supply of money. Many other factors are relevant. Whereas the monetary authority primarily seeks to control the average rate of interest, the Treasury, through management, largely controls the structure of rates. Thus issues of long-term securities tend to raise long-term rates. It is not considered sound policy to issue large amounts of long-term securities during a recession period; for the result is likely to be absorption of funds by the government and pressure towards higher rates.*

* Cf. Chapter 11 on the national debt.

An example of how not to sell government securities is revealed by the table below. In the recession period, July 1957—April 1958, the Treasury sold $7 billion of long-term securities, thus intensifying the difficulties of lowering rates; and in the recovery period it actually reduced long-term issues. During the period April 1958—May 1960, the expansion period, the government relied exclusively on short-term issues. Some expansion of long-term issues was the appropriate policy.

U.S. GOVERNMENT MARKETABLE SECURITIES OUTSTANDING,
JULY 1957—MAY 1960
(billions of dollars)

		Short Term	Bonds
	July 1957	$ 77.9	$80.8
Recession	⎰ April 1958	78.3	87.7
Period	⎱ May 1960[a]	102.5	85.1

[a] Twenty-five months of expansion from the trough.

In the recovery of 1961–1963, secretaries Dillon and Roosa were careful not to repeat the mistakes of 1957–1960. Depending on a technique of advanced refunding, the Treasury in 1961–1963 was able to increase the long-term debt and yet not deprive the money market of substantial amounts of investment funds.

Another approach to reduced interest rates is for the government to depress rates in imperfect markets. Thus because of its guarantee of housing mortgages, the government can exploit its relations with the housing market, and where rates on mortgages seem excessive under current market conditions, the government can depress rates. Insurance then becomes available only if mortgage rates are below x per cent. The Kennedy administration has been more disposed to depress rates in such markets than was the Eisenhower administration. Indeed, if rates are kept too low in relation to other markets, the penalty may well be a drying up of funds for the mortgage market.

A prime objective of low rates is the expansion of investment. But there are paths to rising investment other than reduced rates of interest. One is improved prospects of returns on investment.

In its program of investment credit and liberalization of depreciation allowances, a Democratic administration had greatly improved profit prospects for businessmen. Such a program initiated by a Democratic administration is more likely to be a success than if introduced by a Republican administration. Just as legislation in support of labor has a much better chance of approval if introduced by a Republican Congress—for Democrats could not afford to oppose it—so legislation in behalf of business initiated by a Democratic administration is almost certain to be passed.

In short, monetary policy under Kennedy was much more expansionist than under Eisenhower. The concern over the external position of the dollar and possibly an unwillingness to disturb business confidence led the President to be less persuasive in bringing rates down in 1962 and 1963 than one might have expected from the expression of early views. He believed that in view of the balance of payments problem, monetary policy would have to play a smaller part and fiscal policy a larger part in stimulating the economy.

The President did not attack the independence of the Federal Reserve. In fact he affirmed it. But in practice, through early criticism of monetary policy and later by making clear that despite high short-term rates, long-term rates must be protected and even depressed through operations of the Federal Reserve, debt management, and direct measures to reduce mortgage markets rates, he made it clear that whatever he said about independence, he would allow the Federal Reserve independence only within limits. It is possible that long-term rates would have fallen more in the absence of higher short-term rates. But the administration and the Federal Reserve had a considerable success nevertheless. From 1960 to October 1963, despite an increase of 52 per cent on three-month Treasury bill rates, the rate on prime commercial paper and on corporate Aaa bonds declined. Moreover, despite the need of keeping short-term rates up, in four successive recovery periods of twenty-seven months bank rates on short-term loans had increased by 30.2, 23.0, 19.2, and (from February 1961 to April 1963), by only 0.8 per cent. The record in the current recovery has indeed been remarkable. The President, as well as his Secretary of the

Treasury and the Council of Economic Advisers, had insisted on the importance of keeping long-term rates down; and by offsetting higher short-term Treasury bill rates by increasing the availability of funds, even short-term rates in the private markets had been stabilized to a remarkable degree. Moreover, despite recommendations of the Bank for International Settlements and others, the administration refused to support higher long-term rates as a means of improving the balance of payments.

Federal Reserve policy in 1961–1963 was not like that of 1952–1960. At the early stages of recovery in the 1950s, the Federal Reserve, overly sensitive to inflationary dangers, aborted recoveries. Whether the explanation was a growing conviction that inflation was no longer a threat, or whether it was an awareness that the Kennedy administration would not tolerate stifling monetary policies, the Federal Reserve made no serious attempts to deflate the economy after 1960. In fact, in 1963, Mr. Martin boasted of the large contributions made to expansion.

An examination of rate movements; of purchases of securities by the Federal Reserve; of reductions in reserve requirements; and of inclusion of vault cash as reserves as a means of offsetting gold losses; of financing increased currency in circulation and of providing a base for more money creation; and also the high volume of free reserves of commercial banks—all of these point to a degree of cooperation of the Federal Reserve which was lacking in the 1950s. Indeed, as Senator Douglas pointed out, free reserves may not be as expansionist as claimed, for they are largely concentrated in the country banks.

On one issue the Federal Reserve may still be suspect: a premature tendency to insist on financing the 1963–1964 deficit through savings instead of created money. The Federal Reserve ought to take into account a view presented persistently by James Tobin, of the Council of Economic Advisers, that deficits create income equal to a multiple of the deficits, and this rising income provides the savings required to absorb the new securities.

I 3

Unemployment

JOBS AND GNP

In the first half of 1961, seasonally adjusted unemployment averaged close to 5 million or almost 7 per cent of the labor force. In 1962, unemployment had fallen to 4 million, and 5.6 per cent of the labor force. In 1963, unemployment was slightly higher than in 1962.

One of the great disappointments to President Kennedy was the continued high level of unemployment.

Few would have anticipated early in 1961 that with an anticipated rise of gross national product of almost $100 billion in current dollars, and $75 billion in stable dollars over a period of three years that unemployment would still fluctuate around 4 million and 5.5 per cent. In his first presentation to the Joint Economic Committee, Walter Heller pointed out that should unemployment drop from 6.4 to 4 per cent, total output should rise by 8 per cent. Yet with an increase of output of about 15 per cent, unemployment was still around 5.5 per cent in the latter part of 1963.

In a speech before the Communications Workers of America, on June 12, 1963, Dr. Heller dramatically expressed the issue:

> To close the output and employment gap by the end of 1964 would take an average rise of $14 billion per quarter. Yet . . . the economy has been advancing by only a little more than $8 billion per quarter so far this year. At that rate . . . it would take roughly 10 years to close the gap and reach 4 per cent unemployment. . . .

122

Apparently the additional GNP consistent with a million additional jobs has risen greatly in the last few years. The improvement in GNP has been more than satisfactory; that in unemployment, disappointing. In a study of the three last recovery periods, including 1961–1963, I found that the increased GNP consistent with an *additional* million jobs increased from an average of $18 billion in two earlier periods of recovery to $33 billion in the period of February 1961–July 1963. In stable dollars the increase was 100 per cent. The Budget Bureau (letter from Budget Director Kermit Gordon of September 12, 1963), in reply to a request from the writer, revealed increases from $17.6 to $19.4 and $22.7 billion (stable dollars) over periods of one year in three successive recoveries.* In the current recovery I find a rise of GNP roughly equal to that in the two previous recoveries accompanied a rise of only 60 per cent as many jobs.

THREE RECOVERY PERIODS, 1954–1963, RELATION OF RISE OF GNP
TO RISE OF JOBS
(dollars in billions)

Period of Recovery	Rise in GNP		Rise in Employment[a] (millions)	Rise in GNP per Added 1 Million Jobs	
	Current Dollars	1962 Dollars		Current Dollars	1962 Dollars
August 1954—July 1957	$80	$56	4.27	$19	$13
April 1958—May 1960	70	50	4.15	17	12
February 1961—July 1963	81	64	2.47	33	26

NOTE: My calculations. Because of the need of interpolating and also variations in methods of presenting figures, the results are subject to a margin of error, but they are reasonably close to reality.
[a] Civilian and armed forces.

It is not easy to explain the recent rise of GNP in relation to X additional jobs. It may be that manhour productivity has risen more rapidly than usual. In manufacturing, productivity seems to have improved by more than 4 per cent in both 1961 and 1962, and

* The budget director limits his analysis to *one year,* to nonagricultural employment and GNP, and to stable dollars. I treat the periods on the basis of *monthly* figures for two to three years, *total* GNP and employment, and current and stable dollars.

greatly in 1963, an unusual occurrence. Possibly due to the strain of unsatisfactory profits, more inefficient or unnecessary labor may have been weeded out. But this should have been reflected in rising productivity, as should any shifts to more productive employments —that is, to occupations requiring higher levels of education. A relevant factor is the rise of numbers on the labor market as prospects for jobs improve.

ANALYSIS OF UNEMPLOYMENT

Some economists tend to stress deficiency of demand as the explanation of the shortage of jobs and the excess of unemployment. Others emphasize structural unemployment, that is, an absence of equilibrium in labor markets—such as an excess of unskilled workers, a deficiency of skilled and professional personnel, or unfilled vacancies in parts of California and a heavy concentration of unemployment in the coal mining areas of West Virginia and Pennsylvania.

The President's Council of Economic Advisers believed that the major explanation of rising unemployment was inadequacy of demand. *A number of observers have noted that at the peak of the cycle unemployment has risen over the last few cycles.* The Council has repeatedly argued that in recent years there has been little change in the proportion of the unemployed among nonwhites, the unskilled, the less educated, youths, and employees in manufacturing industries. Supporting themselves on such statistics, the "demand" school argues that the explanation of rising unemployment is, therefore, to be found in a deficiency of demand rather than in rising structural maladjustments.

In a talk to the American Council on Education (October 4, 1963), Heller dwelt on structural and demand unemployment: ". . . measures to expand our plant capacity and our brain capacity must be matched by measures to expand the purchasing power of consumers and the investing power of business. . . ."

But he was clear that demand was crucial: "Indeed, though total unemployment has been consistently higher since 1957 than in the years before, its general pattern has not changed significantly, nor in directions supporting the structural thesis. If automation were generating a new surge of technical unemployment, it would surely be reflected in rising relative unemployment of those with low educational attainment and shrinking relative rates for those with college education. But the evidence is to the contrary." Thus the proportion of the unemployed with an eighth-grade education or less fell substantially in the years 1957 to 1962.

In a report for the Joint Economic Committee, *Higher Unemployment Rates, 1957–60: Structural Transformations or Inadequate Demand,* James Knowles in general supported the position of the Council of Economic Advisers. The emphasis was on demand, not on structural transformations. Productivity had not risen more than in earlier periods, and hence unemployment could not be fully explained by automation. Hence the report concluded that a correction of the unemployment situation through rising demand would not be more difficult than in the past. "The weakening of demand had a highly uneven but pervasive effect." With adequate demand workers would have sought available jobs in other places or occupations. The author admits that there may have been some rise in frictional unemployment; but this was not an important factor.

I agree on the whole with the council and the committee, though I would perhaps stress structural unemployment somewhat more. I would not, however, go along with Gunnar Myrdal; in *Challenge to Affluence* (1963), he admits the need of adequacy of demand, but concentrates primarily on structural unemployment, which he would treat through education, vocational guidance, etc. What he does not seem to realize is that the gains of structural therapy are limited by the number of unfilled vacancies. If, for example, there are 4 million unemployed and 1.5 million unfilled vacancies, the latter puts an upper limit to the reduction of unemployment to be had through a policy of dealing with structural unemployment. When the educational achievement and skills of the unemployed are on the average much less than the skills required and the location of unfilled vacancies far away from the homes of the unemployed, then 1.5 million unfilled vacancies may ultimately provide no more than (say) 500,000 additional jobs. Moreover, with say 6 per cent unemployment the number of unfilled vacancies is likely to be relatively small. Once unemployment is down to about 3 per cent, then policies to treat structural unemployment, such as education, vocational guidance, and financing transportation, may become increasingly effective. This explains the greater recourse to structural measures in some Western European countries, where unemployment is 1 to 3 per cent. And it is correct to argue, as the writer of the committee report contended, that with rising demand mobility would improve. A good example is the experience in World War II when unemployment dropped from 14.6 per cent in 1940 to 1.2 per cent in 1944.

But the President also stressed structural causes. He devoted a major speech in Chicago on March 21, 1963, to the unemployment problem:

> It is strange that jobs . . . the great issue of the thirties, when we were in a depression, should also be the great concern of the sixties when we enjoy a relative period of economic prosperity. . . . In the thirties . . . there was an inordinately low supply of jobs. . . .
> The difficulty now is the tremendously high manpower demand which exceeds the supply of jobs. . . .

Among the factors inducing unemployment, the President emphasized (1) the technological revolution in farming, with one farmer producing food and fiber needed for twenty-five Americans as compared to only seven at the turn of the century; (2) the expected rise in the youthful population, in the 1960s of 40 per cent in excess of the 1950s (they now account for less than one-fifth of the population but more than one-third of the unemployed); (3) the association of unemployment with inadequate education and, hence, the problems of the 7.5 million of the 26 million new younger workers who will enter the labor market in the 1960s without a high school education; (4) "finally, underlying all of these trends is the phenomenon [of] . . . the technological advance, known loosely by the name of automation." In support of the relevance of this cause of unemployment the President noted that in manufacturing output rose by 20 per cent in six years with 800,000 fewer jobs, with white collar jobs not filling the void. In coal mining the President said that 46 men achieve what 100 did in 1947: ". . . Our civilian labor force grew by nearly 12 million jobs during the last 15 years. But the number of jobs grew by only 10 million. In the last five years we saw an annual increase of only 175,000 private jobs, outside of agriculture, compared to 700,000 in each of the previous ten years. . . ."

I agree substantially with the demand school. I am impressed by the fact that for eight industries that lost one-third of their jobs (7.5 to 5 million) over a period of thirteen postwar years, the annual losses were eight times as large in four years of recession (inadequate demand) as in nine years of prosperity (high demand). Demand is crucial. Again unemployment declined by 600,000 and 900,000 in 1955 and 1959 when GNP rose by 7–8 per cent, and rose by 1.7 million and 750,000 in 1954 and 1958 when GNP declined by 2 per cent. That is to say, unemployment is associated inversely with GNP.

But the demand school sometimes seems to underestimate the significance of structural unemployment. The Council of Economic Advisers could be criticized for this at the beginning of its activities under Kennedy. Perhaps this is a necessary offset to the excessive attention given to structural unemployment by Mr. Martin, the chairman of the Federal Reserve Board, and the Republican party generally, inclusive of its most distinguished economist, Arthur Burns. Those who are fearful of fiscal or monetary policies as stimulants of the economy tend to weigh structural unemployment more heavily than those schooled in modern Keynesian economics who stress inadequacy of demand (see the *Congressional Record,* June 28, 1961).

Unemployment of a structural nature increases insofar as occupations especially subject to unemployment rise. Thus from 1948 to 1956, a rise of white collar and service workers of 163,000 accompanied a decline of structural unemployment of this group by 64,000; but though the number of manual workers, especially subject to unemployment, rose only by 52,000, unemployment of manual workers increased by 274,000. In general, goods-producing industries accounted for 43 per cent of the labor force and 55 per cent of the unemployment.*

A major point made by the demand school is that unemployment in the goods-producing industries, which are especially vulnerable to automation, has not increased more than unemployment gener-

* Joint Economic Committee, Study Paper No. 6, *Extent and Nature of Frictional Unemployment,* 1959, pp. 61–67.

ally. But a breakdown by subindustries and occupations may point to advances in structural unemployment, whether the explanation is automation or increased competition from abroad or declining demand generally. The rising amount of unemployment in utilities, in railroads, and in coal mines are cases in point.

Again, nonwhites are especially exposed. Since the late 1940s unemployment among nonwhites has more than doubled, and the unemployment in this group has risen much more than for all members of the labor market.

Much has been said about the contribution of automation to unemployment. Few would dispute the long-term gains of automation. Yet that it brings transitional unemployment and serious problems for those displaced is also clear. Many of the most serious strikes of late have been provoked by automation. If automation is to make its greatest contribution, then both private employers and government must ease the transition, partly by sharing the gains of automation with those who are injured. A good example of a cooperative effort in the early 1960s to treat the unemployment associated with automation was the effort made to help 35 per cent of the 2,000 employees who were to be displaced by the building of a completely automated plant to replace the Cudahy Meatpacking plant constructed in the 1880s.

The United Automobile Workers raised the issue of considering the interests of those on the outside seeking jobs as well as the insiders with jobs. The Kaiser Steel Corporation and the United Steelworkers agreed that no worker would lose his job on account of automation, and workers would receive one-third of the gains of increased efficiency. But however advanced this agreement, it does not help those on the outside and unemployed.

Secretary Arthur Goldberg told a subcommittee of the Senate Committee on Labor and Public Welfare, on June 7, 1961, that "in the post-war period productivity in the soft coal industry nearly doubled. . . . During this same period the number of coal miners fell by 262,000. Productivity in the nation's railroads . . . rose by 65 per cent . . . ; the number of workers employed by the railroad fell enormously by 540,000."

But these losses of jobs are not to be associated merely with automation. As the President's Advisory Committee on Labor-Management Policy noted, in a report of January 11, 1962, an understanding of the effects of automation requires consideration of the general increase of productivity and unemployment. The net effect of automation is not known since it is greatly complicated by such factors as the recession of 1960–1961, chronic unemployment in distressed areas, changing consumption patterns, the changing nature of jobs—e.g., a 58 per cent rise of the number of skilled technical and professional workers in the 1950s, the unusually high entrance rate into the labor market, discrimination against some workers, and the large migrations from the farms.

A given amount of unemployment is much more costly if it is heavily concentrated on particular groups. The large number of young entrants into the labor market, the decline of jobs formerly available to the young, and the serious dropout problem are among the most important causes of unemployment among the young. The President's Youth Employment Committee reported, in April 1963, that about

One in six of all the unemployed who are out of school are 16 to 21 year olds, although this age group makes up only about 1 in 14 of the nation's labor force. Unemployment among teenage Negro youth is double that of white boys and girls.

With a tremendous increase of numbers entering the labor market— 26 million in the 1960's—and with almost 30 per cent without a high school education—the problem becomes increasingly serious.

President Kennedy, in his message of February 14, 1963, on the nation's youth, noted: "And in terms of the number of youth in the potential labor market bracket, ages 14 to 24, the amount of the increase in this decade over the previous decade—some 6 million youths—is nearly 15 times as high as the increase which occurred in the 1950's."

And in his June 19, 1963, message on civil rights and job opportunities President Kennedy remarked that: "Unemployment falls with special cruelty on minority groups. The unemployment rate of Negro workers is more than twice as high as that of the working force as a whole. In many of our larger cities, both South and North, the number of jobless Negro youth, often 20 per cent or more, creates an atmosphere of frustration, resentment and unrest which does not bode well for the future."

The variations in unemployment vis-à-vis representation in the labor market are suggested by the following from a Labor Department survey of June 1961 of 928,000 workers unemployed twenty-seven weeks or more.

	% Unemployed of Total Unemployment	% Total Civilian Labor Force
White	24.6	88.8
Negro	25.4	11.2
Professional and technical	2.4	10.4
Unskilled Industrial Workers	19.2	6.2
Manufacturing	39.4	24.7
Finance, service	12.6	22.3
Construction	12.9	5.7

There are a few more cheerful aspects of the unemployment situation. Many have remarked at our acceptance of 6 per cent of unemployment as compared to about 2 per cent in Western Europe without much protest. The explanation of this phenomenon runs along these lines:

A large proportion of families have more than one worker.

Real incomes per capita are more than twice as high as in Western Europe, and hence savings tend to be large. Moreover, per capita disposable income, an index of standards of living, rose by more than 20 per cent since the end of World War II.

Unemployment is frequently of short duration: In 1962, 44 per cent were unemployed four weeks or under, and 72 per cent, fourteen weeks or under.

Concentration of unemployment by areas is much less than in the 1930s and 1940s.

Availability of unemployment insurance is helpful.

Many of the so-called unemployed are not potentially competent members of the labor market.

How Many Unemployed?

Before we discuss therapy, we should comment briefly on the numbers unemployed. According to the official figures unemployment reached a low of 1.87 millions, or 2.9 per cent of the civilian labor force in 1953, and then varied from 4.2 per cent in 1956 to 6.7 per cent in 1961 and 5.6 per cent in 1962. The seasonally adjusted figure varied from 5.5 per cent (August) to 6.1 per cent (February) in the year 1963.

But these are only rough figures. It is especially difficult to distinguish those who are on the labor market and unemployed from those not on the labor market and hence, though unoccupied, not included as unemployed. A Senate Special Committee (in *Employment Problems,* March 1960, p. 116) observed that:

> ... the measurement of the number of men between the ages of 20 and 55, nearly all of whom are permanently attached to the labor force is generally fairly simple. ... A large number of workers, however—over two-fifths of the work force—including married women, young people and elderly men, have a more intermittent and uncertain attachment to the labor force. ... In 1957, for example, the monthly labor force averaged 68 million persons, but 78 million persons were in the labor force at some time during the year. ...

Yet Ewan Clague, director of the Bureau of Labor Statistics, in a paper given at the Labor Conference at the University of Minnesota (February 1955) said that when the "Census reports that there are 3 millions unemployed, they also report that the true figure ... might vary as much as 200,000 either way."

For many the official figures are misleading. Thus Professor Killingsworth argued, in September 1963, that unemployment was in fact more than 1 million in excess of the official figures, because had there been as many on the labor market as in 1950 by age groups, then unemployment would have been much higher. Undoubtedly poor employment prospects keep down the numbers on the labor market. In 1962, labor force participation was 57.5 per cent as compared with 58.3 per cent in 1959 and 1960, a decline of about 1 million. In response to improved conditions, the numbers on the labor market rose by 10 million from 1940 to 1944. But it is not exactly correct to count the discouraged as unemployed. To be so counted they must be seeking work.

The National Planning Association, in a release of April 3, 1961, put unemployment at 7.1 million: 4.9 million, official figures seasonally adjusted; 1.2 million, involuntary-part-time equivalent; 1.0 million, equivalent of underemployment of marginal farmers.

Unemployment in the United States in recent years has been much higher than in Western Europe. One explanation is undoubtedly the impact of a large backlog of demand, a backlog which has been largely used up in the United States. Another relevant point is that Western Europe has used fiscal policy more effectively than this country. Improvements have been marked. For example, from 1932 to 1959, over-all unemployment in Great Britain declined from 19 to 2 per cent in developed areas; in depressed areas, from 38 to 4 per cent.

The Presidential Committee on Measuring Employment and Unemployment reported, in September 1963, that contrary to usual views, differences in methods of measuring unemployment "do not materially affect the comparability of unemployment rates among the industrial countries surveyed." The committee found that its adjusted figures ranged from 5.6 per cent unemployment in 1960 for the United States to 1 per cent for Germany and an average of 2.1 per cent for five major European countries. The differences are explained especially by social and legal factors as well as economic. Thus a worker is more closely tied to his job in Western Europe.

The amount of structural unemployment is unknown. If we had statistics for unfilled vacancies, we could estimate structural unemployment, though the volume of unfilled vacancies is related to fiscal and monetary policies: They tend to fall with improved demand.

The numbers unemployed in areas of surplus labor give some indication of the structurally unemployed, as do the numbers unemployed over long periods of time. There has been some tendency for the numbers of those unemployed 15 to 26 weeks and over and 26 weeks or over and for the average duration of unemployment to rise absolutely and relatively since 1957.

	Total Unemployed (millions)	Number Unemployed 15–26 Weeks	Number Unemployed Over 26 Weeks	Average Duration of Unemployment (weeks)
1957	2.94	321,000	585,000	10.4
1962	4.01	534,000	239,000	14.7

SOURCE: *Economic Report of the President*, 1963, p. 199. See Joint Economic Committee, Study Paper No. 23, *The Structure of Unemployment in Areas of Substantial Labor Surplus*, 1960; also see Hearings, *Ibid.*, 1961.

An estimate of structural unemployment by the National Planning Association (NPA) has not been widely supported. The NPA starts with the unemployment at the peak of the cycle and deducts transitional unemployment, estimated at 2 per cent; and the remainder is estimated as structural unemployment (*A Joint Statement on the Rise of Chronic Unemployment,* 1961). Their figures are: third quarter 1953, 0.5 million; fourth quarter 1956, 1.5 million; first quarter 1960, 2 million.

Unfortunately, the 2 per cent for transitional unemployment is only a guess. Moreover, part of the unemployment at the peak may be seasonal or even cyclical. It is doubtful, for example, that by the the first quarter of 1960 the authorities had stimulated the economy to a point where all cyclical unemployment was eliminated. The large amount of excess capacity in the first half of 1960 and the stability of prices in 1960 do not suggest a degree of demand stimulation sufficient to exclude all cyclical unemployment.

Much of structural unemployment is in the surplus labor or depressed areas. Thus in a recent year these areas had twice as many unemployed for twenty-six weeks or more than other areas. They also had relatively more factory workers and a smaller participation in the labor market. In the same employments, they also tended to have more unemployment.

Here are a few examples:

% INSURED UNEMPLOYMENT—DISTRIBUTION JULY 1956—JUNE 1957[a]

	Depressed Areas	Other
Mining	7.4	1.6
Manufacturing	62.8	57.8
Transportation equipment	20.0	4.6
Trade	7.6	12.3
Semiskilled	42.7	31.5
Unskilled	25.0	30.3

SOURCE: Joint Economic Committee, Study Paper No. 23, *The Structure of Unemployment in Areas of Substantial Labor Surplus,* 1960, pp. 20–27.

[a] These figures do not add up to 100. Transportation equipment is part of manufacturing and semiskilled and unskilled, a breakdown (not all inclusive) of manufacturing and trade; other items omitted.

Unemployment is a costly disease, partly because of its heavy concentration in some cities and regions. Hence the significance of the surplus labor areas. Unemployment also tends to be higher in the large urban centers—e.g., in early 1963, unemployment was 5.1 per cent in urban sectors but 5.7 per cent in thirty-five large cities. These cities accounted for one-fifth of the nation's population and one-quarter of the unemployment. In some parts of these cities, such as Harlem, in New York, unemployment is of course much higher.*

THERAPY

Treatment of unemployment depends partly upon the diagnosis of the disease. The Council of Economic Advisers, impressed by the insufficiency of demand, as has been the Organization for Economic Cooperation and Development, sought a cure in the stimulation of demand through appropriate monetary and fiscal policies. The council also supported structural approaches, but rightly put the greater emphasis on general measures. No practical deficit program will, for example, solve the problem of unemployment in the New England textile industries or the West Virginia coal mines. The expansionist fiscal policies will contribute towards declining unemployment in these pockets of unemployment, but a massive deficit and much inflation would prevail before general measures would solve these problems of structural unemployment.

In introducing such programs as vocational education, manpower training, and area redevelopment, the Kennedy administration tried to treat structural unemployment. The President, as a result of his Congressional experience in representing a state which was losing major industries to the South and Middle West and, hence, experiencing much structural unemployment, was well aware of the need of measures to contend with structural unemployment. From 1946 to 1960, the President fought for increased federal contracts for Massachusetts, minimum wages to improve its competitive position vis-à-vis the South, quotas on textile imports, fair transportation rates for New England, unrestricted imports of

* Based on U.S. Department of Commerce *Memo of Area Redevelopment,* June 26, 1963.

raw materials and oil—all facets of the attacks on structural unemployment.

In his message on recovery and growth of February 2, 1961, the President already realized the need of a two-pronged attack: ". . . Government action is also necessary, not only to maintain an environment favorable to economic growth, but also to deal with special problems in communities and industries suffering from economic dislocations. . . ."

In his first manpower report (March 1963), the President again dwelt on the contributions of general measures as well as on the special structural measures: ". . . Clearly, our manpower program must be designed not only to balance the needs and resources of the present but also to project those needs and resources so that current investment in manpower is shaped to future needs."

In urging the passage of the Manpower Development and Training Act, the President said:

. . . A growing and changing economy demands a labor force whose skills adapt readily to the requirements of new technology. When adaption is slow and occupational lines rigid, individuals and society alike are the losers. . . . A few hundred dollars invested in training or retraining an unemployed or underemployed worker can increase his productivity to society by a multiple of that investment. . . .

The message on civil rights and job opportunities (June 19, 1963) included similar comments on the need of both general measures to stimulate growth, and specific measures. Negro unemployment, he argued, would respond especially to greater economic growth: "Recent studies have shown that for every *one* percentage point decline in the general unemployment rate, there tends to be a two percentage point reduction in Negro unemployment."

The President continued: "The unemployment rate for those adults with less than five years of schooling is around 10 per cent; it has consistently been double the prevailing rate for high school graduates. . . ."

One final point. It would be helpful if the government in deciding upon alternative expenditures would consider as a relevant factor the number of jobs to be expected from each kind of outlay. Since there is a job shortage, we should consider the employment effects of policies just as we now consider the impact of expenditures on international reserves. Employment effects should, of course, not be a decisive consideration. The budget director has assured me that more attention will be paid to this matter.

What is so frequently ignored is that the structural approach to reducing unemployment is much less costly than the deficit route. Indeed, its use is limited by the magnitude of unfilled vacancies. But within these limits, the greatest possible use should be made of these approaches. If $1 to $2 billion were so spent, it might yield 500,000 jobs or reduce excess unemployment by one-third. Hence it is surprising that many of the congressmen who especially seek economical management oppose the "structural" measures and therefore put greater burdens on the more costly fiscal policies.

Here are some rough figures:

Deficit Route

> $10 billion deficit = + $30 billion GNP = 1 million jobs
> or cost of 1 job = $10,000 (Net gain)
> Manpower training costs $1,000 per additional job
> Area redevelopment = $2,000–$3,000 per additional job

We should at this point summarize a few major points:

1. The state of demand is crucial. Since the rise of productivity in 1961–1963 was unusual even for a recovery period and since the number of new entrants into the labor market was substantial, unemployment is likely to rise unless GNP per year rises by about $35 billion to $40 billion in stable prices. (Possibly in a later stage of recovery, e.g., 1964, the required rise may be less.) To get rid of excess unemployment would require an even larger rise of GNP. Since increasing productivity and accessions to the labor market and a rise of weekly hours bring a vast increase in potential output, it is imperative to match this rise with a corresponding increase of demand, or suffer the penalty of unsold goods, declining profits, and rising unemployment.

2. Hence the emphasis on any measures such as expansive monetary supplies, rising public expenditures, and tax cuts as the road to sufficiency of demand.

3. Structural unemployment is important. But its significance is

reduced, in that any measures taken to stimulate demand will also reduce structural unemployment. Demand-inducing measures will not be greatly impaired by structural unemployment.

4. But a residue of structural unemployment requires therapy. General, i.e., demand measures will not greatly affect this residual. The special direct measures to treat this residual are all the more necessary because the costs of adjusting supply of labor to demand in different labor markets through educational and similar measures is much less costly per job added than the demand approach. Moreover, excessive reliance on the stimulation of demand to cure residual structural unemployment is likely to mean excessive deficits and inflationary pressures.

5. Structural medicine is limited in its effects, because with substantial unemployment, unfilled vacancies are not numerous; and the magnitude of unfilled vacancies sets a limit on the gains through structural measures.

6. As the Council of Economic Advisers has argued many times, there is no clear evidence that structural unemployment is on the increase. In some areas, such as nonwhite unemployment, it may be; in some manufacturing occupations, in mining, and in some branches of transportation there may also be an upward tendency in structural unemployment; but this is not necessarily true, for example, for the less educated.

7. Restraints on general measures to stimulate buying arise in later periods of recovery as wage demands escalate and bottlenecks emerge. This may well be a problem in 1964 or 1965.

14

Wage Problems and Collective Bargaining

WAGE AND PRICE POLICIES

One of the fundamental objectives of the Kennedy administration was price stability. The President sought to dissociate himself from the view that the Democrats are the party of inflation. Continued weakness of the dollar abroad only confirmed this view that price stability was absolutely necessary. President Kennedy succeeded in stabilizing the price level, and prices rose little despite substantial federal deficits and a relatively easy money policy.

In the midst of a sluggish economy, the President was not greatly concerned over the possibility of an excess of demand bringing about inflation. Rather, the problem that concerned him was a cost push induced by wage rises that exceeded the improvement in productivity. He was aware of the substantial wage push in the middle 1950s which had contributed to a substantial price rise. He did not want that kind of development in his administration, since either it would bring higher prices or, if the Eisenhower policies had been continued, there would be restrictive monetary, and possibly fiscal policies, which would increase unemployment.

In a speech to the United Automobile Workers, on May 8, 1962, the President revealed he was aware of the issues: "To return to a policy of halting inflation by curbing demand [Eisenhower's policy] would be self-defeating; but to expand the forces of demand by feeding the fires of inflation [wage inflation and its effects] would be equally dangerous and delusive."

In announcing wage guidelines the Kennedy administration was in fact seeking goals to be reached with the help of proper wage policies. First, the administration wanted a noninflationary wage policy, with gains in equity, for inflation injures some at the expense of others. Avoidance of inflation also improves the competitive position of American producers. Second, the wage policy should contribute towards a desired allocation of resources. By requiring adjustments upward or downward in wage rates as workers are in short supply or in excess, the Council of Economic Adviser's guide was contributing towards a needed influx or efflux of labor. Third, the distribution of the nation's product should stimulate growth. All should share in the gains of productivity. Profit incentives should be adequate, but profits should not be so high as to contribute to inflation. Labor's gains may be achieved through either rising wages and stable prices or stable wages and declining prices (the most desired approach and the most difficult to achieve) or finally, by the usual trend, through rising prices and wages increasing even more. Fourth, the council's guidelines support equity not only as indicated above, but also in allowing adjustments in wages when, on the basis of training required and the tasks performed, wages are too low in comparison with wages elsewhere. Fifth, wages and profits should respond in an anticyclical manner. Thus, in terms of classical economics, it was generally assumed that a decline of wage rates would pull an economy out of a depression; but more recently it has been stressed that falling wage rates reduce spending and thus aggravate conditions in a depression.

These considerations help explain the guidelines for wage policy first presented in the January 1962 report of the Council of Economic Advisers to the President. In introducing the guidelines the council was courageous and helped improve the understanding of the issues involved. The guidelines probably also contained the increase of wages during the Kennedy administration. One cannot be sure of its exact contribution to noninflationary wages, for the large amount of unemployment also tended to restrain trade union leaders in their demand for higher wages. At any rate, it is clear that in 1961–1963 wage rates had risen substantially less than in the Eisenhower years. Perhaps trade union leaders are more restrained when Democrats, rather than Republicans, are in power.

What were the guides? Ordinarily, annual wage rates should not rise more than the average increase of manhour output in the economy. This means, on the whole, that a rise of wage rates above 3 per cent would generally be excessive. But there are some reservations. On grounds of equity, adjustments have to be made for workers whose pay is low vis-à-vis other workers with similar abilities and responsibilities. Again, where workers are in excess even in periods of full employment, the rise of wages should be less than that indicated by over-all productivity guides; and when workers are in inadequate supply, a case can be made for wage rises in excess of that given by the increase of productivity. In this manner, wage policy would contribute to the adjustment of supply to demand. Still another problem arises when attention is paid to the productivity trends of individual industries or occupations. When productivity is relatively high, the case is strong for price reductions, and when productivity rises little or even declines, price rises are justified.

These guidelines raise all kinds of problems. First, it is not clear that movements in wage rates are an adequate measure of inflation potential. More important are wage earnings (with the assumption of no decline in hours). The difference between wage rates and wage earnings are given by modifications in fringe benefits (probably implicit in the guidelines) and other factors making for wage increases, and sometimes referred to in Great Britain as the "wages drift." In a recent book (*The British Economy,* 1963) Sir Roy Harrod lists as the four components of the wages drift, that is, the excess of rise of earnings over wage rates, as (1) an increase of overtime, (2) excess of wages over those fixed in collective bargaining paid by some employers in order to attract workers, (3) upgrading of workers, (4) effects of operation of piece rates when improved machinery and management result in larger output.

Second, controversy in the interpretation of the guidelines broke out early on the issue of the distribution of income between workers and management. The Council of Economic Advisers did not seem to rule out a redistribution of income between labor and capital so long as no rise of prices was involved. But the President had said that fights to secure a larger slice of the economic pie "by forcing wages up ahead of productivity can only weaken our efforts to expand the economy." In a letter to the *New York Times* (July 7, 1962) Nat Weinberg of the United Automobile Workers argued with some effectiveness that it was a proper task of a trade union to try to get a larger share of the output. Also, capital's share might justifiably increase when the improvement in product stems from larger relative inputs of capital or management.

Third, in practice, wage negotiations had not always followed the guidelines. Thus textile wages have risen much less than electronic wages, in part because productivity within the industry determined wages to a substantial degree. In bituminous coal, wages rose by 161 per cent from the end of the war to 1962, a rise substantially higher than that for manufacturing. Yet on the basis of productivity increases *in the economy,* the increase should have been much less, and a fortiori when allowance is made for the massive losses of jobs in coal mining. But John Lewis and the collieries agreed on raising productivity and, correspondingly, wages, in relation *not to general increases in productivity,* but to those in coal mining.

It is not clear that major agreements were always consistent with the guidelines. An agreement with the nonoperating railroad workers in 1962 seemed to be excessive on the guideline criteria, especially if allowance is made for the fact that the numbers of workers was excessive, and hence the rise of wages should have been less rather then in excess of the increase given by the gains in general productivity. In the stoppage of work by longshoremen, the Morse Committee appointed by the President pressured the employers to accept an agreement which also apparently provided for wage increases beyond that suggested by the rise of productivity in the economy. Here undoubtedly an inflationary wage increase might be the lesser of two evils, the other being the effects of the unfortunate strike on the economy and especially on the balance of payments.

From the very beginning of his administration President Kennedy called out against inflationary wage increases, especially because of the unfavorable effects on the balance of payments. In a letter to the steel companies as early as September 6, 1961, the President warned them of the dangers of rising wages and prices:

In the years preceding 1958, sharply rising steel prices and steel wages provided much of the impetus to a damaging inflation in the

American economy. From the beginning of 1947 to the end of 1958, while industrial prices as a whole were rising 39 per cent, steel mill product prices rose 120 per cent. Steel wages also rose rapidly, causing employment costs per ton of steel to rise by about 85 per cent. The international competitive position of American producers was impaired, and our balance of payments was weakened. . . .

Then the President commented on price stability since 1958, the absorption of wage increases by the industry, the high profits and values of the common stocks of the industry. Since iron and steel are each a bellwether of, as well as a large factor in, industrial costs, a rise of steel prices would invite price increases elsewhere. But if the steel industry should keep prices stable, the case would be strong for moderate rises in wages under the impending wage negotiations of the steel industry. That the President forced the companies to retract is well known.* The costs of the President's steel price policy were heavy. He had no alternatives but a showdown with the industry. Moreover, the President has every right to seek from steel companies, trade unions, and other vital forces in the economy policies that take into account the needs of the nation. In this period, policies that induce inflation and weaken the dollar are against the interest of the nation.

In groping towards a solution, the President used moral suasion on both labor and capital. But the costs in time and energy for the President and his aides, the resulting hostile reaction of business interests, and the difficulty of applying similar techniques to other groups negotiating wage rates—all of these raise questions concerning future attempts to rule out wage and price inflation.

In his April 11, 1962, press conference, the President ended his comment on the steel episode by saying:

Price and wage decisions in this country, except for a very limited restriction in the case of monopolies and national emergency strikes, are and ought to be freely and privately made, but the American people have a right to expect in return for that freedom a higher sense of business responsibility for the welfare of their country than has been shown in the last two days.

In 1963, the steel companies announced another price increase. The President did not object, partly because the rises were selec-

* Cf. Chapter 5.

tive, and also because there was a disposition to hold that in the competitive world the steel companies might not be able to maintain the 1963 rise.

But in April 1963 he had warned against a general increase in steel prices. On April 19, in reply to a question of the newspaper editors, he insisted that he had responsibilities in the price field: " . . . Price stability . . . is the best thing for the steel industry, and wage stability is the best thing for the unions." He noted that the 1 per cent average rise in 1963 would only offset the decline since 1959, and he hoped a large part could be absorbed by buyers, e.g., automobile manufacturers.* In the fall of 1963, further increases were being pressed.

The case for presidential opposition to price increases that were likely to be costly to the economy in a period of crisis was great. Yet in the absence of war, direct controls are not acceptable. The President sought to use moral suasion instead of asking for controls. But even in wartime moral suasion is not too effective. Moreover, questions of equity arise. With a limited amount of purchasing power, price containment for some industries, e.g., steel, means more purchasing power available to others to validate their wage and price increases, and in particular for the employments over which moral suasion is likely to have little effect—teachers, construction workers, defense workers, service workers.

The President was concerned over his rift with the steel companies and their business allies. At his April 18, 1962, press conference he volunteered that the government could not and should not control prices (and) or wages. But "we can attempt . . . to bring before the parties in the most effective way possible, the public interest that is involved. . . ."

At the same time he said that ". . . this Administration harbors no ill will against any individual . . . or segment of the economy. Our goals of economic growth and price stability are dependent upon the success of both corporations, business and labor, and there can be no room on either side in this country at this time for any feelings of hostility or vindictiveness." The President continued that he was aware of the need of the steel industry for profits, modernization, and investment capital.

In a speech to the United Automobile Workers, on May 8, 1962,

* But prices seem to have risen 2 to 3 per cent in 1963.

the President admitted that "we can suggest guidelines for the economy but we cannot fix a single pattern for every plant and every industry." And he said, "But we possess and seek no powers of compulsion, and must rely primarily on the voluntary efforts of labor and management . . . to make sure . . . that the national interest is preserved."

In 1963–1964 the guideposts for wage and hence price increases continued to be a source of friction between President and labor and industry.

COLLECTIVE BARGAINING

When President Kennedy took over, the position of trade unions had greatly weakened. Evidence of corruption, pressures for inflationary wage increases, strikes and threats of disruptive strikes, undemocratic administration, protection of the interests of the employed against those of the unemployed—all of these and other factors had aroused much resentment toward the trade union movement. The public ignored the fact that many of the abuses were concentrated among a minority of trade unions and members, and that the movement was still led mainly by such highly moral leaders as Walter Reuther.

It was one of the President's duties to impress upon labor leaders their public responsibilities; for example, support of non-inflationary wage policies and avoidance of strikes which might seriously damage the economy in the midst of a period of crisis. That the trade unions were having their difficulties obviously would make them sensitive to Presidential pressures, especially since the President had had their support in the election. It was no secret that labor leaders were not pleased with the guidelines of the Council of Economic Advisers.

In 1961 and 1962 a number of strikes broke out which concerned the administration. On June 22, 1962, the President criticized the flight engineers for refusing to accept binding arbitration after a period of seventeen months, in which a settlement had been sought under the Railway Labor Act. The railroad telegraphers, who had refused to accept the proposal of a presidential emergency board, that the union withdraw its demand that no telegraphers be dropped without consultation with the union, were also criticized by the President. The President pointed to the damage of a strike to the economy of nine states.

A series of strikes in the aerospace industry was an occasion for several pronouncements of the President in September 1962 and January 1963. Here the big issue was the union shop. Following the recommendations of a board which he had appointed, the President pressured the companies to accept the union shop, which, he pointed out, had been the rule in major industries for many years. At one press conference, he was accused of being antibusiness because of this action. But the President was determined to prevent strikes in an industry which would "substantially delay our vital missile and space programs and would be contrary to our national interest." In January 1963 he rebuked the Boeing Company for refusing to grant the union shop, especially since the workers had accepted a *modest* rise in wages.

The longshoremen were a particularly troublesome group. They virtually closed the Atlantic and Gulf ports and further weakened the balance of payments. Here again the President forced an agreement on management and labor through the Morse Committee, which was told that if it could not settle the strike it should suggest other ways of opening the ports. The workers gladly accepted the Morse proposals, which provided a rise of wages beyond that given by the guidelines; management accepted with reluctance.

Perhaps the railroads were the greatest source of concern. On several occasions (e.g., June 15, 1963), the President reprimanded both parties to the railroad dispute for failing to bargain. On July 22, 1963, the President, reacting to the stalemate, sent a special message on the railroad rules dispute to the Congress:

This nation stands on the brink of a nationwide rail strike that would, in very short order, create widespread economic chaos and distress. After more than three and one half years of constant, but fruitless, attempts to achieve a peaceful settlement between the parties through every private and public means available, this dispute has reached the point where only prompt and effective Congressional action can assure that serious injury to the public will be prevented.

". . . New and complex issues relating to changes proposed by the carriers and the brotherhoods in work rules" were the major problems. A commission and a board had agreed on reductions of personnel but with provisions for compensations and retraining. The brotherhoods would not go along.

The Emergency Board, mindful of the need of efficient operations by the railroads, also took account of the burdens of dislocation on the workers. Railroads and society should share the burdens, which, in addition to dollar payments, "involve education or retraining for new jobs at the expense of the carriers, supplemented by public funds. . . ."

In his July 22 message the President, basing his views on a Council of Economic Adviser's estimate, warned that after thirty days of a general railroad strike 6 million nonrailroad workers would have been laid off, that unemployment would reach 15 per cent for the first time since 1940, and that the decline in our rate of GNP would be four times as great as in the worst prewar recession.

Struck by the problems raised by automation, the President devoted much space in his Congressional message to this issue and its treatment. He showed much sympathy for the firemen, who were hurt by the replacement of steam locomotives by diesel engines for 97 per cent of all freight tonnage. Admitting the great gains of technological change, the President reminded the Congress that the displacement of manpower is a problem that should be treated by public as well as private interests.

15

The Dollar Problem

POLICIES

Concern over the dollar makes it difficult to rely on expansionist policies as a means of treating unemployment. The need of watching the balance of payments was particularly vexing for an administration that had come in on the promise of maximum growth and adequate spending for welfare and security.

President Kennedy issued one of his first state papers in 1961 on the problem of the balance of payments and the dollar. As the President said, on February 6, 1961, ". . . the United States must, in the decades ahead, much more than at any time in the past, take its balance of payments into account when formulating its economic policies and conducting its economic affairs."

THE DOLLAR: EXPANSION OR CONTRACTION AT HOME?

Within the government and outside there are disagreements on how to manage at home in order to protect the dollar. There are those who hold that an expansionist policy at home is the only safeguard for the dollar. They insist that this kind of policy, with large creations of money and federal deficits, will bring prosperity and inflows of capital, a reduction of outflows of capital, and even lower costs and, hence, induce an improved competitive position. Indeed, the President in his message stressed the need of "maintaining competitive costs, improving productivity, and stabilizing, or,

147

where possible, lowering prices." But it is clear from numerous statements of the President that he believed that the balance of payments restrained expansionist policies.

The President's position was the classical one, namely, that the way to induce a favorable balance of payments is to keep costs low, with exports rising and imports declining; nor is it inconsistent with the neoclassical view, namely, that as incomes rise relatively here, we tend to import more and export less. Moreover, excessive federal deficits suggest to many a loss of confidence in the dollar which is expressed by outward movements of capital. Many see in these large deficits a possibility that the dollar will depreciate in relation to gold (i.e., resultant conversions of dollars for gold may induce inconvertibility).

But there are differences of opinion here. Some hold that confidence suffers more if the recovery is anemic and the economy tired than if as a result of expansionist policies the economy becomes healthy. Professor Alvin Hansen, in a letter to the *New York Times,* in May 1962, argued that the road to equilibrium in the dollar market is domestic expansion. He stressed especially the decline of costs as the economy approached and reached full employment. Undoubtedly, in the first and probably the second year of a recovery, unit costs fall as excess capacity declines and rises of wages tend to lag. But possibly by the third year, and certainly by the fourth, the emergence of bottlenecks and the pressure for wage increases are likely to bring rising, not declining, prices. In 1961 and 1962, and even 1963, events seem to have supported the views of the rising productivity school. We shall have to wait for history's verdict for 1964 and 1965.

PRESIDENTIAL POLICY: 1961–1962

The President emphasized especially the need of treating the balance of payments directly—through reducing costs, encouraging foreign travel to the United States, putting greater burdens of defense and aid on our allies with surpluses in their balance of payments, and tying aid to purchases in the United States.

By the middle of 1962 the President seemed to be less sure of the necessary tactics. He inquired whether substantial deficits in the federal budget were really incompatible with large growth and surpluses in the balance of payments. Here he was impressed by European experience, where growth twice as large as here seemed compatible with large favorable balance of payments.

As a result of numerous measures taken and also the favorable effect of trade recession (less imports) the loss of reserves was substantially cut in 1961. In fact the loss of gold and convertible currencies and the rise of short-term debt to foreign interests had declined from about $4 billion in 1960 to $2.5 billion in 1961. Balance of payment deficits were still too high, especially since the trend of deficits rose in the latter part of the year.

In submitting the *Report to the President by the Secretary of the Treasury on the Balance of Payments* to the Congress, the President, on March 28, 1962, admitted that "much still remains to be done. . . . We must work with our friends and trading partners to achieve a more equitable sharing of the burdens of aid and defense, and to build a stronger international financial system. Above all, we must harness the energies of all our people—in labor and management as well as government—to the vital task of keeping our industry competitive and expanding our exports."

IMPROVEMENTS IN 1962

In 1962, there was an improvement in the balance of payments, with deficits down to $2.2 billion, though if allowance is made for special transactions (e.g., prepayment of debts) the correct figure is roughly $3 billion. At a meeting with the American Bankers Association, of February 25, 1963, a questioner charged the administration with losing gold largely because of the giveaway programs inclusive of military aid. The President replied:

. . . The fact of the matter is that private industry in this country has invested about $2¼ billion over the last ten years, and that is a dollar drain. . . .

. . . If the Ford Motor Company spends $350 million two years ago to buy Ford in Great Britain that can end up as a dollar loss, and can end up, as Britain keeps nearly 100 per cent of its reserves in gold, that can end up as a gold loss. . . .

We lose a billion dollars in tourists every year. . . . We have attempted to tie our purchases as much as possible, to our military expenditures—we now tie about 80 per cent of our aid to expenditures here . . . and we are trying to do even better. . . .

On the whole the record of 1962, though somewhat improved, was not satisfactory. And conditions did not improve in the first half of 1963. In fact the deficit in the second quarter of 1963 reached a record amount in excess of $5 billion (annual rate). But the second half of 1963 and early 1964 showed promise.

THE JULY 18, 1963, STATEMENT

On July 18, 1963, the President issued his second impressive statement on the balance of payments. He reassured the country:

. . . Rejecting a choice between two equally unpalatable alternatives —improved employment at home at the cost of a weaker dollar abroad or a stronger dollar at the cost of a weaker economy and nation—we sought a new course that would simultaneously increase our growth at home, reduce unemployment and strengthen the dollar by eliminating the deficit in our international payments. . . .

The President then emphasized the substantial growth achieved and the improved balance of payments. But he also noted the special transactions, which could help only temporarily. Despite the problems, the President assured the world that this country would continue its liberal trade and investment policies, seek solutions to its growth and unemployment problems, and maintain the fixed dollar-gold relationship.

It was necessary to concentrate on short-run palliatives and long-run correctives. The nation needs "inroads into the hard core of our continuing payments deficit—augmenting our long range efforts to improve our economic performance over a period of years in order to achieve both external balance and internal expansion—stepping up our shorter-run efforts to reduce our balance of payments deficits while the long range forces are at work. . . ."

The President here stressed increased investment, rising productivity, continuing cost and price stability, and also faster growth. He did not raise the issue of the relation of more rapid growth and the possible adverse effects on the balance of trade. But he noted that price and wage stability accompanied by some inflation abroad would be a "powerful force working to restore our payments balance over the longer run. . . ."

In this statement the President supported an increase in the short-run rate of interest. But he was careful to point out that

when liquid savings are growing rapidly, and when there are no accompanying restrictions on credit availability nor parallel increases in the interest rates on bank loans, home mortgages or other long-term obligations the rise of short-term rates should have little, if any, adverse effects on our economy. The unprecedented flow of liquid savings should largely insulate the longer term markets from the effect of higher short-term rates. I have been assured by both Treasury and Federal Reserve officials that they intend to do everything possible through debt management policy and open-market operations to avoid any reduction in domestic credit availability and any upward pressure on long term interest rates while the economy operates below capacity without inflation. . . .

The President supported this position on the basis of the trend of long-term and short-term rates from February 1961 to July 1963.

The President urged foreign countries to remove restrictions on the export of capital, and asked American officials to redouble their efforts to find new markets for United States products. He hoped that the improved economic conditions here would reduce capital exports from this country and increase the inflow.

The President's most significant proposals were to save about $1 billion on military and civilian expenditures abroad, about half from military and the other half from AID. The President estimated that within eighteen months, the reduction of military and civilian expenditures abroad and the effects of higher short-term rates (to treat an outflow of $1.6 billion of capital in 1962), and the new 1 per cent tax on foreign securities purchased by Americans would yield savings of about $2 billion in all per year. He had also mentioned a few other items that might save a few hundred millions. Such savings, if consummated, might well close the major part of the gap. This proved an excellent forecast.

THE EXPORT OF CAPITAL

President Kennedy's willingness to support the tax on foreign securities sold to Americans reflected the concern over the rising sales of these securities and the failure of earlier attempts to deal with this problem. The President had noted increases of sales of portfolio securities from $850 million in 1960 to $1,200 million in 1962 and $1,500 million in 1963. In fact a level of almost $2 billion (annual rate) had been reached by early 1963. As late as April 24, 1963, Secretary Dillon still hoped to avoid extreme measures:

" . . . We are working with our European friends in the OECD [Organization for Economic Cooperation and Development] to liberalize their control on capital movements, and we are urging them to develop their own internal capital markets so that they will not have to rely heavily on our capital market. . . ."

In the years 1961–1963, the administration had taken numerous steps which, it was hoped, would reduce the deficit on capital account. Among these measures were the investment credit and accelerated depreciation allowances which would make investment in the United States relatively more attractive. The tax cut was expected to contribute towards a more prosperous economy, and hence attract capital here and discourage its export. Tax measures of 1962 against tax havens were also helpful. But these were inadequate or slow in their operation.

In the meantime the rapid increase of sales of foreign securities to Americans had become the most important new factor in the situation, and threatened to offset a substantial part of the gains associated with other measures. The appetite for new capital in Western Europe seemed unlimited. In their report of April–May 1963, the Chase Manhattan Bank revealed that though the Common Market countries had only about one-eighth as large a volume of securities outstanding as this country, their new issues in 1962 were two-fifths as large—statistics pointing to rapid expansion.

It is not surprising, then, that the Treasury proposed an interest equalization tax on purchases of foreign securities. As Secretary

Dillon made clear in his statement before the Ways and Means Committee on August 20, 1963, the tax, roughly equal to 1 per cent, would divert security issues away from the United States. The Secretary admitted, however, that where capital was not available, dependence on our market would continue. Moreover, it was necessary to exclude Canada, dependent on our markets, even though Canada accounted for about one-half of the foreign securities purchased by the United States. But the government required scrutiny of new issues by Canada. Nevertheless, Dillon hoped to reduce the purchases from a $2 billion annual rate and from even higher rates threatened later, to about $600 million, the annual rate of the years 1961 and 1962.

This tax, in Dillon's view, was the equivalent of a rise in the rate of interest to foreign sellers of 1 per cent. It was in fact an alternative to raising the long-term rate of interest here by 1 per cent. The alternative, namely, a direct attack, through an increase in the long-term rate of interest in an underemployed and excess capacity economy, would have been most unwise.

Capital movements have undoubtedly been the most important single factor in the deficit of the United States, and they were tending to become more serious. They have been more of a burden than military expenditures. An excess of exports of goods and services varying from $4,275 to $5,309 million from 1960 through 1962 was not enough to offset military expenditures abroad, other aid, and long- and short-term capital exports, inclusive of unrecorded transactions. The last is generally considered largely short-term capital, a fact supported by the sudden shift of a billion dollar credit into a deficit of $683 million in 1960, the year of the great crisis in the balance of payments.

Capital movements (net) are roughly equal to the net credit on trade and service account, and in the two years 1961 and 1962 were about twice the over-all deficit (kept down by special government transactions). Short-term capital movements and unrecorded transactions, totaling $2,121, $2,380 and $1,741 million in the years 1960, 1961, 1962 were about as troublesome as the long-term capital movements. It has often been said that these are reversible; but it is of some interest that they continued for three years and accounted for $6,200 millions of deficits. In the nine years 1951 to

1959, the errors and omissions were a credit item of $4,693 million and short-term capital was a debit of $2,037 million, or a net change (credit) of $2,656 million, i.e., roughly $300 million annually as against an average $2 billion deficit in the years 1960–1962. In a sense there is no limit to short-term capital movement except that set by an ultimate rise in the price of gold or foreign currencies. Theoretically, a conversion of a large part of the total money supply in this country and of assets convertible into money might prevail. But in practice, long before this occurs, corrective measures would be taken. Undoubtedly the outflow is related in part to speculation of a devaluation. An export of dollars with pounds sterling at $2.80, for example, would yield a profit of $1.20 once the dollar declined to £1 = $4.

In some respects, we are overstating the burden of capital movements. First, because against these debit items we should put earnings on private foreign investments of $2,283, $2,962, $3,327, $3,488 million (annual rate) for 1960, 1961, 1962, and the first quarter of 1963. An offset is the roughly $600 million in income paid to foreign interests on foreign investments in the United States. Ultimately sound investments yield earnings in excess of new investments each year. But in the early years when investments are being made the debits on payments exceeds earnings remitted. Thus the roughly $12 billion of capital exported in 1960–1962 after three years would at the most yield $600 million per year of remittances; but in the meanwhile $12 billion would have been sent abroad.

Moreover, the remittances tend to be relatively less helpful from the developed countries, which are gaining disproportionately from capital exports from the United States. Thus from 1956 to 1960 I estimate that against a capital outflow of $5.4 billion to developed countries remitted income was $3,895 million, and hence the net cost to the U.S. balance was $1.5 billion. For the less developed countries income remitted exceeded capital outflow by $4.0 billion. Moreover, the rise of sales from foreign auxiliaries of U.S. corporations in the countries of operation and to third countries greatly exceeds the rise of exports from the United States relative to direct investments abroad.

Second, the losses related to capital exports are overstated because there is some relation of capital exports and the rise of merchandise and service exports. The more capital exports, the more the exports of commodities and services. But the relationship is not necessarily close, and there are important lags. Moreover, large proportions of foreign loans, as Secretary Dillon noted on August 20, 1963, are for purely domestic use abroad. According to classical theory, capital exports reduce purchasing power at home and thus tend to reduce prices and costs and, therefore, to expand exports and curtail imports. But in an economy where foreign trade is but 4 per cent of the GNP and wages and prices are sticky even though substantial unemployment prevails, the net price effect is not likely to be large, and especially when the monetary authority determines monetary supplies on other criteria.

INTEREST RATE POLICY

Beginning in 1961, the U.S. authorities have sought to keep the short-term rate of interest up—the Federal Reserve, through recourse to the usual weapons; and the Treasury, through issue of Treasury bills. These authorities had been impressed by the large movements of short-term capital in response to high rates abroad. Thus in the middle of 1960, three-month Treasury bills yielded 2 per cent in the United States, 5 per cent in Germany, and 5.5 per cent in the United Kingdom. It was held that the high short-term money rate policy in the United States in 1961 and 1962 reduced, despite large increases in trade financing, the short-term and unrecorded deficits from $2,121 million in 1960 to $1,741 million in 1962. These movements of short-term capital were held to be so crucial as to justify high short-term rates. But the hope was that long-term rates might be insulated. So far (1963) this hope had largely been fulfilled.

Among economists there is some difference of opinion on the sensitivity of short-term capital movements to relative interest rates. In a statement to the Joint Economic Committee (*Compilation of Studies Prepared for the Subcommittee on International Exchange and Payments,* 1962) Professor Philip Bell related short-term capital movements to trade trends. But even Bell admitted that in some areas, such as balances of nonfinancial corporations, the relative rates of interest were of some importance. Professor Peter Kenen, in a study for the Treasury, October 1962, stressed the relation of interest rates to capital movements. Kenen concluded that most of the outflow of short-term capital "was probably autonomous—the consequence of international interest rate differences, disparities in the availability of credit, and outright speculation." Kenen could not find a high correlation of the short-term capital movements and trade. But he concluded that there was a close association between relative interest rates and investment by foreigners in Treasury securities and other money-market assets. Moreover, Kenen found "a significant relationship between the U.K.–U.S. differential and U.S. lending to Continental Europe; also between the Euro dollar–U.S. bill-rate differential and U.S. lending to Latin America."

In still another study (*A Survey of Capital Movements and Findings Regarding Their Interest Sensitivity*, July 1963) for the New York Federal Reserve Bank, B. J. Cohen found a significant sensitivity. He concluded that a substantial relative rise of rates here might be associated with a reduction in our balance of payments deficit by as much as $750 million in a year. Moreover, Cohen noted that private foreign holders of dollars are very much interested in relative interest rates. He stated that a rise on rates here might reduce private switching out of dollar assets by as much as $600–$700 million. This would involve corresponding relative gains for our gold stock.

TIED ASSISTANCE

Another aspect of the President's program requires some elaboration. Perhaps the most important gains relate to the increasing use of tied assistance, that is, requiring that aid dollars be spent here. Many disapprove because this is a protectionist device. Indeed it is. But the alternative is less assistance. What is important here is that the gain from tied aid may not be so great as it appears. First, because more tied sales, where supply conditions are not elastic, may result in reduced exports to other countries, and second, because there is an important component, e.g., raw materials of exports. In periods of large excess capacity the resultant loss of other exports associated with tied assistance may not be great. But second, there is another factor, namely, that countries receiving aid and required to purchase in the United States may divert other purchases from the United States to other countries. How large these leaks may be it is difficult to estimate. But it is important to realize that unlike the conditions in the early postwar period, when our competitors were not able to provide the goods which were the counterpart of our aid, in more recent years they have been prepared to validate *our* capital exports by providing the required goods. Yet tied aid makes a significant contribution to easing our dollar problem.

COMPETITIVE POSITION

Above all, an improvement in the strength of the dollar awaits a rise of exports of commodities and services vis-à-vis imports. There are other solutions, such as reductions of economic aid and military expenditures abroad. But these are largely offset by reduced voluntary or compulsory purchases in the United States. Hence cuts would not substantially favor our balance of payments.

Another way out is to reduce capital exports, as is intended by the interest equalization tax. Here there may be some substantial gains, for capital exports are not offset by corresponding rises of exports or reduction of imports. According to the classical theory, a rise of capital exports brings a reduction of purchasing power at home; hence reduced prices; and hence more exports and less imports to match the rise of capital exports. Then increased capital exports would not be a burden on the balance of payments.

But this relationship of capital and merchandise and service exports may be a tenuous one, as the British discovered in the 1920s. In the United States of the 1960s there are special reasons why a rise of capital exports, and especially through purchase of portfolio investments, may not yield corresponding exports, and hence why a reduction of capital exports may favor the United States balance of payments. Among these factors are: (1) The fact that monetary supplies are determined on the basis of the needs of the economy; and, hence, diversions of dollars to foreign borrowers would probably not be at the expense of the nation's purchasing power needed for domestic purposes. (2) Since the United States exports but 4 per cent of its GNP and only 17 per cent of the world's exports, the transfer of dollars to foreigners may well not have a great effect on its export sales. (3) Not only may the borrowers buy in other countries than the United States but may use the proceeds for purely domestic purposes. Finally, it is well to stress the point that if exports of capital of $4 billion had been offset by corresponding exports or reduced imports, the dollar would not in 1963 be in serious trouble. Surely aid and military outlays are not at fault, for they are very largely tied.

But despite these reservations, the crucial problem is the United States competitive position, an improvement in which should increase the excess of exports over imports. In 1963 prices of United States exports were too high vis-à-vis those of her competitors to achieve an excess of exports of about $7 billion, an excess which would largely have wiped out the deficit in the balance of payments. A rise of these proportions from the 1962 excess of $4.8 billion (exclusive of military transactions) would have secondary repercussions of significance, and notably a rising confidence in the dollar which would greatly reduce the outflow of short-term capital related to expectations of a devaluation.

Another way of discussing this issue is to say that the dollar is overvalued. That simply means that export prices are too high in the United States vis-à-vis those of her competitors to wipe out the deficit in the balance of payments. In one sense the dollar is not overvalued, for exports exceed imports by $5 billion and on this ground our competitive position is strong. But in two other ways, the dollar is overvalued. First, because at the current cost of the dollar in foreign currencies the dollar is priced too high for the United States to achieve an excess of exports today of $7 or $8 billion. Second, because even the current international deficit is held down by imposing on the country monetary and fiscal policies that are not nearly as expansionist as they would be in the absence of the constraints of the balance of payments. In other words that GNP is less and unemployment greater than they would be with exclusive attention paid to domestic requirements is evidence of an overvalued currency.

How does one measure a deterioration of competitive conditions?

One approach is to study the share of the world's export market accruing to the United States. This test is subject to some reservations. First, losses may be associated with increased discrimination against United States exports. But this is not a valid reservation now. In fact, in recent years markets have been increasingly opened to the United States, and hence any decline of our share to that extent understates our losses. (The development of the Common Market probably operates in the reverse direction.) Again, the deterioration of our position may be associated with the fact that the economies of our best customers, in short, the Western Hemisphere, have grown less slowly than Europe, and our relative rise of export trade reflects the modest gain of our best customers. This has been an important factor. But these misfortunes are relevant in assessing competitive position. If one's customers lose relative economic status, the effects are the same as if the sellers experienced relatively high rises in prices.

Western Europe and Japan improved their competitive position vis-à-vis the United States, if the guide is to be a share of the world's markets. Thus, from 1953 to 1962 the United States share of world exports of manufactures among highly industrialized countries dropped from 26.2 to 19.9 per cent. Only the United Kingdom had an equally bad record. West Germany, France, and Italy increased their shares from 13.4, 3.3, 3.8 to 20.1, 6.1 and 7.5 per cent respectively. What is perhaps even more surprising is that despite the relative price stability here and inflation abroad since 1960, the *rate* of loss for this country from 1960 to 1962 exceeded that for the nine years 1953 to 1962. An examination of United States exports of all commodities reveals similar disappointments. From 1953 to 1962, despite the upward relative trends for industrialized countries, United States exports dropped from 21.8 per cent of world exports in 1953 to 17.4 per cent in 1962, a relative decline of 20 per cent. Even from 1960 to 1962, the share of the United States fell from 18.2 to 17.4 per cent.

PRICE AND COST TRENDS

A few examples of trends of prices in Western Europe, Japan, and the United States follow (1953=100):

	Unit Value of Manufactured Goods		Machinery and Vehicles	Metal and Metal Products
	1959	1962	1959	1959
United States	116	122	124	121
United Kingdom	110	117	—	—
France	94	99	—	93ª
West Germany	99	106	106	108
Italy	80	80 (1961)	95	91
Japan	93	89	—	—

ª Adjusted for devaluation.

This table reveals a deterioration of the United States price position. The major explanation is rising productivity abroad. Again, whereas hourly earnings from 1953 to 1960 rose in the basic metal industries in France, Germany, Italy, and Japan by 49 per cent (unweighted average) and 37 per cent in the United States, labor costs rose by 20 per cent in the United States and declined by 10 per cent (unweighted average) in the four countries. The explanation was of course much larger increases in manhour output in Europe: 15 per cent in the United States, and an average of 93 per cent for the four countries.

Losses in export markets are generally associated with rising relative costs and prices in the countries experiencing these relative losses. It is necessary to take into account not only wage rates but also productivity, and not only wholesale prices, or the price of the GNP but especially export prices. Unfortunately the last are not all that they should be. Despite substantial price and wage increases exceeding those in the United States, Western Europe and Japan gained on the United States in the 1950s. The crucial factor was relative rises in productivity related to a changeover to larger scales of production; great expansion of capital which was, in turn, associated with the import of American capital; and substantial advances in technology, again tied to increased recourse to large-scale output and to American technology. A large part of the explanation of our losses lies in the large considerable advance in Western Europe in a relatively few industries, such as automobiles and iron and steel, where our exports had been important.

The movement of dollar prices per metric ton of steel was as follows:

	May 30, 1953			January 1, 1961		
	European Coal and Steel Community	United Kingdom	United States	European Coal and Steel Community	United Kingdom	United States
Merchant bars	$ 93	$ 96	$105	$100	$113	$134
Sections	93	105	104	94	109	132
Plates	115	127	104	99	115	127
Sheet	147	128	134	148	145	157

Whereas the European countries (exclusive of the United Kingdom) experienced a small *average* decline in these eight years, the United States suffered substantial rises of prices. The competitive position of the United States in iron and steel deteriorated greatly.* From exports of 5 million net tons in 1956 and imports of more than 1 million tons, by 1962 exports had declined to 2 million tons and imports had risen to about 4 million tons. From 1954–1956 to 1961 the United States share of iron and steel exports declined from 11 to 3.5 per cent in Europe.

Competitive position is not given merely by a comparison of export prices. Such factors as level of output—such as the large increase of capacity in Western Europe and Japan, which yields large relative gains in exports at any given price relationship—delivery dates, salesmanship, accommodation of product to the preferences of the markets affect the competitive position. Undoubtedly Europe and Japan gained on the United States in response to nonprice advantages. Moreover, they are more export-oriented and tend to pursue more flexible export pricing than the United States.

* I have depended especially on the Brookings Institution report, *The United States Balance of Payments in 1968,* 1963; essays by B. Balassa and Seymour E. Harris in Joint Economic Committee, *Factors Affecting the United States Balance of Payments, 1962;* an essay by R. Cooper in *The Dollar in Crisis,* Seymour E. Harris (ed.), 1961.

How to Improve Our Competitive Position

In a survey of policies designed to ensure that American products are competitive in world markets October 4, 1962 the President's Advisory Committee on Labor-Management Policy reported to the President on the measures necessary to improve the competitive position of the United States. The emphasis was on special measures to stimulate exports, such as "designing and pricing of products for foreign markets," increases of productivity, and wage policies suggestive of the need for over-all price stability and improvement of the competitive position of the United States. In other discussions of the issue, the importance of rising productivity was stressed. But if these gains are absorbed wholly in rising incomes, and not in depressing prices or containing rises, then the increased productivity does not contribute to an improved competitive position. Improvement of competitive position would yield, according to this committee, more jobs, more stable employment, higher labor incomes, profits, and standard of living, and a stable currency.

Failures to Gain

Since 1960 the government has vigorously sought to improve the competitive position of the United States. Among the important measures taken were aggressive selling policies abroad, extended credit on exports, and pressures to keep wages and prices down. Partly through persuasion by the United States government, Germany and the Netherlands raised the value of their currencies by 5 per cent, thus making dollars and United States exports correspondingly cheaper. Moreover, this country was helped by some removals of restrictions on trade abroad: This has an effect similar to an improved competitive position. A slowdown in the gains of productivity and rising pressures on wages and prices abroad also should have contributed greatly to an improved competitive position of the United States.

Thus in 1961 hourly earnings in manufacturing rose by 2.33 per cent in the United States and by 8, 15, 7, 9, and 6 per cent in France, Germany, Italy, Japan, and the United Kingdom, respectively; and labor costs showed a decline of 1 per cent in the United States and changes of 0, 12, 5, −4, and 5 per cent for these countries. Hourly earnings in the second quarter of 1962 vis-à-vis 1961 showed similar trends. According to Oscar Altman of the International Monetary Fund, in 1962 wage rates rose by 3 per cent in the United States and by 8, 9, and 12 per cent in Italy, France, and Germany, respectively. Moreover, the United States profited from a rise of productivity reflected in labor costs (above) in the first two and a half years of the Kennedy administration—in part a response to natural recovery and in part induced by governmental policies.

In view of these facts, one might have expected large improvements in the United States competitive position in 1961–1963. In 1963 these gains were not evident.

The United States share of total exports and of manufactured exports continued to decline in 1961 and 1962, facts that suggest either weaknesses in the price, wage, and labor cost indexes, or the deviations of export indexes from others, a lagged response of exports to price and cost trends, or the importance of nonprice considerations.

In one sense, however, an improvement was observed: The excess of exports of goods and services (military excluded) was as follows: 1960, $3,769 million; 1961, $5,444 million; 1962, $4,826 million; and 1963, 5,275 million.

These were substantial improvements over 1960. The deterioration in 1962 vis-à-vis 1961 undoubtedly reflected the effects of *relative* growth of imports. In 1961, the gain was primarily in rising exports. In 1962 there was an equal rise of exports; but whereas imports of goods and services declined by about $350 million in 1961, they rose by more than $2 million in 1962, a rise associated with a GNP gain 2.5 times as great in 1962 as in 1961. But if the United States trade and service statistics reveal improvements, shares of trade among industrial countries do not yield similar conclusions on competitive position.

It is useful to remember the net relation of trade and service movements and the balance of regular transactions (i.e. excluding special governmental transactions, such as borrowing abroad and prepayment of debts by foreign interests), as shown below (in billions of dollars; net changes, year to year):

	1961	1962	1963[a]
Balance of trade and services	+1.7	−0.6	+0.2
Deficit on regular transactions	−0.9	+0.5	+0.1

[a] First quarter only, at annual rate.

In 1961 about one-half of the improved trade and service position was reflected in an over-all gain; in 1962, a deterioration of roughly one-half billion dollars was accompanied by a similar rise of the over-all deficit.

CORRECTIVES

The administration in its first three years relied especially on measures that would increase exports vis-à-vis imports, and through raising the short-term rate of interest and adhering to "respectable" monetary and financial policies and thus inspiring confidence, the administration tried to discourage short-term capital movements. The latest move has been a proposal for a differential tax that should cut purchases of foreign portfolio securities by United States investments.

The Kennedy administration also attempted to put part of the burden on the surplus countries, which responded to some extent: They reduced their short-term rate of interest, contributed more to aid and military programs, cooperated with our tied aid programs, and in two instances raised the value of their currencies. Moreover, the administration was hopefully looking eastward for rising wages, a decline in the advance of productivity, and higher prices—all of which should strengthen our export-import balance.

In addition, the administration relied on special measures to treat speculative attacks on the dollar or spasmodic short-run rises in the external deficit. Adopting measures in large part the creation of the Treasury's brilliant and imaginative theorist as well as practitioner, Robert Roosa, the United States government began to hoard and purchase foreign currencies, provide for exchanges of currencies so that in times of stress foreign currencies would be available to neutralize some of the effects of dumping of dollars and thus strengthen the dollar. Also, the Treasury began to operate on the exchange market and especially on the futures market, which, being relatively thin, could respond to moderate operations: Large premiums on foreign currencies could then be averted and, thus, holders of dollars would be encouraged not to dishoard. Finally Roosa led the effort to add $6 billion of additional resources to be advanced to the International Monetary Fund.

But the administration, greatly influenced by Roosa's views, was hostile to large moves to increase international liquidity. Over the three years the general view was that the introduction of such programs as those proposed by the British Chancellor of the Exchequer or by Harold Wilson or Robert Triffin would distract from the measures required to attack the fundamental disequilibrium. Even in his July 18, 1963, statement the President continued to stress the importance of an appropriate cost-price policy as a *sine qua non* for solving the dollar problem.

Roosa was much more emphatic on this point. In a speech to the American Bankers Association, on May 17, 1962, he would "build further the outer defenses around the liquidity of the IMF. . . .

". . . But explorations along these lines are far more preferable . . . to the often proposed types of action . . . that basically involve an oath of allegiance by all governments and Central Banks to a synthetic currency device, created by an extra-national authority bearing neither the responsibilities nor the disciplines of sovereignty. . . ."

In an able statement before the Joint Economic Committee, on December 13, 1962, Roosa related the seekers of substantial increases of international liquidity ". . . with the yearning that has always been expressed by those who feel that more money, and the facilities for creating it, would assure expansion and prosperity within a particular country."

In Roosa's view, this type of new institution was likely to break down because new money would have to be created through provisions of credit. It would have to be possible to work out terms agreeable to both creditor and debtor countries, and this Roosa believed would be the barrier to successful operation. The automaticity of credits, as assumed by the adherents to the new institution, is not likely to be forthcoming. In the discussion of the Triffin Plan similar criticisms were made: The Triffin Plan seemed to many to be a plan for creating credit for underdeveloped countries, with the strong currencies thus gradually being replaced by the soft currencies.

As Roosa told the American Bankers Association on May 17, 1962:

Let me make it absolutely clear, again, there is no thought that foreign exchange operations can provide the solution to the United States payments deficit. More fundamental corrections are necessary for this end. . . . [We are] moving forward toward a restoration of equilibrium and surplus in the American balance of payments.

In the future, the issue of a more ambitious program for raising international liquidity is likely to receive serious consideration. One reason for this is the disappointments in the first three years with the results of the thirty or more significant measures already taken by the United States government. In his July 18, 1963, balance of payments statement, the President, after commenting on the helpful results of the Dillon-Roosa programs, added that the

U.S. will continue to study and discuss with other countries measures which might be taken for a further strengthening of the international monetary system over the longer run. The U.S. interest . . . is not a result of our current payments deficit—rather it reflects our concern that adequate provision is made for the growth of international liquidity to finance expanding world trade over the years ahead. . . . One of the reasons that new sources of liquidity may well be needed is that as we close our payments gap, we will cut down our provision of dollars to the rest of the world.

This statement reflected the pressure to which the President had been subjected. The Treasury consistently held out, as did businessmen and some economists, for limited measures to raise liquidity, lest the country fail to take the long-run measures which are crucial. The Council of Economic Advisers and, to some extent, the State Department, high officials of both British parties, and many economists (such as Triffin and those of the Brookings Institution) have urged larger measures to raise international liquidity. The latter are fearful of a lack of liquidity as trade increases and the United States balances its account; some are also fearful of the steady accumulation of short-term debts by the United States, an important source of liquidity, which makes the economy vulnerable to withdrawals of gold; and the relation of restrictive or inadequately expansionist policies associated with inadequate reserves.

To these arguments Roosa had at least one valid reply, namely, that no country confronted with large deficits in the balance of payments has experienced the low money rates of the United States, and only Switzerland and the Netherlands among Western Europe surplus countries had rate levels as favorable as ours. He could also show that in contrast to earlier recoveries, free reserves of banks remained at high levels in 1961–1962. Moreover, one could also argue that federal deficits were not exactly modest.

CONFIDENCE IN THE DOLLAR

Undoubtedly monetary and fiscal policy was oriented to the objectives of excluding a substantial inflation and assuring continued confidence in the dollar. It is not easy to assess the varying rates of confidence. One measure is the extent to which surpluses of foreign interests were taken in dollars, such as in investments in short-term assets in the United States, or in gold. Conversion of dollars into gold is held to suggest lack of confidence in the dollar, that is, a fear of the depreciation in the dollar vis-à-vis gold. On this score the record in the troublesome years, 1958–1960, with deficits of $11.2 billion (annual average of $3.7 billion) was roughly the same as for the twenty seven months ending March 31, 1963, with deficits of $4.4 billion (annual average of almost $2 billion). The ratio of losses of gold (and convertible currency) to total deficit from 1958–1960 was 42 per cent; from 1961 to the first quarter of 1963, it was 39 per cent.

In view of the large deficits of 1958–1960, it might appear that foreigners had more confidence in the dollar in 1958–1960 than in 1961–1963. But a continuation of deficits for two and a half more years, despite large measures taken, even if accompanied by smaller annual deficits may well reduce confidence in the dollar and hence result in large conversions of dollars into gold. In the course of the first great defense of the dollar the ratio of gold withdrawals to deficit of the United States declined from 43 per cent in 1960 to 30 per cent in 1961; but in 1962 the ratio soared to 58 per cent, almost equaling the record 65 per cent in 1958. To some extent, the withdrawals in gold depend on the country favored by large surpluses: Some convert almost automatically and some tend not to convert. Furthermore, the division of dollar gains between private and official sources is relevant. Private interests may not convert into gold; but they can put balances at the disposal of their own central bank and thus contribute to conversions.

Undoubtedly withdrawals of gold would have been much larger had not the United States aggressively tried to protect the dollar since 1961 and had not cooperation of foreign central banks been enlisted. Foreign monetary authorities have a large stake in a strong dollar. In view of the passage of three additional years with substantial deficits, I would argue that with a reduction of the ratio of gold losses to deficits confidence in the dollar has been at a somewhat higher level since 1960 than in the preceding years.

Confidence in the dollar is an important objective of United States policy, for without confidence foreign interests will reduce their holdings of dollars to an absolute minimum, with the result that gold reserves would be inadequate to maintain the convertibility of the dollar at $35 per ounce. (In May 1963, the total of short-term liabilities to foreign countries amounted to $22.3 billion against $15.8 billion of gold reserves. Of the $22.3 billion, $12 billion were official.) This situation explained to some extent why American authorities have urged a policy under which central banks would agree to hold a given proportion of their reserves in currencies of a designated number of countries. Then a guaranteed market for dollars would prevail; and insofar as other currencies were held as reserves, the burden on both the dollar and available gold reserves would be reduced. But it will require much persuasion to get some Western European countries to agree to hold less gold and more foreign currencies for reserves.

Still another approach to raising confidence in the dollar is the proposal to guarantee any foreign holders of short-term dollar assets against a devaluation, that is, if the dollar is devalued by 50 per cent, the foreigner would receive twice as many dollars for his dollar balance. But there is not much enthusiasm for this solution in official United States. First, the Congress is not likely to be enthusiastic about guarantees. Nor can one be sure that the Congress would appropriate the necessary sums to validate such a guarantee. In fact, the criticisms of numerous plans to set up a supranational bank, to which dollar liabilities to foreigners would be transferred, are related to unwillingness of Congress to offer such guarantee, a necessary condition for the transfer of liabilities in dollars to this bank.

Second, there is a reluctance to concentrate guarantees on one class of holders of dollars, thus favoring foreigners against nationals. Third, many are fearful that serious talk about a guarantee would raise doubts about the dollar. Fourth, a guarantee to be meaningful must be accompanied by adequate domestic policies to keep the dollar strong, and would probably invite some foreign control of our domestic policies.

OTHER PROPOSALS

Many have not agreed with the government and have offered proposals not acceptable to the government. Thus the Bank for International Settlements in its 1962–1963 report could find evidence only of excessive liquidity, not a shortage, and contended that this excess precluded effective policy to deal with the United States deficit. Had $9 billion of short-term dollar liabilities not accumulated in the years 1958–1962, and had gold flown out instead, pressure for restrictive measures would have been much greater. Its major proposal was high rates of interest as a means of reversing the flow of capital; but the emphasis was on long-term rates and more audacious fiscal policy. Rises in long-term rates were unacceptable to the Kennedy administration, partly because they were not prepared to put an excessive burden on fiscal policy.

As might be expected, the American Bankers Association, in its highly publicized *Statement on the Balance of Payments of July 1963,* emphasized the need of stabilizing federal expenditures, thus inspiring confidence and helping to stabilize prices; of adequate tax relief to stimulate investment and thus reduce costs; and of the avoidance of excessive liquidity.

Both the Joint Economic Committee, in its *Report on U.S. Payments Policies* . . . of December 26, 1962, and the Brookings report on *The United States Balance of Payments in 1968* recommended major measures to increase international liquidity, and opposed the use of higher rates of interest to treat the balance of payments. The Brookings report recommended a volume of international reserves which would cover deficits over several years associated with "structural factors, such as changes in technology, competitive position, relative productivity . . . or the structure of world demand for a country's products. . . ." These, in the view of the Brookings authors, are the problems the solution of which requires a great increase in liquidity. The creditor countries are to hold balances at a central institution available to be used by debtor countries both automatically and under some restrictions, but in a way that would not bring deflationist policies by the debtor countries in the process of adding liabilities. In the absence of availability of such reserves, the countries in difficulty, according to Brookings, would contend with their deficits through exchange controls (and) or increased restrictions on trade and the like, all measures that would increase the malallocation of resources. The Brookings report does not discuss whether the creditor countries would be willing to undertake these responsibilities and transfers. They argued that their solution would relieve the United States of the burden of being a reserve center.

But the authors were aware that the kind of improvement wanted by the United States, that is, greater willingness of Europe to hold dollars, may not be acceptable to European countries. Hence the Brookings study offered even more radical measures. They would introduce flexible exchanges with a British–United States axis and a European Economic Community (EEC) coalition. Exchanges would fluctuate freely between these two groups of countries but be fixed within each group. Exchange flexibility would reduce the need of reserves, and would offer almost automatic adjustments to a worsening of the balance of payments: A depreciation of the exchanges would increase exports and reduce imports as prices of commodities rose less than the price of foreign currencies. Unfortunately the Brookings report did not explain how, for example, France and Germany would agree on their exchange rates or, for that matter, what should be relatively simple, how Canada and the United States would do so. Is it likely that the United States, United Kingdom, and others tied to this axis vis-à-vis the EEC will be prepared to abandon current controls and allow exchange rates to respond to strength or weakness in the balance of payments?

The Brookings report also recommended a somewhat greater range of exchange rate fluctuations under the fixed exchange system. This would give countries more freedom in fixing interest rates and discourage short-term capital movements. This is a most desirable modification, though a current range of 2 per cent, as provided by the International Monetary Fund, may be adequate for the time being. Brookings suggested larger variations.

The Brookings authors did not consider devaluation as a solution. No case can be made for devaluation on their premises that the balance is likely to improve. Devaluation would then lead only to an undervaluation of the dollar and trouble for others. Moreover, a devaluation, because of the effects on the desire to hold reserve currencies, may well reduce reserves rather than increase them.

With the large reserves available, and the many attacks for treating the dollar problem, the appropriate policy is to use these reserves, totaling at least $18 billion, while the various measures are allowed to have their impact. Indeed the cost of restrictive policies may become so great and the effectiveness of therapy so disappointing that a devaluation may be the only way out. But there is every hope that we shall not come to this impasse. It is useful to remember that the case for devaluation in the 1930s under worldwide deflation is not nearly so strong as when the world is prosperous and inflation is a threat.

Sir Roy Harrod's suggestion for a substantial rise in the price of gold and, hence, increase reserves is interesting. His case rests largely on the assumption of inadequate supplies of money: In three years, he points out, the supply of money in this country rose by 2.5 per cent and income by 16 per cent. From 1948 to 1960, short-term rates in important countries rose by 40 per cent, with adverse effects on investment. Moreover, the shortage of reserves contributed, in Harrod's view, to the stock market collapse and the squeeze on profits.

FOREIGN AID

Foreign aid is a burden on the balance of payments. As noted earlier, tying foreign aid reduces this burden, though there are offsets: More foreign aid means more imports, and the act of tying encourages foreign countries to divert other purchases from the American market. The effect of aid on the deficit may not be large, though the Clay Committee Report on Foreign Aid (March 22, 1963) and others seemed to stress the adverse effects on the balance of payments. This can be overdone; but when the Brookings Institution estimate that a rise of foreign aid from $4 to $6.5 billion from 1961 to 1968 will bring a rise of deficits of but $300 million, they seem to be rather optimistic. (This is aside from the fact that on the basis of 1963 development, a 60 per cent rise does not seem likely.)

I believe that the importance of foreign aid is likely to decline as a factor increasing our international deficit, partly because of the growing criticism of aid, partly because of the tying process, and partly because of the increased emphasis on aid to Latin America where additional dollars made available are largely used to purchase in this country.

The trend of foreign aid in relation to GNP and the exports of goods and services is clearly downward:

FOREIGN ECONOMIC AID AND RELATION OF ECONOMIC AID TO UNITED STATES
GROSS NATIONAL PRODUCT EXPORTS, 1946–1963
(dollars in billions)

	Economic Aid	Economic Aid as Percentage of GNP	Economic Aid as Percentage of Exports of Goods and Services
1946–1949	$5.8	1.7%	34%
1950–1955	3.8	1.0	22
1955	2.6	0.5	12
1961	3.9	0.7	13
1963[a]	3.5	0.6	11

[a] Estimated.

From the viewpoint of American policy and particularly of our security, the declining stress on economic aid is unfortunate. The Clay Committee is partly responsible. Many of its criticisms were justified: inadequate contributions from abroad, failure of self-help by the recipients, excessive aid for unjustified political reasons, overextension geographically, and many others. But in urging substantial reductions and overstressing what might be accomplished in a short time, in insisting that United States aid should be oriented to the principle of free private enterprise, and, in general, by overemphasizing the deficiencies, the Clay Committee contributed to the unfortunate cuts of 1963. They were not alone responsible. But they shared an opposition to governmental spending, a fear of public deficits, an exaggerated view of the adverse effects of aid on the balance of payments, and some disappointments at the visible results.

TRADE

The balance of payments is related to trade policies. The reduction of tariffs as provided in the Trade Expansion Act (TEA) should not necessarily reduce the deficit. But in providing improved techniques for negotiating with Western Europe, the TEA should at least keep us from losing markets. On the basis of past experience we would be fortunate if we were not outbargained in our negotiations. In one sense, our deficit should be cut. When dollars were short we allowed Europe to raise her barriers vis-à-vis the United States. In a similar manner, with dollars in excess supply, we could now demand larger concessions by Europe.

In securing passage of his TEA in 1962, President Kennedy achieved his greatest domestic triumph. There were indeed complaints. The President had made too many concessions to special interests as the price of passage. But this criticism is not merited: Without these concessions an adequate act would not have been passed. Still another criticism was that the President had been misled on the gains of employment associated with the trade act. This is fair. Reduction of tariff barriers is a way of increasing productivity and thus reducing jobs. The support for the program lies in other directions.

United States policy toward Western Europe and particularly toward the European Economic Community (EEC) has been subject to much criticism. In *Challenge to Affluence,* Gunnar Myrdal is very critical of the United States for encouraging the Common Market and pushing the United Kingdom to join it. In his view the European Free Trade Association (EFTA), consisting primarily of the United Kingdom and the Scandinavian countries, should have been the partner of the United States, for the United States and the EFTA seek reduced trade barriers whereas the EEC wants discrimination in its favor and control of its economies by supranational bureaucrats, objectives unacceptable to the United States.

Because of its reduced internal tariff and the increase of its external tariff, the EEC promises to contribute more to restricting trade than the higher incomes associated with growth will contribute toward expanding trade. In a careful estimate for the Joint Economic Committee (*Factors Affecting the United States Balance of Payments,* 1962) and for the Brookings study, L. B. Krause concluded that the EEC, through its discriminatory policies, would cut United States trade annually by $750 million.

The rift between the EEC and the United Kingdom has of course reduced the likely benefits of the Trade Expansion Act. In particular, the possibilities of arriving at helpful solutions through GATT are reduced. In negotiating for the United States under GATT, Christian Herter has already encountered serious obstacles in opening markets for our agricultural products and in obtaining acceptance to our proposals for linear percentage reductions in tariff. Moreover, the possibility of a complete erasure of duties when the cooperating countries account for 80 per cent of the trade in commodities is impaired by the failure of the United Kingdom to attain entry into the Common Market.

THE FUTURE

On the whole the improvements in the balance of payments during the Kennedy administration were few. Despite the major attention given to the dollar problem and the innumerable measures taken, the over-all deficit continued at about $3 billion per year.

Clearly, there must be a substantial improvement in the next three to four years or more drastic measures will be required. The failure of the trade and service balance to improve more despite the much larger price and wage increases abroad in 1961–1963 has been both puzzling and disappointing. Yet by 1964, the relative price trends may well begin to pay off in gains in the balance of trade, though an offset may be adverse factors associated with greater growth here relative to the experience since 1952. By the middle of 1964, substantial improvements have emerged.

The Brookings study on the balance in 1968 is optimistic. I am inclined to agree with their estimates of large gains by 1968, but they seem to overdo our competitive gains in prices and the reduction of capital exports. From the Brookings statistical presentation, one might have expected that the policy recommendations would have been largely directed to keeping costs down and finding export markets. But instead they concentrated on massive increases in liquidity to exclude any constraints at home and, as a second best, floating exchanges.

The Brookings authors underestimated the difficulties of correcting the disequilibrium associated with the proposed massive rise in liquidity, and they failed to allow adequately for the difficulty and disruptions resulting from the introduction of fixed exchanges within the two blocs of country and floating exchanges between the two galaxies. Nevertheless this was a pioneering study of great value.

16

Growth

Growth with minimum inflation was the major economic objective of the Kennedy administration. Growth is generally defined as the dollar rise of gross national product per year. Where population increases greatly, the rise per capita may be small or even negative. In examining growth for the purpose of assessing our military potential, the total GNP is the more relevant concept. In the study of the welfare of the average individual or family, per capita rates of growth are especially significant. Growth in current dollars may be misleading in periods of price instability, and for that reason it may be well to adjust GNP by a price deflator. As a general rule the GNP price deflator, that is, the price level of GNP, rises at a minimum of about 1 per cent per year. Hence in anticipating, say, a rise of GNP of 4 per cent a year in stable dollars we may be reasonably sure that the GNP would rise by 5 per cent; and a 5 per cent GNP projected in current dollars is likely to mean at best a rise of but 4 per cent.

One problem in assessing output is the gap between actual and potential output, estimated at from $30 to $50 billion in the first years of the Kennedy administration. This gap may be explained by the failure to maintain cyclical peaks; but in the later 1950s and early 1960s it was also associated with a sluggishness in the economy reflected in a rising level of unemployment at the cyclical peak.

Aside from the gap, the country is interested in the rate of growth. Elimination of the gap would yield a higher rate of output at any one time; an increase of the growth rate would shift the entire curve of output upwards.

Growth has become a large political issue between the parties; the Democrats are articulate on this issue, and the Republicans have reluctantly received the challenge. At first the latter tended to minimize its significance, but later they criticized their opponents' espousal of increased rates of growth, associating the proposed Democratic gains with more government spending.

The more rapid our rate of growth, the more resources are available for private spending for food, clothing, housing, and so on; also more is available for the necessary services that only government can provide. With adequate growth, the economy can provide higher standards of living, as well as increased services by government.

With greater growth, we could also have more resources for defense. For example, if our growth in the years 1952 to 1959 had matched that from 1947 to 1952, we would have had $70 billion more of gross national product in 1959. This would have yielded $12 billion more of federal government revenue. With these resources, we could easily have spent the few more billion dollars necessary for defense and yet put no additional burden on the taxpayer. We could also have done a more adequate job in health, housing, education, urban redevelopment, and the like.

Varying rates of growth are reflected in large differences in GNP, for the compound interest law is at work. Thus, assume a 2 per cent rate of growth for one country and 7 per cent for another. In twenty years the increase is not 40 per cent (20×2) and 140 per cent (20×7) but 49 and 287 per cent (the former, roughly the Eisenhower rate), and 14 per cent for the country gaining 7 per cent a year (the Russian rate).

The following figures give a further idea of how the compound interest rule works. At a 2 per cent rate of growth, the gross national product would rise by 22 per cent in ten years, but at a 4.5 per cent rate of growth, which is a probable rate here with good management and no recourse to controls, the increase would be 55 per cent; and at the Russian rate of 7 per cent, the increase would be 97 per cent. In twenty years the respective increases would be 49, 141, and 287 per cent, and in forty years 121, 482 and 1,398 per cent.

In more concrete terms, we could take former Vice President Richard Nixon to task for having made fun of "growthmanship," and having said that the Russian output could not possibly exceed American output even by the year 2000. Actually, at the Eisenhower rate of growth, the United States by the year 2000 would have a GNP of over $1,200 billion, while the Russians, starting with a GNP in 1960 of less than half that of the United States, but growing at their 7 per cent rate, would have a GNP of $3,375 billion. Even a 5 per cent rate for the USSR would yield a GNP roughly equal to ours in the year 2000 if we continue the Eisenhower rate of growth. This suggests how important it is that we keep our rate of growth at 4 to 5 per cent. Incidentally, the Russians are not likely to maintain a 7 per cent rate for a long period of time. We cannot allow them to grow much more rapidly than we do, especially since they, through their system, can achieve a much more effective use of their resources for the development of their military machine.

Much depends on management. Thus we had the resources from 1929 to 1933, but output declined by 29 per cent, and unemployment rose to 13 million, or one in four unemployed. Management was bad.

From 1933 to 1952, our growth averaged 7 per cent a year, or 4.5 per cent compounded. This was good management, especially if we consider the heritage of a stubborn depression in the 1930s. From 1947 to 1953, annual growth averaged 4.6 per cent; but from 1953 to 1960 the growth rate was about 3.4 per cent.

Most experts agree that we can have a GNP of around $750 billion in 1970 compared to more than $600 billion in 1964. But good management is assumed. In fact, the National Planning Association, one of the best research organizations in the country, has estimated that we could well have a GNP of $790 billion by the year 1970. The Republican Committee on Programs and Progress said in 1960 "that by wise private and public policies, we should attain sustained growth in the vicinity of 4 per cent a year. . . . It would give us a $900 billion economy by 1976."

Actually from 1961 to 1963 GNP rose by $100 billion. At this rate GNP would rise by $330 billion by 1970 or to $830 billion. Increases of the percentage rate of 1960–1963 would yield an even larger rise of GNP in the 1960s. But it will be difficult indeed to continue the 1961–1963 base throughout the 1960s. Such a continued rise would require imaginative and sensible management.

The following is an interesting exercise in arithmetic. Compare actual GNP in 1953–1960 with that under growth levels achieved from 1947 to 1952. In stable dollars, the loss in the 1953–1960 years was $305 billion; in federal revenues, $44 billion; and in man-years of employment, 43.5 million. The last exceeds the amount of unemployment, and thus allows for the rise of numbers on the labor market associated with improved employment prospects; and does not allow for the transitional loss of jobs associated with rising productivity. This is the roughest of calculations; but it has some significance.

A continuation of a growth rate of 2.5 per cent would yield us only $713 billion by 1975 as compared to a yield of $971 billion, or $258 billion more, if the rate of growth should be 4.5 per cent, the record of the years 1947–1953.

To understand what has to be done we must realize what determines growth. Among the important factors are the rate of scientific and technological advance, the rate of investment, the average age of our capital plant, our standards of education, health, and welfare, the rise of population, the ratio of the labor force to the population, the percentage of unemployment, changes in the number of hours of work, and the quality of business and government management.

We should not underestimate the importance of public policy. For example, in 1957–1958 we had a recession which was partly brought on by unwise monetary policy, and was prolonged by a failure of the monetary authority to reverse its policies. When, early in 1958, private spending was declining at an annual rate of almost $20 billion, the President had proposed an increase in spending of only $1 billion (annual rate), and refused to support a cut in taxes. For various reasons, a rise of spending and a reduction of tax receipts, despite the failure to act, brought a $12 to $13 billion deficit in fiscal 1959. Had the government moved more quickly in increasing monetary supplies and in giving help through increased public spending and reduced tax rates, the recession would have been much shorter and the loss of income much less. A modern recession, even if it is not a depression, may well cost the economy $30 to $60 billion. Hence, if we are to have maximum output and therefore minimum unemployment, we must above all provide the nation with adequate supplies of money.

The nation's goal should be one of keeping the rise of prices down to less than 1 per cent a year. With a 5 per cent rate of growth an inflation of less than 1 per cent could be feasible. With a 5 per cent rise of output per year and a rise of prices of less than 1 per cent, most Americans would receive increases of income several times the losses due to inflation. And there are ways of protecting those in need and those whose incomes do not respond to rising prices.

In short, if we concentrate on the ingredients of growth, namely, keep our investment up, work hard, manage our economy so that we have maximum output and minimum unemployment; and on top of that increase our productivity through adequate education, improved health, adequate and proper allocation of research funds, improved housing, more effective use of the old and women on the labor market; rid the economy of monopolistic features; and also provide adequate demand through a proper tax and spending program, then we would have growth of 4 or 5 per cent. The difference between 5 and 2.5 per cent would be tremendous in our competition with communism, and would also provide the underprivileged with the minimum standards of living that they should have. Unless we grow by at least 3.5 per cent a year, not only do we fail to reduce unemployment, but it actually increases.

In general the Democrats have been much more disposed to stress growth than the Republicans, though Nixon in the 1960 campaign devoted some attention to the issue. But like most Republicans, he emphasized that "right policies to get growth are not through relying upon Government action . . . but through increasing opportunities and incentives for expansion of the private sector of the economy."

In the years 1956–1960, when the Democrats emphasized the growth issue, the Republicans tended to be silent or highly critical.

There were some exceptions. Nelson Rockefeller was a notable exception, and he contributed greatly to the dissemination of the growth thesis. By the middle of 1959, the Republicans began to take note of the problem. The Task Force on Economic Opportunity and Progress and the Nixon report on price stability and economic growth (1959) both acknowledged the need of growth, but also emphasized the recourse to private incentives, for example, reduction of high-bracket tax rates, as the road to greater growth. "Our Republican program seeks a strong rate of *economic growth* by fostering private initiative, not by resorting to vast public spending and loose money policies. . . ."

By July, 1960, even President Eisenhower had to enter the debate. Complaining of the great amount of misinformation on GNP, the President boasted of a 25 per cent rise of GNP in seven and a half years; and, he added, ". . . during the almost eight-year duration of the prior, Democratic administration, the GNP actually declined in every single peacetime year save one." This is an inaccurate and misleading statement.

In the famous Rockefeller Panel Reports, *Prospect for America,* first issued in the later 1950s, the Rockefeller Brothers initially presented a carefully documented report on what a difference growth rates of 3, 4, and 5 per cent made over a ten-year period— a difference of $124 billion in 1947 dollars was involved. At that time Governor Nelson Rockefeller gave government a very important responsibility in stimulating growth—in fact, a 50 per cent rise of public expenditures in a period of ten years.

Incidentally, the rise of cash expenditures of all governments from 1957 to 1962 (calendar) was an average of 6 per cent; for seven years of administrative expenditures for the federal government, an average also of 6 per cent. The governor's projections check well with what has happened, for the expenditures deflated by price rises increased roughly 5 per cent a year.

In a speech to the Governors' Conference on accelerated economic growth, as late as June 1, 1960, the governor still advocated growth with enthusiasm. But he stressed government's contribution much less. In fact government seemed to play a minor part. In explaining why suspicion attaches to those who plan for a 5 or 6 per cent growth, he said that part of the skepticism "derives from the fact that the advocates of faster growth often have been persons with no real belief that the institutions of private enterprise could be depended upon to produce it. Hence their advocacy was accompanied by proposals for central planning implemented by government interventions and controls. . . ."

Republicans in general have not urged growth as a fundamental objective of policy, partly because once the goal is set, government is likely to become more activist. Republicans raised questions on the significance of GNP, the measure of growth, and also the lack of comprehensiveness in coverage of growth, for many of the gains in well being do not come under the rubric of growth.

GROWTH UNDER KENNEDY

In some respects growth in 1961–1963 was disappointing, though not in the total gains, however. From the first quarter of 1961 to the third quarter of 1963, GNP in stable dollars rose by 14.1 per cent, a gain of 5.6 per cent per year. From the second quarter of 1960 to the second quarter of 1963, the total gain was 11.1 per cent; the rate per year, 4.4 per cent.

For the almost three years of the Kennedy administration, the average gain was around 5.5 per cent, an excellent record on any criterion. The average for the eight Eisenhower years was 3 per cent or somewhat less. Even if the rise for the Kennedy administration was somewhat inflated because the base was low, the record was still very good. And if the test of satisfactory performance is the ratio of increase of GNP to rise of prices, the Kennedy achievement was still distinguished. For the Eisenhower years, 1952–1960, the ratio was 150; for the Kennedy years, first quarter 1961—fourth quarter 1963, the estimated ratio was 420.

Yet the President expressed disappointment at the rise of GNP. In an address to the American Bankers Association, February 25, 1963, the President, after criticizing those who held that growth is too abstract a concept and too theoretical to be a basis for proposals to the Congress, said:

I do not see anything abstract or academic about economic growth. It means finding 1,200,000 additional jobs every year for the men and women pouring into our labor market. . . . It means preventing the periodic recessions which have hit our nation, three times in the last 10 years. It means ending the persisting lack which has kept our unemployment rate at five per cent or above for 62 out of the last 63 months. It has kept output $30 billion to $40 billion below our productive capacity.

There is nothing academic about pushing our economy to four per cent instead of three per cent, which might total over the next ten years in today's prices more than $40 billion more in output of goods and services. . . .

Then why all this distress about the rate of growth? One reason for disappointment was, as the President implied, the unemployment problem. In 1961, the Council of Economic Advisers had estimated that if unemployment were reduced from 6.4 to 4 per cent, output would rise by 8 per cent. A 2.5 per cent decline of unemployment would account for a much larger increase of output because productivity would rise and hours would increase, and numbers on the labor market would respond. Actually in a period of two and a half years during which output increased by 11 per cent, unemployment had slightly increased, despite a rise of numbers on the labor market of about 800,000 below expectations. In a Kansas City speech of June 12, 1962, Heller expressed disappointment that in a year in which GNP had risen by $28 billion unemployment had gone up from 5.5 to close to 6 per cent. Then why the very satisfactory gain of output? The causes were rising productivity and the increase of numbers and hours of work—in that order.

It is of some interest that the GNP divided by employment and military personnel gives an average of about $8 billion per million employed. Then why does it require, say, $50+ billion additional per year to assure a million fewer unemployed? The explanation is mainly the increase in productivity, inclusive of shifts to employments of high productivity, accessions to the labor market, and also in periods of improvement, longer hours.

For example, from 1960 to the third quarter of 1963, GNP (in 1962 prices) rose by $64.4 billion or by 11.3 per cent. Unemployment actually was higher in the third quarter of 1963 than in 1960. But civilian employment was up by 2.4 million. In other words a rise of $27 billion (64.4 divided by 2.4) was consistent with 1 million additional civilian jobs. This is explained by the substantial increase of productivity and the rise of hours of work by almost one hour in this period. If, for example, productivity rose by 4 per cent the gain of GNP per year would be $18 billion and a rise of hours by one would increase output by about $12 billion additional. (Actually the increase in hours would be about one-half per year). In periods of rising activity, employers tend to extend working hours of the labor force already occupied and get rid of unproductive workers. That productivity also advanced greatly is suggested by comparing (1) an 11 per cent rise of GNP in stable prices with (2) an increase of civilian employment of 3 per cent and of hours of 3 per cent.

If a $27 billion expansion of GNP corresponds to a million additional jobs, then it would be clear that a rise of $25 billion would still be consistent with increased unemployment. For in the 1960s the average rise in the labor force is estimated at 1.3 million. Then the needed increase of GNP to cover 1.3 million jobs would be of the order of $35 billion. In addition, a rise of productivity of only 2 per cent would require an additional $11 billion of GNP, or, say, $46 billion to exclude a rise of unemployment.

Unfortunately the ratio of the increase in GNP to that of additional employment is not generally of these proportions. (The figures are in stable dollars.) In current dollars larger amounts would be required. One can easily find larger increases of GNP per additional million jobs than given below. For calendar year 1962, the figure is $25.5 billion. And elsewhere larger rises in later recovery periods occur than suggested in the figures below.

INCREASE OF GNP (STABLE DOLLARS) PER MILLION ADDITIONAL CIVILIAN
AND MILITARY PERSONNEL EMPLOYED
(billions of stable dollars)

1949–1960	= 20
1949–1953	= 17
1954–1957	= 15
1958–1960	= 19
1960–1962	= 23

The disappointing results for employment in 1960–1963 were partly the result of an increase of productivity substantially in excess of 2 per cent, and partly because GNP rose only about $29 billion per year in the two and three-quarter years from the first quarter of 1961. That the country will face serious problems is attested by the increase of GNP (in 1962 prices) in the post-war period considerably below what is required to keep unemployment from rising.

The largest increases were (in billions of 1962 dollars):

$$1950 = 28*$$
$$1951 = 30*$$
$$1955 = 33$$
$$1959 = 31$$
$$1962 = 28$$

* Related to war.

Over the sixteen years 1946–1962, GNP in 1962 prices rose by $225 billion or a $14 billion average per year. We shall need considerably more than a $25 billion rise per year in stable dollars to stabilize our unemployment.

I believe that a very large rise of GNP is required to stabilize unemployment, and an even larger increase to bring unemployment down to 4 per cent—the excess of unemployment over 4 per cent in 1963–1964 being about 1 million. This is suggested by a comparison of the increase of GNP (1962 dollars) and the accompanying rise of jobs. Here is a possible way of looking at the problem:

Rise of GNP due to:

1. An increase of productivity of 2.5 per cent with a $610 billion GNP in 1964 = $15 billion.

2. A rise of hours of one-half per year in recovery, or roughly $5 billion (1/140 of $610).

3. An increase of 1.3 million new workers per year would need a rise of GNP of $17 billion = 1.3 × 13. Here I assume that $13 billion will yield 1 million additional jobs—I leave out such factors as the rise of productivity for the 70 million workers roughly (estimate of Council of Economic Advisers).

4. One million × 13 million = $13 billion to bring unemployment down to 4 per cent. Hence a rise of $15B + $5B + $17B = $37 billion (1962 prices) would be required in 1964 to keep unemployment stable. Should we assume a larger rise of productivity (as we have elsewhere for 1961–1963) the amount required would be larger.

This is one way of putting the problem. The President's Economic Council, in a first-rate statement before the Subcommittee on Employment and Manpower of the Senate Committee on Labor and Welfare (October 28, 1963) preferred to put the matter in a different manner. They consider the rise of productivity irrelevant for determining the amount of additional GNP required to yield a million additional jobs, and they eliminate any rise of GNP associated with cyclical rises of GNP: "One must not mistakenly attribute to increases in employment those increases in output which should properly be attributed to the growing productivity of workers already on the jobs . . ."

I have no objection to this approach. It suggests, for example, that a gain of $12 to $14 billion of GNP will provide a million additional jobs. Hence, an $11 billion tax cut resulting in a rise of $30 billion of GNP should yield 2 to 3 million additional jobs. That is why the council, on numerous occasions, has contended that a gain of $30 billion in GNP associated with the tax cut would provide 2 to 3 million additional jobs. The council approach is consistent with their net gains of jobs.

My approach, which says that it will require, say, $37 billion to stabilize unemployment and $54 billion to bring unemployment down by 1 million, also has its advantages. It tells us that very large increases of GNP are required to assure even stable levels of unemployment. It also underlines the importance of demand. A rise of productivity of, say, 2 to 3 per cent is not very helpful if a deficiency of demand results in large volumes of unsold goods and reduced profits. My approach, like the council's, points to the underlying importance of demand and, hence, of the tax cut. But the council approach may fail to allow adequately for the element of demand and, hence, rise of GNP required to offset the rise of productivity and the increase in the number of workers.

Heller effectively expressed the attitude of the administration in a speech on November 14, 1962, on fiscal and monetary policy for economic stability and growth:

Do we accept 5½ per cent unemployment, a 2½ per cent growth rate, 83 per cent utilization of our manufacturing capacity (McGraw-Hill Survey, November, 1962), profits leveling off $8 or $9 billion below the full employment norm, and an output gap of nearly $35 billion between actual and potential production of the U.S. economy . . . [and] do we dismiss this as perhaps statistical trickery, or as a natural and normal concommitant of growth and maturity, or as an allegedly necessary cost of containing the price-wage spiral and reducing balance of payments risks?

But though the President complained of the gap between actual and potential output and the high level of unemployment, when challenged, he was quick to stress the large gains of output made. At a press conference on August 1, 1962, in reply to a criticism by Senator Goldwater, the President expressed hope that with Congressional cooperation, the economy would rise to the target of $570 billion GNP for 1962. Yet in the press conference the preceding week he had agreed with a statement of Gunnar Myrdal, the Swedish economist, who had stressed the state of stagnation in the nation. The President said, "Well, I think it is regrettable that we have not been able to develop an economic formula which maintains the growth of our economy. If we were moving ahead at full blast today of course we would have full employment. . . ."

But the President was careful, in his State of the Union Message of 1961, to point to disappointing growth during the anemic recovery of 1959–1960 and in his 1962 State of the Union Message to emphasize the satisfactory rate of growth.

On August 13, 1962, he reassured the country on the growth issue. GNP under his administration had increased by 10 per cent; industrial production, by 16 per cent; unemployment had declined by 23 per cent; wages and salaries were up 10 per cent; and corporate profits, higher by 26 per cent.

Before the New York Economic Club, on December 14, 1962, the President reiterated the facts on the nation's growth, though once again he expressed regret at the gap. ". . . America's rise in the century since the Civil War has reflected more than anything else our unprecedented growth. . . ."

In the January 1963 report to the Congress, the President not only revealed the substantial gains in GNP, the drop in unemployment, the improvement in wage and nonwage income, but he also pointed to the continued high level of unemployment and the poor record of growth in the United States compared to that in Western Europe.

That the President shifted from the optimism induced by the substantial improvements from 1961 to 1963 to the pessimism based on inadequate growth is explained by the caution with which a President must move in these matters. He must be optimistic enough to inspire confidence among businessmen and maintain his political position, and yet must be sufficiently gloomy about the shortcomings so that he can get some action out of a recalcitrant Congress. In pushing his tax program, for example, President Kennedy had to underline the many disabilities of the economy which the tax program would cure.

THE GAP

The gap between actual and potential output displeased the President. If the gap were reduced output would be higher and unemployment less. The Council of Economic Advisers in particular called attention to the gap. But even earlier the Joint Economic Committee had alerted the country to the gap, and in its January 1961 *Report on the Economic Report of the President* it estimated the gap at $30 to $35 billion for 1960. In its 1963 report the JEC noted a widening gap between total demand and potential output. Whereas demand was about 2 per cent above potential output late in 1955, at the next cyclical peak, in 1960, actual output was about 6 per cent below potential output and "the ratio of actual to potential output has been stable or drifting downward since the fourth quarter of 1961."

The gap is troublesome because, reflecting output below potential, it is also responsible for part of the unemployment. Not only has actual output been below potential but in the 1950s, with declining rises of productivity, the annual rise of potential output had been falling.

The President was obviously torn between his satisfaction at the rate of growth and the unhappiness at the rate of unemployment. In the years 1957–1962, the council stated in its 1963 report, the gap totaled $170 billion in 1962 prices, or an average of $34 billion.

But there are many critics of the gap analysis, partly on ideological and partly on economic grounds.* Recognition of the gap means that government will try to do something about it. For this reason some question the analysis. Others hold that the excess plant capacity, upon which the theory of the gap partly rests, is largely nonexistent. The unused plant is held to be largely obsolescent plant. Some of the critics express satisfaction with the growth rate and the number of jobs, stressing the high level of employment against resultant transitional unemployment.

Perhaps the size of the gap has been exaggerated. One should not assume that the gap can be eliminated without some inflationary pressures. These in turn may require a check on rising output before the gap is eliminated. Keynes in his *General Theory* was careful to stress the inflationary pressures as output expands, even though he believed in expansionist policies. As more money is manufactured, part is used to put idle men and machines to work; but part is consumed in higher prices. The fact that resources are not homogeneous and hence not substitutable, one for the other, means that returns (productivity) will decline to this extent: Bottlenecks emerge especially in the later stages of recovery. Moreover, real wages rise when money wages do not reflect the decline in productivity, and in fact money wages rise as output and profits grow. Once we allow for the lack of homogeneity of resources and the early tendency of wage rates to rise, the effect of increasing effective demand associated with expansionist policies will be diluted to some extent, and output will rise less than might be suggested by any crude measures of excess capacity and gaps.†

A matter of concern has been the tendency of growth, total

* See chapter on conservative critics.
† In the "Papers and Proceedings of the American Economic Association," *American Economic Review,* May 1963, the reader will find an interesting discussion of capacity, the various estimates of capacity, and some of the theoretical problems raised in arriving at estimates of capacity output and hence of the gap.

and per capita, as well as the rise of productivity and potential productivity to decline in recent years. In its 1962 report the Council of Economic Advisers put it thus:

| | Percentage Change Per Year | |
	1947–1954	1954–1960
GNP, billions of 1961 dollars	3.8	3.2
Labor input:		
Labor force	1.3	1.3
Employment	1.1	1.3
Potential employment	1.3	1.3
Billions of manhours	.6	.9
GNP per capita	2.0	1.4
Productivity		
GNP per worker	2.7	2.0
Potential GNP per worker	3.1	2.2
GNP per manhour	3.4	2.4
Potential GNP per manhour	3.8	2.6

It is clear that the villain is declining potential and actual productivity, which is partly related to some sluggishness in the economy. The contribution of manpower actually rose in the later vis-à-vis the earlier period. As might be expected both total and per capita growth were less satisfactory in the later than in the earlier period.

In its 1962 report, the council estimated that actual production in 1961 was $40 billion below potential. With demand adequate to assure full employment, lower unemployment would contribute $15 billion; a larger labor force in response to greater demand, $4 billion; longer hours associated with higher utilization, $5 billion; greater productivity per man hour associated with higher utilization, $16 billion.

FUTURE GROWTH

In early 1963 the council was hopeful that improved demographic factors, i.e., larger numbers added to the labor market and treatment of the unemployment problem would yield a growth rate in excess of 4.5 per cent in the 1960s and an average rate of growth of potential output of 4.3 per cent. If unemployment were brought down to 4 per cent, the rise of GNP would be from $511 billion (1961 prices) to $825 billion, or an annual gain of 4.9 per cent in GNP and 4.3 per cent per year in potential GNP. Higher productivity, increased accessions to the labor market, and reduction of unemployment would contribute to the happy result, not, however, promised by the council.

In the ministerial agreement of the Organization for Economic Cooperation and Development (OECD) countries, the ministers set 4.4 per cent of GNP as a collective target for annual growth in the 1960s. The United States had done substantially less well than the other four major countries in the 1950s, except for the United Kingdom, and relied much more on gains of employment as against improved productivity than the others. An achievement of 4.4 per cent of growth from 1960–1970 was thought possible for the United States only because almost 40 per cent of the gain stemmed from a rise of employment (more workers and less unemployment) as compared with 17 per cent for the four other countries. Larger contributions by increased numbers on the labor market also mean that the improvement in the United States to this extent is reflected in gains of total GNP rather than in the more significant rise of GNP per capita.

In the United States much, perhaps too much, has been made of the greater rates of growth in Western Europe and Japan than in the United States. I would expect higher growth rates in these countries. The Common Market, the great inflow of American capital and management, the high level of investment related to the last but also to the stage of economic development, greater recourse to planning, the greater stress on consumption taxes, more effective monetary and fiscal policies, the transition to much higher levels of output and hence increased productivity—these are among the explanations offered for the large relative growth abroad. It should not be expected that the rate of growth in the United States at our stage of development should match Europe's. But we can learn something from the European experience. It will indeed be surprising if this country achieves an average rate of 4.4 per cent, the rate projected for the five large countries of the OECD.

COMPETITION WITH THE USSR

Earlier, I commented on United States versus Russian rates of growth and examined the possibility that the USSR might produce more than the United States. This is not, however, a likely outcome, for there is hope for improvement for the United States, and it is not likely that the USSR could maintain a 7 per cent rate for forty years. But it is useful to note here that the Russians have one advantage over the United States, namely, dictatorial power to allocate for security.

In a more realistic treatment, Gerhard Colm, in a paper for the Joint Economic Committee (September 1959) projected a 6 per cent rate of growth for the USSR and a 4.4 per cent rate for the United States for the years 1957–1970. Soviet GNP would then rise from 40 to 48 per cent of United States GNP—$378 billion and $790 billion, respectively, in 1970. On the whole this is a more favorable projection for the United States than is justified. For example, from 1957 to 1963, the estimated over-all rise in stable dollars was only 19 per cent, or about 2.5 per cent per year compounded.

In a recent study for the Joint Economic Committee (*Dimensions of Soviet Economic Power,* December 1962, page 52) Professor Holland Hunter, on the basis of a paper by S. H. Cohn, estimated that the Soviet GNP would rise from 46.7 in 1962 to 56.5 per cent of United States GNP in 1970. This is a substantial improvement for the USSR. That it is not higher is related to the tendency of retardation of the rate of growth for the USSR.

EXCESSIVE OPTIMISM ON THE RATE OF GROWTH?

In some respects the President's advisers in 1960 oversold him on the growth thesis. In 1960, too little was known about the possibilities of increasing growth from 3 to (say) 5 per cent per year. In retrospect, one could explain growth by studying the rise in capital and labor force and the gains of productivity. Thus in a speech before the Economic Club of Detroit, on February 19, 1962, Heller said that "if [real] GNP per person employed had been the same in 1961 as it was in 1929, we would have had a GNP of some $305 billion instead of $521 billion." This indeed underlines the great significance of rising productivity.

In the last few years, as a result of work of the National Bureau of Economic Research, Denison, and others, it has become clear that it is not easy to raise growth from say 3 to 5 per cent. Edward Denison, in trying to explain the greater increase of output over input, an index of rising productivity, has provided relatively precise values for the various inputs, such as labor, education, capital, and also for the factors accounting for the residual, that is, the excess of output over input. Thus, he concludes that education accounts for about 40 per cent of the rise of productivity. There are some difficulties in these estimates as Denison himself is well aware, and as others, and in particular Moses Abramovitz, Nicholas Kaldor, and John Vaizey have shown.

It is clear that there are many roads to increased rates of growth. In a rather full statement the Committee for Economic Development, in its 1962 report (page 111) listed the important factors as follows:

(1) The number of people available for employment, the number of hours they wish to work, their incentives and motivations, and their health, general education, occupational desires, and vocational skills;
(2) The stock of new and old plant and equipment, and its composition by age, type, and location;
(3) The terms on which the economy has access to natural resources, whether through domestic production or imports;
(4) The level of technology, covering the range from managerial and organizational competence to scientific, engineering, and mechanical understanding;
(5) The efficiency with which resources, domestic and foreign, are allocated to different economic ends, and the extent of monopolistic or other barriers to the movement of labor and capital from low-productivity to high-productivity uses.

These basic determinants interact in complex ways. For example, advanced machinery is of little use without skilled labor to operate it; advanced technology often requires capital equipment to embody it.

But of course these are not the only relevant considerations. A restrictive monetary policy or an inadequate fiscal policy will contribute to more frequent and deeper recessions and add to the sluggishness of the economy. Adequate demands related to these policies are of great importance. What a spectacular rise of demand can achieve is suggested by a 61 per cent rise in GNP (stable prices) in the 4 years 1940–1944. A recession every 3 to 4 years that costs the economy $30 to $50 billion means slower rates of growth. If we could maintain output at full employment levels at all times, output would be perhaps 2 per cent above what it otherwise would be. But this is a once and for all gain, and this contribution to growth declines as the number of years covered increases. The major improvement of growth will not be found to any large degree in getting rid of the business cycle.

President Kennedy was criticized for supporting his 1963 tax cut both to prevent (and) or soften the impact of a recession and to raise the rate of growth. The emphasis should indeed be on growth; but the cyclical indispositions are of some relevance for growth and are unwanted for other reasons as well. A $10 billion tax cut, which, according to Heller, would raise GNP by $30 to $40 billion, will surely extend the recovery, shorten and weaken recessions, as well as contribute to growth. But once the $30–$40 billion are added to output then with time its contribution to growth becomes less important. The level of output is, however, much higher. It is not only how much we grow that counts; but also from what base. A higher base in itself means greater output, and a given percentage of growth yields a larger gain the higher the base. Here the United States has a great advantage over the USSR even though the latter has a much higher rate of growth. A 3 per cent rate of growth in the United States and a 7 per cent in the USSR both yield gains of about $15 billion currently.

Undoubtedly satisfactory rates of growth are a proper target of government. With the reduced rate of growth since 1955, much attention was given to increasing this rate. On the whole the experience of 1961–1963 was favorable, and one that the Kennedy administration underplayed. This conclusion holds even if the rate of growth is somewhat less if related to the boom period of early 1960 than to the end of the recession in the first quarter of 1961.

In stressing the unsatisfactory level of unemployment and the substantial gap, the Kennedy administration drew attention to the fact that a rate of growth, however pleasing, was nevertheless not adequate to solve our unemployment problem. Some rough calculations point to a need of additional GNP per year of about $35 billion (in stable dollars) in the next five years if unemployment is not to rise. This failure of unemployment to respond is the cost of large accessions to the labor market and unusual gains of productivity. Elimination of the gap would help, though the net beneficial effect on growth per year declines as the period covered is extended.

Perhaps growth has had too much attention. It is not a full measure of welfare or even of economic welfare. Yet there is no other measure equally significant. Concentration on rate of growth, moreover, helps to attract attention to a variable of great significance for giving the nation adequate security and welfare, and especially to the most important approach for treating unemployment. Those who underemphasize growth are less inclined to apply the necessary fiscal and monetary therapy. Even Arthur Burns tended to underemphasize fiscal policy as the solution, and in 1961 predicted a full employment economy in fifteen months without special measures of government. He took the position even though he associated the premature termination of the recovery in 1959–1960 with a dramatic changeover from a very large deficit to a substantial surplus in the federal budget.

I7

Welfare

SOME GENERAL ISSUES

At the outset, President Kennedy depended to a considerable extent on spending programs, both to stimulate the economy and to help the disadvantaged. Clearly this was 1961 policy. In fact he objected to a tax cut in 1961, partly because he feared that it would be more difficult to get through his spending programs. In his March 24, 1961, message on the budget and fiscal policy the President said that "we can afford to do what must be done, publicly and privately, up to the limit of our economic capacity—a limit which we have not even approached for several years."

This does not mean that the President was not concerned about costs and deficits. He was. But he proposed use of trust funds, such as unemployment compensation and Medicare, with resultant savings for the administrative budget; he asked for substantial sums but the expenditures were to be strung out over several years; he distinguished between capital and current outlays, though the budget did not; and he urged use of backdoor financing, not to avoid the discipline of annual checking by the Congress, but to provide plans over several years.

Unsatisfactory economic conditions forced the President, with Congressional cooperation, into telescoping several significant measures into a short period of five months. By June 30, 1961, the Congress had approved temporary unemployment benefits, an area redevelopment program, liberalization of social security benefits, aid for dependent children with unemployed fathers, and an omnibus housing bill. He had moved much more rapidly than Eisenhower had in the 1958 recession.

But the welfare programs lagged after 1961. A most important reason was the rising financial demands of our defense program after the 1961 Berlin crisis. A second significant factor was the rising interest in a tax cut. Increasingly the President had to scrutinize expenditures as the price to be paid for acceptance of a tax cut and a substantial deficit. It may even be said that the net contribution of the tax cut to strengthening the economy is greatly reduced just because the squeeze had to be put on expenditures, and especially on welfare outlays.

The President often expressed the hope that with the tax cut and higher incomes state and local governments would assume heavier welfare burdens. In fact this had been the trend. From 1952 to 1961, for example, the rise of state and local expenditures had been relatively three times as great as for federal expenditures.

It is of some interest that on April 19, 1963, in the midst of pressures to reduce expenditures, speaking to the Society of Newspaper Editors, the President discussed "less than 30 priority measures. And it is not expensive—inasmuch as their total elimination would reduce next year's $12 billion deficit by less than $2 billion."

The President discussed a hypothetical subdivision of Random Village: recreation facilities were inadequate; many of the children dropped out of school; families were confronted with a shortage of doctors, dentists, and hospitals; the facilities for the mentally retarded were most inadequate; one-fifth of the houses were deteriorated or dilapidated; one out of eight families had incomes of $3,500 or less; the housing, job availabilities, and education were especially deficient for the Negro population.

Perhaps the most important factor in the lag of welfare programs has been the rising demands of the military. Defense, space, and related expenditures account for about 75 per cent of the increase of expenditures under Kennedy through fiscal year 1964 (estimated).

In the fiscal years 1962 to 1964 (estimated), the Kennedy administration increased its outlays on welfare programs more than the Eisenhower administration. In all major categories this conclusion holds, with the exception of agriculture and housing.

But the relatively smaller rise for housing outlays under Kennedy may be related to the sale of mortgages to the market and the difficulties of liberalizing mortgage terms once the Eisenhower administration had advanced far in this direction. Whereas from fiscal 1954 to 1962, agricultural outlays increased more than $400 million per year on the average, they declined by about $200 million per year under Kennedy. The rise for welfare for the two years (and the rise will be less in several categories to the extent that Congress did not accept the plans and proposals of the administration given in the 1964 budget) has been as follows:

RISE IN EXPENDITURES, FISCAL YEARS 1962–1964

	Millions of Dollars	Percentage Change
National resources	+356	17
Agriculture and agricultural resources	−199	−3
Commerce and transportation	+614	+23
Housing and community development	−73	−22
Health, labor, and welfare	+1089	+22
Health services and research	+514	+56
Education	+461	+43

SOURCE: *U.S. Budget, 1964.* My calculations.

Over these two years the increase was but $2.76 billion, an outside figure since to a small degree some of these items include nonwelfare expenditures. This gain of welfare outlays is roughly estimated at but 5 per cent of the rise of GNP.

Grants-in-aid by the federal government include an important part of federal welfare outlays. In the two years under consideration, the rise was $1,211 million, an annual average roughly equal to that of the Eisenhower administration from fiscal 1954 to 1962. (I assume that fiscal 1953 was primarily the responsibility of President Truman and fiscal 1962, of President Eisenhower.)

Developments in fiscal 1963 and 1964 have been along expected lines. The Democrats have consistently been responsible for major advances in welfare programs—social security, housing, resource development, hospital construction, etc. The Eisenhower administration did liberalize old-age survivors and disability insurance (OASDI) periodically. But OASDI is financed out of a trust fund, not at the expense of the general taxpayer. Insofar as payments exceed earnings of annuitants—as they do to a considerable degree—the administration is indulging in deficit financing.

EDUCATION

I now turn to welfare programs, and first to education. Through 1963, though some progress was made, the results were, on the whole, disappointing. The House Rules Committee was an obstacle in 1961. In 1962, the intrusion of the religious issue and the inclusion of a scholarship program in the Senate, unacceptable to the House, killed a higher education bill at the last moment. In 1963 a new tack was tried. The President did not try to bypass the religious issue; but the proposed legislation made it clear that construction aid would not be given for buildings used for religious instruction. Partly in order to appease the House, the 1963 omnibus bill omitted the scholarship provisions. (This omission may also be related to a lack of enthusiasm, especially among public institutions, for scholarships against subsidies to institutions, and also to growing pressure on the government to retrench on expenditures.)

The 1963 omnibus bill (Program for Education, January 29, 1963) was an unusual package. Undoubtedly, the theory behind it was that a bill which offered help to the schools, to the junior colleges, to other institutions of higher learning including graduate centers, to adults in need of further education and training, for fellowships for graduate students and especially for scientists, to libraries, for aid for training of teachers, for continued assistance for the federally affected areas—such a bill, it was assumed, would win the approval of all relevant interests. But it did not. The Congress was not pleased with the resultant omelet, and soon began to concentrate on the items with political appeal, notably vocational guidance and help for institutions of higher learning.

Another interesting feature of the bill was the attempt to be selective; that is, instead of giving over-all grants, to concentrate help in special areas where a given outlay would be especially effective:

A *selective* application of Federal Aid—aimed at strengthening, not weakening the independence of existing school systems, and aimed at meeting our most urgent educational problems and objectives, including quality improvement; teacher training; special problems of slums, depressed and rural areas; needy students; manpower shortage areas such as science and engineering; and shortages of education facilities. . . .

The President had stressed the drop-out problem; the educational contribution to some 40 per cent to the nation's growth and productivity in recent years (a degree of precision not really supportable by empirical analysis); a tripling of educational costs in the 1940s and a doubling in the 1950s; by 1970 a doubling of college enrollment; and a rise of 50 per cent in the enrollment in secondary schools. The President also spoke out eloquently on the needs of higher salaries and more classrooms. On the salary and construction issue, the attack was selective: He emphasized: "increasing starting and maximum teaching salaries, and increasing average teaching salaries in economically disadvantaged areas, [as well as] constructing classrooms in areas of critical and dangerous shortage. . . ."

In view of the great emphasis the President put on education, the question can be raised whether the proposed program would be adequate, especially in view of the varying capacities of the states to finance education. On June 6, 1963, the President reminded his San Diego, California, listeners that the average current expenditure per student in California was $515 and in Mississippi $230; the average salary for classroom teachers $7,000 and $3,600 respectively.

The 1964 budget provided for a doubling of new obligational authority to a total of $3 billion, with the bulk for new legislation. But for fiscal year 1964, expenditures would rise only by $176 million, of which $144 million would be under new educational programs.

These were not large sums, and many would criticize the President for his failure to recommend adequate expenditures. In the 1960s *all* educational expenditures are almost certain to rise by at least $15–$20 billion or $1.5–$2 billion per year. A contribution by the federal government of even $500 million per year eventually is a rather small one.

But in defense of President Kennedy, it can be said that even the modest sums asked seemed to be too much for the Congress to approve. The religious issue, civil rights, the tax cut, concern over the rising deficit, fear of federal control—all of these made approval of large educational outlays by the federal government unlikely.

For the schools, the religious and civil rights controversies make enactment of federal aid especially difficult. In a June 27, 1962, press conference, the President said:

In my opinion, there are very clear limitations based on the Supreme Court decisions on aid to non-public schools in the secondary field. But in those fields the attendance is compulsory, it is universal. There is a particular tradition connected with our public school system which has placed it in a special place in the tradition and constitutional life of our country. This is not true of higher education. . . .

But even in higher education, it does not seem that federal contributions are likely to be large. Current costs of higher education are likely to rise by at least $600 million per year; and capital costs, by $200 million additional. (Institutions of higher learning—IHL—are likely to need at least $2 billion yearly for plant as compared to expenditures of $1.2 billion in 1958.) It is possible that state and local government, students, and private philanthropy will provide the additional sums, at least for current operations. That state and local governments doubled their total outlays in stable dollars in the 1950s is a good omen. But the burden on these governments and on students could be eased through larger federal contributions, a large part of which might be in loans. (I consider federal outlays on research for IHL as payments for services.) In 1958, the federal government contributed $774 million in all, inclusive of $534 million for research—out of current income of IHL of $4,675 million.

In fiscal 1964, the budget called for outlays of $213 million (housing loans) and $119 million for defense education—student loans, fellowships, language and area centers. This was a large reduction from 1963.

But nevertheless substantial progress was made in 1963. The Congress approved not insignificant outlays for facilities for higher education and loans for students, some help to health schools, and an important bill on vocational education. The great disappointment was failure to help with public school education.*

HEALTH AND MEDICINE

On February 9, 1961, February 27, 1962, and February 7, 1963, the President sent health messages to Congress, urging enactment of comprehensive health programs. He stressed the need of additional health facilities and also (related) increased flow of health personnel, extension of research, medical insurance for the aged under social security, community health protection— ". . . threats to the physical well-being of our families from the contamination of food, air and water, and from hazardous drugs and cosmetics, must be dealt with more promptly and more effectively"—and numerous other items such as improved vocational rehabilitation and child and maternal health.

All three programs were different. By 1963, the President abandoned his proposals for medical scholarships, and substituted loans for students in health schools. The American Medical Association seemed opposed even to loans. At least in the area of medical facilities and medical personnel the Congress, after failing to pass a bill each year since 1951, approved in 1963 a modest bill for federal sharing in the cost of facilities and loans for students.

Education of doctors and dentists is indeed costly, and the students pay a small part of the costs. But despite that fact, the high costs to the students and family result in a disproportionate share of the medical students coming from the high-income families. Medical education is costly partly because instruction is generally in small groups; teachers are expensive because of the high incomes available for practicing physicians; and the medical school is a small operation with an average undergraduate student body of about 400—hence high unit costs.

Shortages prevailed also for other members of the health team. Whereas by 1975 the number of physicians graduating would have to rise by 50 per cent in order to maintain current population-

---

* I have discussed educational issues fully in *More Resources for Education,* Harper & Row, 1960; and *Higher Education: Resources and Finance,* McGraw-Hill, 1962.

physician ratios, the rise would have to be 100 per cent for dentists. The President was also looking forward to a very large increase in the number of nurses, a goal that can be reached only by helping build nursing schools and providing aid to students and potential teachers of nursing.

Another facet of the medical program was, of course, Medicare; that is, insurance under social security for limited hospital benefits for the aged. Low incomes of the aged, heavy incidence of chronic diseases, and heavy costs of medicine, limited availability of insurance to the old—all alerted the President to the need of Medicare. In 1960, despite AMA vigorous opposition, the Senate failed by only four votes to pass the Anderson-King bill for Medicare. In 1962, despite a strong campaign by the President, the bill again failed of passage. On July 17, 1962, the President commented:

. . . A switch of two votes in the Senate would have provided, I believe, for its passage.

. . . This is a most serious defeat for every American family, for the 17 million Americans who are over 65. . . .

. . . nearly all the Republicans and a handful of Democrats joined with them to give us today's setback. [He later said two-thirds of the Republicans voted against the bill.]

. . . I hope that we will return in November a Congress that will support . . . Medical Care for the aged, a program which has been fought by the American Medical Association and successfully defeated. . . .

In other areas the President had some success. Progress was being made in legislation for improving mental health and mental retardation facilities. But on air pollution control the President, in his 1963 message, expressed great concern: " . . . the cost of air pollution is estimated at $11 billion per year, but we are spending but 10 cents per capita to deal with a condition that costs $65 per capita per year."

Health research continued to advance, with the federal government spending about two-thirds of the $1.5 billion being disbursed each year. The President had no trouble convincing the Congress of the need of increasing outlays. In Senator Hill and Congressman Fogarty he had two knowledgeable allies who not only tended to accept presidential recommendations but even persuaded the Congress to spend more than the President had proposed.

Some experts have asked whether in view of the shortage of teachers and research workers, the government was not expanding its research operations too rapidly, and thereby, bringing about an inflation of costs rather than a corresponding gain in scientific advances. The rapid rise of operations may well help explain Congressional investigations of the National Health Institutes. The large research funds available contribute to increasing funds for instruction, an important by-product of these research outlays.

The Kefauver hearings, in 1962, brought out many weaknesses of the drug industry. Profits have been at a record level compared to virtually every other industry; conditions have often been monopolistic or oligopolistic (few sellers). Selling costs are excessive and advertising often misleading if not dishonest; side effects are frequently concealed and drugs dispensed without adequate prior testing. Despite many conditions that required correction, Senator Kefauver was not able to get acceptance by the Senate Judiciary Committee of necessary legislation. But the crisis over a drug that produced malformed babies enabled the government to get drug legislation in 1962 that gave the public greater protection.

One of the worst problems in recent years has been the shortage of hospitals and the rising price of hospital services. The Hill-Burton Act, passed early in the postwar period, has greatly increased hospital facilities in the country and especially in rural communities. Possibly the large expansion in smaller communities has been overdone. With improved transportation there is much to be said for the patient moving to the hospital instead of the hospital being brought to him. The costs of the small hospital are very high, and they can provide only limited service. They have, however, had one helpful effect, namely, inducing physicians to practice in smaller communities.

President Kennedy, in his 1963 message, urged necessary revisions in the program, which had never yielded beds on the basis of needs. As chronic diseases became more and more important, the Hill-Burton Act had failed to provide the beds needed for long periods of illness and, moreover, the stress on hospitals in small communities had resulted in the neglect of the large city hospitals.

To deal with chronic illness the President asked for many more nursing homes, and to improve the situation in the large cities at minimum cost, he wanted to spend for modernization of the old and often dangerous city hospitals.

All in all, the President made progress in his medical programs: in air and water pollution, in research outlays, in medical facilities and personnel, in drug legislation, in community health facilities, and in vocational rehabilitation. His disappointment was especially the failure to push through Medicare.*

UNEMPLOYMENT AND UNEMPLOYMENT COMPENSATION

Unemployment was perhaps the most troublesome domestic problem for the President. The trend of unemployment had been upward for more than ten years, and each succeeding cyclical peak seemed to entail larger amounts of unemployment. Moreover, duration of unemployment tends to increase relatively.

Concerned over the unemployment problem the President succeeded in getting approval for a temporary unemployment compensation (U.C.) bill in record time in early 1961 and in May 1961 proposed radical advances in the permanent system. But the Congress did not cooperate.

U.C. was one of the great achievements of President Roosevelt. But its development has been disappointing. Benefits have not kept pace with the rise of wages, partly because of ceilings on weekly benefits and the failure to raise the taxable weekly wage in a period when wages rose by more than 200 per cent. As Richard Lester shows, the benefits cover only about 20 per cent of the loss of wages resulting from total unemployment. Experience rating, under which the programs provide reduced rates for employers with low unemployment, has greatly cut taxes and induced competition among states for minimum benefits and minimum taxes. States especially vulnerable to unemployment have experienced declines of reserves far below a safe level. Pennsylvania, for example, had reserves at the end of 1962 equal only to 60 per cent of benefit payments in that year. Its tax rate was 3.3 per cent, compared

* I have discussed many of these problems fully in *The Economics of American Medicine*, Macmillan, (1964).

with an average of 2.4 per cent. Yet there were eighteen states with rates of 1.5 per cent and less.

On May 14, 1963, the President sent proposals to the Congress for the improvement of U.C., which largely followed the unapproved version of 1961. Within a few years the President wanted benefits raised from less than 40 to 50 per cent of wages. By 1970, the minimum would be 66.7 per cent of wages. Troubled by the rising trend of long-term unemployment, the President wished to extend U.C. from twenty-six to a maximum of thirty-nine weeks. He desired to finance the additional U.C., as well as special grants to states experiencing much unemployment, by an additional payroll tax to be collected in all states but to be used to bolster the financial position of states needing help to treat long-term unemployment, (and) or experiencing a general heavy incidence of unemployment. By setting minimum standards of U.C. and providing for additional payroll taxes for use outside of the states of collection, the President was treating the abuses that have developed as a result of concentrating responsibilities on the states and as a result of the introduction of experience rating. Minimum federal standards and federal responsibility for part of the financing would improve the benefit standards and reduce interstate competition for minimum rates and benefits.*

AID TO AGRICULTURE

Agriculture and resource development are more than welfare programs. But to a substantial degree they can be included under welfare.

Few economists would approve of agricultural policies under either Republicans or Democrats. Economists might support farm price or income policies on political or ideological, not economic grounds. They would also hope that in return for government outlays to keep farmers' incomes up, that the farmer in turn would

* See especially Richard A. Lester, *The Economics of Unemployment Compensation,* 1962, Princeton University Press, Chap. 3; *Congressional Quarterly,* March 29, 1963; Seymour E. Harris, Study Paper No. 7, *The Incidence of Inflation; or Who Gets Hurt?* 1959, Joint Economic Committee, Chap. 6; and Seymour E. Harris, *The Economics of the Political Parties,* 1962, Macmillan, Chaps. 24, 29.

agree to restrict output. Hence, output and government surpluses would be reduced gradually. In 1962, the Committee for Economic Development proposed to the House Agriculture Committee that the farmers be supported for a transitional period on the condition that they gradually reduce their output, partly through migration. Virtually the whole committee repudiated this approach. President Eisenhower's Secretary of Agriculture, Ezra Taft Benson, who wanted a free market and hence was even less friendly to farm policies of the last generation than most, also had little success.

No one would contend that President Eisenhower's farm policy was highly successful, especially since it was so costly to the Treasury, creating a burden that was especially troublesome to an administration which was hostile to extensive government spending. In fiscal 1954, the expenditures for agriculture and agricultural resources was but $2,573 million. By 1959, the cost had risen to $6,590 million, and the average for 1955–1962 was $5.2 billion. Roughly three-quarters of this cost was for farm income support and production adjustments.

Yet despite these large outlays, income from farm operations declined by 20 per cent from 1952 to 1960, a period when all personal income rose by 47 per cent, or a relative loss for farming income of about 45 per cent. In this same period the parity ratio (ratio of prices received by farmers to prices paid) declined by 20 per cent. The Eisenhower policy tended to favor measures that would induce farmers to abandon their farms. The soil bank reserve plan, which cost $1.32 billion in two fiscal years, was abandoned mainly because its impact was especially to force small farmers out. In the eight years 1952–1960 farm population declined by 30 per cent, a record figure. The Democrats were less disposed to support measures that would drive farmers off the farm.

When President Kennedy took over, he was confronted with a crisis in farming, with costs to the federal budget way out of proportion: 8 per cent of the population was receiving about one sixth of nondefense federal outlays just for support of their prices and incomes.

President Kennedy's general approach was a generous price support program, but on the condition that the farmers would submit to serious control of output and marketing. President Roosevelt had not been too successful in espousing such a program. What greatly disturbed President Kennedy was the accumulation of inventories, the high cost of servicing them, and the high costs of the whole program. But he was confronted with numerous other problems, many of which had also plagued his predecessors. In cotton, for example, there was a conflict between industrialists, who wanted cheap cotton, and the farmers, who wanted high prices; between the farmers in the Southeast, who sought restrictions on output and high prices, and the Western growers, who wanted large outputs and moderate prices. The President had some success in diverting farms from the production of feed grains. But in a wheat referendum of 1963 the President suffered a serious defeat. The strong campaign of the American Farm Bureau, which opposed stringent controls of marketing; the Republicans, who fought the wheat policy of restricted output and high prices; and the adverse votes of the small farmers, who for the first time had a vote—killed the President's wheat plan in 1963.

In his press conference of June 27, 1962, the President explained the defeat of his important farm bill of 1962. He blamed the Republicans who, with the exception of one member, voted against the bill, the vested interests that favored rising surpluses, those who wanted cheap feed, and then those who wanted to plant more corn. With this setback the President added that the farm bill would cost $7.5 billion in the next budget instead of $6.5 billion as he had hoped.

In an able message of January 31, 1962, the President had discussed the farm problem at great length. He was pleased with a rise of farm income of $1 billion in 1961 (this total was maintained in 1962), and a reduction of farm stocks for the first time in nine years. He warned of the dangers of the old policies and the contribution of new patterns of demand to a deterioration of markets, e.g., reduced consumption of milk.

Our rapidly growing capacity to produce far outruns the growth of our domestic and foreign demand for food and fiber.

. . . Instead of a shortage of cropland, as many have long predicted, it now appears that by 1980 we will need 50 million fewer acres than we have today.

Removal of farm programs, the President warned, would slice wheat prices by almost one-half, barley by 28 per cent, dairy by 17 per cent, livestock by 24 per cent, and eggs by 20 per cent.

The President urged his ABCD program: A—to make maximum use of our *abundance* at home and abroad; B—seek *balance* between production and demand (e.g., as in rice, tobacco, and peanuts); C—*conservation*—where land and water are not needed for food they should be diverted for other purposes; D—*development*—"To initiate and expand programs for the *development* of human resources and renewal of rural communities." The President stressed here the need of policies to ease the transitions.

Under his 1963 wheat program the President suggested price supports of 75 to 90 per cent for the domestic allotment for marketing and up to 90 per cent for the export allotment: "I recommend a wheat program which will reduce wheat stocks to manageable levels, improve the competitive position of American wheat in world markets, and maintain the income of wheat farmers."

On May 21, 1963, the farmers rejected by a large margin the wheat referendum. This meant that farmers would not receive a high support price. On May 20, the President had warned the farmers that "a vote [of] yes, will mean reduced production but the price will remain for most of the crop at about $2 a bushel and that is the choice . . . that the farmers must make . . . between wheat at $1.10 a bushel or wheat at $2 a bushel. . . ."

The defeat of the wheat referendum suggested that the Congress might not look favorably toward serious controls of output and marketing of dairy products and cotton, feed grains and livestock. It is possible, as the *Congressional Quarterly* noted, that a year of low prices and no controls may convert wheat farmers to a control policy as a similar experience in tobacco had converted the tobacco farmers.

On January 3, 1963, the White House had released a memorandum from the Secretary of Agriculture. The major objectives were held to be a favorable vote on the wheat referendum, fair competitive arrangements with the Common Market, and new legislation on feed grains, cotton, and dairy products. In 1963, the administration, except for feed grain legislation, had failed to obtain these objectives.

But the Secretary could boast of some progress. The distribution of free food had greatly increased. Prices were relatively stable. Gross farm income in 1962 was $2.5 billion in excess of that in 1960. The administration had succeeded in reducing stocks of wheat and feed grains, though stocks of dairy products and cotton were still rising. The 1964 budget would cut outlays for the Commodity Credit Corporation by $1 billion although admittedly the major part is not a net saving. For 1963, the prospects were for stabilization of farm incomes and exports and a reduction of feed grain stocks.

On January 31, 1963, the President delivered a major farm message which followed the outlines of his Secretary's memo. He found gross farm income up substantially since 1960, surplus grain stocks down by 929 million bushels, and the proportion of income required by consumers to purchase food down to a record of 19 per cent of take-home pay. The President warned the farmers that if the wheat referendum were not approved there would be neither supply management nor effective price supports. In this message the President suggested the two-price treatment of cotton (that is, low prices abroad and high at home) to be carried out without eliminating subsidies for exports required for sales abroad or a reduction of domestic prices which would be costly to farmers; and he proposed a dairy program, which would require marketing control and a ceiling on costs to the government. By the end of 1963, most of the major problems had not been solved, though the deterioration of the farmers' position since 1952 had clearly ceased.

In summary, the Kennedy administration pushed a sensible agricultural policy; but neither the farmers nor the Congress as yet seem prepared to accept genuine control of output as the price for supporting farm prices and incomes. Conflicts among farm groups and between farmers and consumers of their products are further obstacles to an adequate farm program.

DEVELOPMENT OF RESOURCES

It has for many years been a Democratic party objective to develop the natural resources of the country. The budgetary figures point to some advances under Kennedy. Whereas in the fiscal years 1954–1961, expenditures on natural resources averaged $1.48 billion, the estimated average outlays for the two fiscal years 1963 and 1964 were $1.72 billion, or a rise of 16 per cent. From 1954 to 1961, the average rise was $48 million; but for fiscal years 1963 and 1964, the average was $178 million. These are not heroic gains and reflect the containment of spending on resource development related both to the increasing demands of security as well as the damper on spending in general made necessary by the recourse to tax cuts. If the Kennedy administration did not propose to spend as much as had been anticipated, this much may be said: Whereas from fiscal years 1953 to 1961, the rise of federal resource outlays was considerably less than that of GNP, from fiscal years 1961 to 1964, they promise to be substantially more.

In a special message to the Congress on natural resources (February 23, 1961), the President warned the country that by

the year 2000 a United States population of 300 million—nearly doubled in 40 years—will need far greater supplies of farm products, timber, water, minerals, fuels, energy, and opportunities for outdoor recreation. Present projections tell us that our water use will double in the next 20 years; that we are harvesting our supply of high-grade timber more rapidly than the development of new growth; that too much of our federal topsoil is being washed away; that our minerals are being exhausted at increasing rates; and that the nation's remaining undeveloped areas of great natural beauty are being rapidly pre-empted for other uses.

At this time, the President repudiated the Eisenhower policy of "no new starts," and asked the relevant agencies to plan a development of natural resources which would meet accumulated needs but also take account of availability of funds. The President also requested expansion of programs to deal with water and air pollution.

In the area of development of water power, the President asked for the cooperation of all interested groups, for by 1980 installed electric power capacity would have to rise by 200 per cent. Public power was one of the great issues of the Eisenhower administration, which on the whole tended to favor private power interests more than the Democrats would. The great debate on Hells Canyon had been settled in favor of the Idaho Power Company. But the administration had favored public development of the upper Colorado River, part of the explanation being that the power potential of this development had little appeal for private interests.

President Kennedy affirmed "that hydroelectric sites remaining in this country will be utilized and hydroelectric power will be incorporated in all multiple-purpose river projects where optimum economic use of the water justifies such action."

On March 1, 1962, the President delivered his major message on conservation. Noting the relation of population growth and rising productivity to increased leisure, the President said:

the obligation to make the most efficient and beneficial use of our natural resources becomes correspondingly greater. . . . But these resources are not inexhaustible—nor do they automatically replenish themselves.

Our national conservation effort must include the complete spectrum of resources: air, water and land; fuels, energy and minerals; soils, forests, and forage; fish and wildlife. . . .

In this message the President boasted of advances in 1961 in water pollution control, flood plan studies, starts on seventy-four major water resources projects and seventy-nine small watershed projects, provision for acquisition of land for federally financed reservoirs to preserve recreational potential of many areas, a ten-year projection of needs and plans for the development of our national projects, and progress with the Tennessee Valley Authority, the Cape Cod National Seashore Area, the Delaware River Dam compact, and other items also.

Now the President wished to integrate the work of more than twenty federal departments interested in recreation, and to provide matching grants for the development of state plans for outdoor recreation. The President proposed the creation of a land conservation fund which would be financed largely by fees collected from those using the facilities and from sales of surplus lands. In the meanwhile, the President would seek advances of $500 million from the Treasury for an eight-year program.

In this paper the President emphasized the need of more water —a doubling of supplies by 1980 and a tripling by the year 2000.

Hence the need for sufficient water of the right quality available at the right time and at the right place. The President wished to set up commissions to study river basins and would help states plan. ". . . We must harmonize conflicting objectives—for example, irrigation vs. navigation, multiple-purpose reservoirs vs. scenic park sites. . . ."

The President also had much to say about improved use of public lands, increased attention to soil, watershed, and range resources, the needed increase of timber and mineral growth: "During the last 30 years, this nation has consumed more minerals than all the people of the world had previously used. Immense advances in technology and exploration have helped greatly in recent years. But present availability of raw materials must not blind us to tomorrow's requirements."

Problems of power development also received the President's attention. Electric power alone had to double in ten years. The objective would be adequate power for all uses at low prices and, therefore, improved planning and exploitation of power from all sources—nuclear energy, hydroelectric energy captured from the tides, etc.

Surely if the economy rises by $30 billion or 4 to 5 per cent per year in the 1960s a case can be made for a rise of at least 5 per cent in outlays on welfare. The Department of Health, Education, and Welfare estimates public expenditures on welfare in 1963 at $66 billion, as compared to $26.5 billion in 1953. A rise of 5 per cent per year would require additional outlays of $3 to $4 billion in the 1960s as compared to $4 billion from 1953 to 1963, one-half to be financed by state and local governments, as at present.

PART IV

Formulation of Policy and the Critics

18

Critics

President Kennedy was subjected to a steady barrage of criticism from the right and left on his economic policy. He was particularly embarrassed by the persistent attacks from his supporters on the left, among them Walter Lippmann, Senator Albert Gore, Leon Keyserling, Oscar Gass, Sidney Hyman, Robert Lekachman, Hobart Rowan, Bernard Nossiter, TRB of the *New Republic,* Walter Reuther, and even such friendly advisers as Paul Samuelson. These critics were not equally vigorous in their comments. Perhaps Keyserling and Gass were the most vocal. They found very little to praise and much to condemn in Kennedy's decisions.

Following are a few quotes from the critics:

In a carefully prepared television program in June 1961, Walter Lippmann said of President Kennedy: What he has done in the first four or five months is "first of all to carry on in all its essentials the Eisenhower economic philosophy. . . . It's like the Eisenhower Administration 30 years younger."

Leon Keyserling, in a reply to the writer in a *New Republic* article of October 9, 1961, entitled "JFK Economics: Should We All Stand Up and Cheer?" said:

Measuring the current recovery properly by the test of how close it is bringing us toward reasonably full utilization of manpower and other productive resources on a sustainable basis (rather than measuring it improperly by the absolute index of the upturn in production

217

from a recessionary basis), the recovery to date has not been substantially more satisfactory than the two upturns after recessions under Eisenhower. . . . [I comment on this later. Moreover, this is not an acceptable definition of recovery, but rather of goals.]

This is a mild version of some of the criticisms by Keyserling of Kennedy economics. He is particularly critical of economists like myself who consider political issues: "When economists soften their economic findings in terms of their own political judgements, they offer the President what he does not need from them."

Elsewhere Keyserling said that the President's "proposed programs fall far short even of compatibility with these excessively low goals. . . ."

In an article in *Harper's* magazine of September 1961, Hobart Rowan, one of the most able writers on the current economic scene, was especially critical of Kennedy's reluctance to spend and of his claims of fiscal integrity. He quoted Samuelson's comment "that we are in the midst of a placebo program for recovery." (A similar position was taken by Rowan in a *New Republic* article of May 25, 1963.)

After surveying Kennedy's policies in 1961, he concluded:

Yet all this falls far short of the bright promise; the nation has had to settle for a limited program which is unlikely to result in full employment or a significant rise in our economic growth rate . . . .
. . . The political strategy can be left to the politicians. . . . In the first year of this Administration too much obeisance has been paid to political feasibility. If economists do not argue cogently and forcefully for their programs, the goals they want to achieve may never become politically feasible.

Oscar Gass, perhaps the most pungent among the President's liberal critics, also had much to say of Kennedy's economic policies in a series of articles in *Commentary* in 1961 and 1962. His summary position: President Kennedy has "projected little and accomplished almost nothing."

The President was frequently criticized for failing to use the Congress more effectively. Both Gass and Hyman made this point. Gass: ". . . The legislator feels the Constitutional separation of powers not as a theorist's simplification but as a painful reality. . . ."

On interest rates, Gass used one word: "Failure."
Kennedy's political music:

> . . . I might call it *immobilism*. . . . It lacks the militant personnel
> and drive to pull a working bloc of Congressional supporters into
> participation. . . . It . . . looks for support to established Republicans,
> to conservative business figures. . . . It naturally finds intellectual sus-
> tenance in the politics and economics of Galbraith and Schlesinger. . . .

This criticism that the President did not appeal to the people or
use Congress effectively is an often repeated charge.

Perhaps the major criticism results from the slow pace at which
the President moved: Unemployment was high; excess capacity
was costly; growth inadequate; and yet the President moved slug-
gishly in the view of critics. Most of these detractors were prepared to admit that his slight plurality in the election might help
to explain the President's reluctance to plunge. But the common
view was that the President paid too much attention to Congress
and failed to use Congress. Some felt that he should have appealed
to the country and moved far ahead of Congress. For example,
Sidney Hyman, the able historian, writing in *Look* early in July
1963, suggested that it was a mistake for Kennedy to diminish his
demands; he should have put the responsibility of cutting upon
the Congress.

To some extent these critics had a case. The Democratic national
platform promised aggressive measures to induce growth and reduce unemployment; and the President adhered to the outlines
of his platform in his campaign speeches. Yet the criticism should
have been directed more to the system rather than to the President.
The presidential candidate appoints a chairman of the Platform
Committee who has virtually dictatorial powers. The candidate
has little time to direct or supervise the writing of the platform.
Moreover, and more important, it does not bind the Congress,
which has little to do with the platform. Former President Eisenhower also failed to adhere to many of the policies outlined in
his platform, such as his promise not to impair collective bargaining. Here again, it was the system rather than the President that
was at fault.

Critics should also remember the obstacles which confronted

the President, some of them unexpected or more persistent than had been anticipated. Among these were the adverse balance of payments, restraining expansionist policies; the strengthening of the coalition between the Republicans and the southern Congressmen; the increased obstacles of the Rules Committee; the unfortunate incumbence of Senator Byrd and Congressman Mills in the chairmanship of the most important committees (at least, it was unfortunate for any President who would embark on expansionist programs); the collapse of the stock market in the spring of 1962; the weakening of the stimulus, available to President Eisenhower, from the large backlog of demand for consumer goods, stemming from the depression and the war; the revolutionary economic changes in Europe; the unavailability of the degree of liberalization of housing credit available to Eisenhower; the sluggish economy inherited in 1961 and the large advance of automation; the Berlin crisis, which resulted in much larger security outlays (a favorable factor in stimulating the economy but adverse in its effects on welfare expenditures).

From 1961 the President's Committee on the State of the Economy predicted high levels of unemployment and stunted growth unless the President (and Congress) moved with energy and dispatch. But though these economists could urge the President on, irrespective of Congressional attitudes, the President had to consider noneconomic factors, including Congressional attitudes.

Even in the first half of 1961, the critics were demanding more audacious measures. Yet the President had moved quickly to treat the recession: He accepted a modest deficit, pressured for more credit and lower rates, accelerated federal outlays, pushed his area redevelopment program, and temporary unemployment compensation program. Despite the affirmations of Keyserling and Gass, the recovery in these early months was most satisfactory, especially if allowance is made for the less than normal preceding decline. The economy began to improve rapidly, after only nine months of recession, due to the President's aggressive measures.

But the critics had a case against the President in that even as late as the Berlin crisis and the beginning of 1962, he was still excessively cautious of large expenditures and deficits. He was not prepared *adequately* to exploit fiscal instruments. But after the first eighteen months of the Kennedy administration, the President underwent a fundamental change. He had become convinced that deficits would stimulate the economy, that with large amounts of unemployment they would not bring on inflation, and that there were some objectives much more important than the balanced budget. Having accepted and even pushed for a $10 billion tax cut which might, on top of a pretax cut $7 billion deficit, have raised the deficit to $12 billion, the President had moved way beyond his predecessors and had taken big political risks. One might have thought this would silence the critics. But it did not.

I agree with the economists who say that the $11 billion tax cut is not enough to bring unemployment down to 4 per cent within the next few years and, hence, is not enough to achieve the goals of the Democratic platform. But I do not agree that the President should have asked for a $15 billion tax cut. If he had, he would probably not have received the $11 billion, and he would have lost prestige with the Congress and the country.

Another point on which the critics were wrong was their contention that the administration's monetary policy was weak. Writing in the *Progressive,* in 1961, Keyserling said: "In monetary policy, the changes thus far do not sufficiently liberalize credit nor sufficiently reduce interest rates; the citadel of excessive Federal Reserve Board power has not been challenged by the Administration."

Gass, in an exchange with me in *Commentary,* in 1962, quoted approvingly a Congressional report which said: "Monetary policy was—and continues to be—largely immobilized in a posture more suited to restraining overemployment than to stimulating recovery."

I do not agree with these statements. The administration in a period of less than three years, during which GNP rose by the large estimated sum of about $100 billion, or about 5.5 per cent a year (in stable dollars), kept the interest rates that count at home relatively stable. The net change was minimal, and during a large part of this period below the rates at the beginning of the recovery. This was a remarkable performance, especially considering the past anti-inflationary bias of the Federal Reserve Board, and also the need of high short-term rates when the balance of payments is weak. The Kennedy administration was against dear money, and in light of the above considerations as well as the substantial rise of federal debt which tends to raise rates, it is striking that long-term rates declined slightly—compare the more than 50 per cent rise under Eisenhower. Keyserling and Gass would do well to compare the steady rise of interest rates in the three previous recoveries from 1949 to 1960, and the stability in 1961–1963. I refer them to the Department of Commerce, *Business Cycle Developments*.

On the subject of anemic recoveries, it is worthwhile to stress that after recoveries lasting 45, 35, and 25 months, the current recovery has now continued for 40 months. The trend has been broken.

The President's critics concentrated on unemployment statistics as the guide to the degree of success in solving our problem. Unemployment is indeed a serious matter. Yet there were other areas of success: the growth of the economy; related, the rise of productivity; the stability of prices; the increase in welfare payments. On all these criteria, the government performed well. Even the unemployment statistics are not so depressing as they at first seem. Sam Lubell, after interviews in twenty-three cities (*Boston Globe,* July 14, 1963) found that among married persons who were unemployed, roughly 40 per cent had husband or wife working; of the unemployed, he found that 60 per cent were not concerned, for they were moving from one job to another. (This seems like a high percentage for transitional unemployment.) Nearly 10 per cent admitted they could get jobs at lower pay than they were prepared to accept.

Admittedly, the economics of national policy called for more vigorous action. In that sense the critics were right, and in trying to convince Americans of the "economic" issues, they were serving their country. But insofar as they expected policy to be based on economics alone, they were inflating the contribution and importance of purely economic considerations.

The liberal critics failed to weigh noneconomic issues adequately, and forgot that the President had to weigh all aspects of a problem. I believe that they were also wrong when they stressed the failure of the President to "use" Congress. Conflicts between the President and the Congress, each jealous of their prerogatives, have persisted for many administrations. In 1963, the critics gave the President little credit for the revolutionary change in his economic thinking and in his proposals. By concentrating on unemployment and neglecting or underestimating the gains in growth, in stability, in the balance of payments, and in welfare programs, the liberal critics did the President an injustice.

CONSERVATIVE CRITICS

President Kennedy's conservative critics charged excessive spending, excessive deficits, inflationary policies, and unwarranted intervention by the federal government. These have been the main points of attack against the Democrats since 1933, if not since 1914. When there was a conflict, for example, Kennedy's tussle with the steel industry for violating an agreement, with the result of greater threats to inflation, the critics disregarded the anti-inflationary aspects of the President's approach and concentrated on his desire to control the economy.

The conservative attacks probably stem more from noneconomic than economic origins. The conservatives particularly want the free market to operate without interference by government. Naturally, their economic analysis is not unimportant, nor is it always correct. It is, for example, economically unsound to argue, as Eisenhower, Hoover, Goldwater, and others have, that the time to reduce taxes is in the highly prosperous periods, when the budget is in balance, or in surplus, and that they should not be reduced when the economy is depressed and the budget in deficit.

Let us begin with President Eisenhower who, early in 1963, wrote an important article for the *Saturday Evening Post,* called "Spending Into Trouble." The ex-President was especially critical of excessive intervention by government and of the vast expenditures and deficits. In discussing the $99 billion 1964 budget, Eisenhower described it as bigger than the wartime budget. But the President did not say that as a percentage of GNP the federal budget in fiscal 1945 was 47 per cent; in 1964, only about 15 per cent.

I say that the time-tested rules of financial policy still apply. Spending for spending's sake is patently a false theory. No family, no business, no nation can spend itself into prosperity. . . . They and their children will pay and pay and pay. In effect, we are stealing from our grandchildren in order to satisfy our desires of today.

In taking this position, Eisenhower showed that his economics is still primitive. For he failed to take into account the large contribution made by the growth of debt and therefore of demand. Inadequacy of demand is a crucial cause of depressions and sluggish economy, and underwriting of demand helps keep the economy flourishing. Spending is no guarantee of prosperity; but it is a necessary condition.

The nonsense about the grandchildren paying the bill is discussed and dismissed in every freshman economics course in the country. I heard this as an undergraduate at Harvard in 1919. Indeed a larger debt bequeathed to our grandchildren in the year 2000 may mean more taxes, which is a burden; but the transfers are made to other (or the same) grandchildren living at that time. The crucial point is that any beneficiaries of government spending receive income and resources not at the expense of our grandchildren but at the expense of those living today. Surely the President never picked up this kind of economics from Arthur Burns or Gabriel Hauge. It sounds more like Senator Goldwater.

. . . But all of us would feel more comfortable and secure if our national leadership exercised the foresight and self-discipline to balance its budget and to begin paying back something on the national debt. . . . Imagine how much better the country would feel if it had no debt at all but a healthy surplus!

Apparently there are still important citizens who believe repayment of the debt is a crucial need. There are times when repayment may be appropriate: in periods of boom as a means of destroying money and reducing demand. But on the whole the occasion for repayment does not come often; and there have been periods—such as 1866–1893, when repayment through the destruction of currency damaged the economy. However, repayment in the 1920s was helpful.

Eisenhower also discussed inflation—he compared Truman's 47 per cent rise of prices in seven years and his of 10 per cent in eight years. But he did not mention the contribution of war and the aftermath of war to Truman's inflation nor the Republican contribution to inflation in their espousal of tax cuts in the midst of inflationary pressures in the late 1940s. Yet in the political milieu one cannot blame President Eisenhower for boasting of what appeared a much better price history.

Even Arthur Burns, one of our most able economists, who was generally on the side of the angels during the Eisenhower period, was critical of Kennedy's spending policies, as were Henry Wallich and Raymond Saulnier, other members of Eisenhower's Council of Economic Advisers. Burns, generally a very cautious economist, predicted in 1961 that the country would reach 4 per cent unemployment in the midst of 1962—and without government intervention.

Saulnier seemed to adhere to a brand of economics rather like Eisenhower's. In a speech at Miami University in Ohio, he argued that the recession in 1957–1958 had little to do with a cut of federal expenditures in 1957. This may or may not be so. But what Saulnier failed to note was that with the rise of GNP of $45 billion in 1956 and 1957, federal expenditures rose only by $5 billion and budget receipts by $9 billion. The receipts rose too much and expenditures too little. From the third quarter of 1958 to the first quarter of 1960, receipts rose by $20 billion and expenditures by $0.7 billion, with disastrous results.

It is therefore not surprising that Saulnier wrote: ". . . As a practical matter, you can't cut taxes and raise expenditures simultaneously without at some point getting into a frightful fiscal mess and I expect this fact of life to be recognized before too long."

Saulnier's last point was virtually Republican doctrine in 1963. A tax cut would be acceptable; but it should be accompanied by no rise of expenditures and by an equivalent reduction in expenditures for many. He does not recognize that what would be gained by the tax cut in stimulating demand would be lost by reduction of spending.

There was a report, on August 14, 1961, on *Comments on the Final Staff Report on Employment in the Dynamic American Economy* by the Committee of 48 Republican Congressmen chaired by Congressman Thomas B. Curtis. In this over forty-thousand-word report, an articulate group of Republican Congressmen (some more liberal than conservative), expressed their views of the Kennedy administration directly or by implication:

A planned economy only hides unemployment. . . . Individual drive and incentive supported by sound governmental policies, are the only sensible answers to the changing job situation.

[Government's contribution is mainly not through expenditures but to promote conditions] favorable to the exercise of individual enterprise and private effort.

[The federal government is] an auxiliary handmaiden rather than a partner in working together with business, labor and state and local government.

Though the committee stressed the need of solving the unemployment problem, structural unemployment received the almost exclusive attention of the Curtis Committee. Though a comment was made that fiscal policy was accepted by "the leading figures of both political parties," it received virtually no attention in the report.

Little comment is needed on some of the absurdities in the accompanying documents. One quote will suffice: ". . . the economic goal of our economy is exactly that dictated by Communist theory —to make every individual a consumer irrespective of what he contributes to production."

Perhaps the most persistent critic of the Kennedy administration was the editor of the *Wall Street Journal*. In reply to my comment on Eisenhower vs. Kennedy, the editor wrote, in the September 25, 1961, *Journal:* ". . . judged by the criteria of prosperity, mildness of intermittent recessions, and avoidance of inflationary excesses, the Eisenhower period compares very favorably with any predecessors. . . ."

The *Journal* complains again and again of excessive public spending. In the September 11, 1961, issue: ". . . and there is only one place where it [inflation] can be created, namely in the Government itself. . . ." Furthermore, ". . . in just a few short months it [the government] has added tremendously to Federal spending. . . . It has converted previously anticipated budget surpluses into heavy deficits, and no man can see the end."

On the steel episode, the *Journal* blamed inflationary policies.

If the government had not created so much money, then neither a wage nor a price rise could be inflationary. The *Journal* asked for a fiscal and monetary policy that would be sufficiently restrictive to exclude any inflation. Hence with rising wages, and rising prices induced by higher wages, the result of such restriction could be inadequacy of monetary supplies and increased unemployment. This was exactly what happened under President Eisenhower in 1955–1958, when the attempt was made to deal with a cost inflation through classical restrictions on the monetary supply: The inflation was nevertheless a record one for peacetime, and yet the rise of unemployment was disturbing.

Perhaps the best indication of the views of the conservative critics appeared in the minority reports of the Joint Economic Committee on the January *Economic Report of the President* for the years 1961, 1962, and 1963, including two papers by Arthur Burns, and an exchange between Burns and the Council of Economic Advisers. Burns' first paper was an address in Chicago, on April 21, 1961 (a summary and the exchange with the council appear in the *Morgan Guaranty Survey* of August 1961). The second paper appeared in the same publication, July 1963. It was written for the Semicentennial Lecture Series of Rice University, and was also published by the University of Chicago Press as *The Nation's Economic Objectives: Roots and Problems of Achievement*. The minority reports were more sophisticated than they had been under Eisenhower, undoubtedly due to Congressman Curtis's mobilization of economic brains and especially the help given by Arthur Burns.

Briefly, here are the criticisms and proposals of the Republicans as revealed by the six documents mentioned above.

A major charge is excessive federal spending plus especially badly timed expenditures, which could do little good and would induce inflation. The 1963 minority report would put a $95 billion ceiling on expenditures. Burns said in 1963 that the major problem facing the country was the increase in the public debt. What particularly vexed Burns was that the Kennedy administration was committing the same errors as Eisenhower had in 1957–1958— a series of badly planned expenditures, wrongly timed and massive in amount.

A second criticism was that the Democrats depend excessively on government. The Republican Minority Committee in 1963 quoted a study by George Terborgh which showed that there was not a high correlation between government deficits and gains of GNP.

Terborgh's analysis shows that there is no general pattern to support the theory that deficits are stimulative and surpluses repressive. In fact, in the post-war period, of 51 quarters with a rising Gross National Product, Terborgh found that 28 were associated with a Federal surplus and 23 with a deficit. . . .

Recovery, in the view of the Republican minority, was the result of natural forces and the contributions of the free market. But no attempt was made to explain the long recovery of 1961–1963, with promise of many more months of rises, or of government's contribution to this recovery.

Perhaps the strongest attacks were related to the "growthmanship" of the Kennedy administration. Both the emphasis on growth and the weapons used to reach the targets received much comment. To the Republican minority, GNP was a most inadequate measure, for it did not account for such factors as improved quality or more leisure. Moreover, the idea of a sluggish economy, or a gap, did not appeal to the minority.

In the first exchange between the President's council and Burns, the issue was largely the size of the gap in current output relative to potential output. The difference stemmed largely from disagreement on the base from which trend lines were taken. Burns' estimate of the gap was less than Heller's.

The minority of the Joint Economic Committee expressed the view that the council was overoptimistic about the gap. Excess capacity may be largely obsolescent plant; hence, the excess capacity, in the minority's view, and the gap between actual and potential output may be smaller than it seems. This position has some merit.

Some questions may also be raised concerning the council's forecast of output. It is based on the theory of substantial rises of numbers on the labor market and continued increases of productivity. When employment prospects were not favorable, the numbers seeking work tended to fall below estimates; and after two years of recovery, rises in productivity may taper off. Hence output may not rise as much as anticipated. Burns stressed such possibilities, and also a likely inflation, which might interfere with growth. Actual developments in the first three years surprised many people. Output rose much more than expected by the government; prices were much more stable than anticipated by Burns; and unemployment, in view of the rise of output, remained generally much higher than had been expected.

Although Burns was concerned over the unemployment problem, he sometimes made little of it. He did not like the 4 per cent goal. Moreover, he asked, why should not the emphasis be on the 95 or 97 per cent employed rather than the 5 or 3 per cent unemployed.

Perhaps the greatest split between the administration and the Republican minority was on how to treat unemployment. The council stressed the deficiency of general demand; hence the need of fiscal and monetary policy to raise demand and reduce unemployment. The minority and Burns both emphasized the structural aspects of unemployment, and hence urged measures to improve the functioning of the labor market, to retrain workers, and similar measures. At times, it seemed that the minority was completely unaware of deficiency of demand. Burns sought adequate statistics on unfilled vacancies, and he would compare unfilled vacancies and unemployment, with the lower of the two indicating structural unemployment. He especially insisted that much unemployment was inevitable irrespective of deficiencies of demand. I am not unsympathetic with this approach. But I do not agree with the Burns-minority position, which greatly overdoes the significance of structural unemployment. In one report, the minority says that "full employment is reached at higher levels of unemployment." When unemployment is 6 per cent, unfilled vacancies will be substantial but certainly not a major factor. The crucial disease is insufficient demand. As I noted (Chapter 12), the large reduction of employment in declining industries in recession years as against prosperous years enforces this conclusion.

Concerned over the balance of payments, the minority in 1961 urged putting a large part of the burden of defense and aid on other countries. But in 1963 the approach was entirely different. Large expenditures, substantial deficits, and easy money were held both by the minority and Burns to have serious effects upon the unfavorable balance of payments. Irresponsible finance, in their view, reduced the confidence in the dollar. All those who were critical of measures to stimulate demand through fiscal or monetary policy tended to overemphasize the effect of fiscal and monetary policy upon the balance of payments. However, the weakness of the dollar was bound to weaken pressures for expansionist measures.

On monetary policy, the minority reports consistently criticized the "nudging" or "twisting" of the Federal Reserve to create more money. Whereas the Kennedy administration feared the effects of inadequate liquidity, and the majority of the Joint Economic Committee criticized the Executive for being too cautious in creating money, the minority group and Burns often lashed out at the Executive for providing easy money, with concomitant dangers of inflation and weakening of the dollar abroad. In their view, the tax cut and the large deficit were also likely to yield further inflation if the securities were sold to the banks and the Federal Reserve provided additional reserves; and to bring higher interest rates to private borrowers if sold to savers. In general, the Executive was concerned that savings might be excessive; the minority thought they would be inadequate. The minority felt that keeping rates of interest down through cheap money would discourage savings.

Obviously, the conservative charge has been the reverse of the liberal: too much government, excessive concern with growth objectives, too much spending and excessive deficits, too much help to consumers, too little to savers, and too much money and excessively low rates of interest. Failure to bring full employment was another source of criticism. The Eisenhower record on government spending, though not nearly as restrictive as had been promised, was in fact mildly expansionist, and was better than the Truman record on extent of inflation. But this view ignores the relevance of war and war's aftermath under Truman, and also assumes that less federal spending is always an advantage. In relation to Kennedy, Eisenhower's inflation record was less impressive; and if the criterion of sound policy is less spending and smaller deficits, Eisenhower clearly had the edge on Kennedy. But whether Eisenhower's advantage is good for the economy is another matter.

PART V

The American Economy in the 1960s

19

1964 and the 1960s

THE KENNEDY-JOHNSON YEAR, 1964

In some respects one might expect from Lyndon Johnson's administration a legislative program that would diverge from the Kennedy program. The business groups support President Johnson much more strongly than they did President Kennedy. Many people believe that after Johnson's early, close affiliation with New Deal objectives, he moved greatly to the right. However, in an interesting article in the *Progressive* of January, 1964, Karl E. Meyer wrote that in the late 1950s [Johnson's] "position on labor, welfare, conservation, and agriculture was one that a progressive Senator like Hubert Humphrey, Minnesota Democrat, could endorse without blushing. . . ."

In its December 13, 1963, issue, the *Congressional Quarterly* examined Johnson's voting record for 1957–1960 on twenty-four key votes. The *Quarterly* concluded that the votes indicated a middle-of-the-road position for Senator Johnson. Three of the Senate's leading liberal Democrats—Paul Douglas, Hubert Humphrey, and Joseph Clark—took Johnson's position fourteen times and the opposing position ten times. Of twenty-four votes Johnson took the liberal position fourteen times, the conservative one ten times. But of the latter, seven votes were on civil rights or liberties.

In economics, Johnson in the late 1950s usually agreed with the liberals: He favored generous borrowing authority for the Development Loan Fund in 1957 and 1959; a liberal program for temporary unemployment compensation in 1958; and authority to the President to extend aid to Communist-dominated countries. He supported a less protectionist position vis-à-vis the use of the escape clause in relation to the trade negotiations; opposed some toughening amendments to the Taft-Hartley Act in the Labor-Management Reporting and Disclosure Act of 1959; and in 1960 favored an amendment to allow federal grants to be used for teaching subsidies.

Thus, Johnson's record from 1957–1960 was mainly a liberal one. He opposed, of course, a reduction of oil depletion allowances, just as President Kennedy, as a senator, supported policies such as serious restraints on imports of textiles which he found difficult to sponsor as President. I do not believe that support of oil depletion was as worthwhile as Senator Kennedy's attempts to reduce the very serious losses of jobs in Massachusetts textiles through various approaches. But it would be difficult for any Texan senator to oppose the oil depletion allowance.

In the degree of emphasis, President Johnson may have diverged from the policies of the Kennedy administration in a few instances, and notably in the modified spending pattern in the 1965 budget and the greater stress on economy.

THE 1965 BUDGET

The cut in the 1965 budget (year ending June 30, 1965) is relevant here. In presenting a budget of $97.8 billion, the President seems to have moved more vigorously than President Kennedy. It has even been claimed that the reduction vis-à-vis the probable Kennedy budget was $4 to $5 billion. Undoubtedly the President felt that economy in government was a policy which would greatly appeal to the voter.

In fact, however, the Johnson budget of $97.8 billion is only $2 billion below the likely Kennedy budget. Yet this is a great achievement if spending cuts are the objective, and especially when consideration is given to Johnson's estimated 3.5 billion built-in increases, such as rises in pay, spending related to new programs, and the like.

Only time will tell whether Johnson's budget is in the pink rather than in the red. The gains occur partly through sales of capital assets, a procedure often used to improve the looks of the budget. A substantial saving on the farm program will occur only if appropriate farm policies and prices emerge. Some additional burden was transferred to the 1964 budget through additions to expenditures or loss of revenue. Yet to cut the 1965 budget by $500 million despite $3.5 billion of built-in increases is an accomplishment.

Even when allowance is made for all these factors, it is clear that the President did wield the axe. Anyone who discussed the problem with high officials or budget officers in departments had to admit that the pressure was on.

Are such large cuts, even if they are not quite as large as they seem, judicious? The tax cut was meant to increase spending and therefore employment in an economy that was underspending. Obviously any reduction in federal spending tends to offset the stimulative effects of the tax cut. President Kennedy was able to get his tax program through the House merely by telling the country that he would scrutinize expenditures. Johnson's further cuts certainly helped to hasten the passage of the tax cut; but the reduction may have been larger than was required.

The large reduction of expenditures raised some issues concerning the health of the economy. An excessive cut reduces the contribution of the tax remission. By a fortunate last-minute change in the proposed tax program, however, the administration protected the 1964 (calendar year) economy. The step was to reduce taxes by an additional $2.5 billion in 1964, a remission at the expense of 1965. We can therefore assume that 1964 borrowed ammunition from 1965, and insofar as 1964 was strengthened, 1965 will be more anemic.

President Johnson's savings were spectacular in the area of defense. It was possible to cut only because Kennedy had bolstered the nation's defense in 1961–1963. Secretary McNamara, in a television appearance soon after the Kennedy assassination, said that President Kennedy often repeated that our defense needs were to take precedence over finance. President Kennedy had learned from the Eisenhower years that priority of finance over defense could be costly.

President Johnson announced in his budget message that he could reduce defense outlays by $1.5 billion because military expenditures had risen by $7 billion since 1961. The country could boast over a period of three years a 100 per cent increase in the number of nuclear weapons available in the strategic alert force; a 450 per cent increase in the number of Polaris submarines; a 60 per cent increase in the tactical nuclear forces deployed in Western Europe; a 45 per cent increase in the number of combat-ready Army divisions; a 35 per cent increase in the number of tactical fighter squadrons, etc., etc.

President Johnson's budget was designed to save as much as possible, especially on military and related programs, and to use the savings for welfare programs.

The 1965 budget calls for large savings in defense but also in many other programs. Significant rises in obligational authority (the ultimate source of expenditures) include $1.5 billion for the Department of Health, Education, and Welfare, related largely to new health and educational proposals; $360 million to finance manpower and youth employment legislation; and $500 million of special appropriations for new community programs to attack poverty. In all, $1 billion of new obligational authority became available for dealing with poverty.

. . . An austere budget need not and should not be a standstill budget. . . . But when vigorous pruning of old programs and procedures releases the funds needed to meet new challenges and opportunities, economy becomes the companion of progress.

. . . It [the budget] cuts the deficit in half, and carries us a giant step toward the achievement of a balanced budget in a full employment, full prosperity economy.

The urgent and necessary program increases recommended in this budget will be financed out of the savings made possible by strict economy measures and by exhaustive screening of existing programs. . . .

How successful the Johnson budget will be depends partly upon the extent to which savings in some areas are offset by spending elsewhere. It does not follow that a deficit reduced by one-half will

yield a balanced budget and full employment in the near future—
as was implied in the budget message.

One of the great advances in the Kennedy administration was
the emphasis on the stifling effects of large federal surpluses at a
full employment level. As the economy approaches full employment, federal revenues tend to rise, and to that extent the private
spending of the economy suffers. The corrective has to be either
a rise of public spending (and) or another tax cut. In fact the
1963–1964 tax cut campaign stems largely from the theory that
rising revenues, unless corrected as the economy moves up, bring
an automatic block to continued recovery. The trouble from the
latter part of 1958 to early 1960 was mainly a stabilization of
federal outlays even as revenues rose by $20 billion.

However, the Johnson budget has not ignored the problem of
large and stifling surpluses in a full employment economy. Thus,
it has been estimated that at a (say) GNP high enough to yield
full employment the surplus in federal revenues would be about
$10 billion. The correction, that is, the elimination of this surplus,
would have to come from a rise of expenditures, plus the tax cut.
Expenditures are to decline modestly in fiscal year 1965, and hence
the tax cut will be the corrective for the surplus. There are those
who hold that since tax relief will precede the reduction of expenditures for fiscal year 1965, the Johnson program may in fact
be inflationary.

Another important factor is the extent to which increasing
expenditures (and) or tax reductions are exploited to prevent
economic declines following recoveries. The case for the tax cut
was that this was the only large stimulative program that could
receive Congressional approval. Many, including myself, would
have preferred a mix of larger rises in spending and smaller tax
cuts if the combination were practical. In other words, I support
strongly the position that Kenneth Galbraith presented so clearly
and effectively in *The Affluent Society*. I wish that Galbraith and
twenty other writers with equally potent pens would continue to
press his position until it becomes a program acceptable to the
American people. That President Johnson pushed the tax cut vs.
the spending formula even more toward tax cuts than President
Kennedy had and that the public services are becoming more and

more starved suggest the need of reconsidering the present combination of tax cuts vs. more spending as routes to increased incomes and more jobs.

I do not mean that the arguments for more public spending are merely ideological. They often can raise total income; and dollar for dollar, it is true that they yield more than tax cuts. But it is difficult to put through the spending programs that should have the highest priority.

A prominent feature of the Johnson program has been the attack on poverty. The Council of Economic Advisers, under the direction of Walter Heller and with the help of Robert Lampman, had been studying poverty problems for some time under Kennedy. President Kennedy was, according to Arthur Schlesinger, Jr., ready to launch such a program. Nevertheless, it was to President Johnson's credit that he enthusiastically accepted the Kennedy-Heller program and incorporated it in his budgetary planning.

It is the kind of a program which has much appeal to many voters; but it is also a program that elicits charges for its creator of being visionary, a dreamer, impractical, and wasteful. That the President produced large economies and yet urged the large advances in numerous welfare programs elicited charges of the "fast deal" from his political adversaries. One cannot as yet judge the merits of these charges. The issues will be resolved when it becomes clear how much additional money will be put in the new spending programs, and how large the budgetary savings prove to be in the next few years. At any rate, in reducing defense outlays and spending relatively more on welfare, the President introduced a pattern of spending which has much appeal.

THE ECONOMY IN 1964 AND 1965

Recovery should continue throughout 1964, which means a recovery of nearly four years, a span much greater than expected by economists early in 1961. This advance is amazing for peacetime, especially with the rise springing from an economy only moderately down early in 1961, and with the small increase of prices accompanying the advance. But 1964 is likely to witness more inflationary pressures than the years 1961–1963.

A big question mark is 1965. Even with government intervention, especially to offset the borrowing of demand of 1964 from 1965, it will require the most skillful management to avert either a recession or continued recovery which is accompanied by an excessive rise of prices.

INFLATION?

Under President Kennedy, the price record was surprisingly good. The new President operates under more difficult conditions than his predecessor. Inflationary pressures are increasing. As excess capacity is reduced and bottlenecks emerge, and as labor, never friendly to the guideposts for wages, intensifies its opposition, the pressure for higher wages gains strength. With rising profits the workers may be able to improve their relative position at the expense of profits, and to that extent the price level will be protected. But there are signs of strong pressures for higher wages, which would yield increases much beyond that allowed under the 1964 guideposts, or likely to be absorbed out of profits, with a resultant upward pressure on prices. The truckers demanded increases of 8 per cent a year but received somewhat less. The transport workers of New York City seem to have obtained a settlement early in 1964 equal to about 6 per cent and the United Automobile Workers make large demands not consistent with a 2 to 3 per cent rise tied to productivity gains.

In its 1964 *Economic Report,* the Council of Economic Advisers presents its guidelines clearly and in an improved form. Given the attitude of the American people, the council seems to go about as far as is judicious in this approach to moral suasion. Again the council relates wage increases to the *general* rise of man-hour output; and price movements to the productivity gains. Where the latter are above average, there is a case for price reduction; and if below, for price rises. The exceptions to the general rule, such as raising wage rates that are low in relation to wages for similar work, again receive approval.

But the guideposts do not have enough teeth to prevent inflationary wage increases; and it would be unfortunate if the President's prestige were committed too often to such episodes as the 1962 steel wage case.

We can then expect some inflationary pressures from the wage side. The monetary authority can preclude corresponding price rises by restricting monetary supplies and thus inducing unemployment—that is, monetary supplies would not be adequate to finance current levels of employment at higher wages.

MONETARY POLICY AND THE FEDERAL RESERVE BOARD

This brings us to the major issue of monetary policy. The Federal Reserve authorities tend to be restrictive, because they are especially concerned with price stability, and, therefore, tend to weigh more heavily than the government should, the *penalty* of rising prices against the *gains* of higher output. This generalization applied to the 1950s but not to the first two and a half years of the Kennedy regime, when the President paid lip service to the independence of the Federal Reserve but insisted on adequate supplies of money.

In the second half of 1963 there were signs of monetary restraint and rising interest rates. Late in 1963 Chairman William Martin told the Senate Finance Committee that with increased demands for credit, interest rates would rise. Recently the chairman, on a number of instances, complained of deterioration in the quality of assets held by the banks.

In an address of December 9, 1963,* the Federal Reserve Board chairman said:

At a meeting twelve months ago—on December 18, 1962, to be exact—the Committee came to the conclusion that it would be dangerously inappropriate to continue further the extensive degree of credit ease that had been long prevalent—since at least the beginning of the 1960's. Accordingly, it redirected its policy toward lessening that degree of ease and toward "accommodating moderate further increases in bank credit and money supply, while aiming at money market conditions that would minimize capital outflows internationally."

During 1963 the Federal Reserve has gradually lessened the monetary ease that had been prevalent for several years. The only dramatic step was that taken in July, when the discount rate of the Federal Reserve Banks was raised from 3 per cent to 3½ per cent and the

---

* Reprinted in the Federal Reserve Bank of New York, *Monthly Report,* January 1964.

maximum rates payable on time deposits with a maturity of three to twelve months were raised to 4 per cent. But over the preceding months, the banking system had been permitted gradually to absorb its margin of uninvested reserve funds.

In short, there has been a real threat of monetary restraints and higher interest rates in 1964. Serious restrictions on monetary supplies and substantial increases in interest rates have been a genuine menace to continued recovery and improvement in 1964. Should inflationary pressures be strong, the Federal Reserve would be justified in raising rates. But with an expected rise of GNP of about 6 per cent in 1964, it would be difficult to justify serious monetary restrictions even if prices were to rise as much as 2 per cent a year. In view of the increased choices of goods and services available to consumers and the improvements in quality not measured in the price index, the genuine rise of prices may be substantially less than the price rise given by the Bureau of Labor Statistics index numbers.

President Johnson comes from a state where populist traditions, including demands for adequate supplies of money and low interest rates, are traditional. The President is an advocate of money-cum low rate of interest. Moreover, it is not likely that President Johnson will allow views about independence of the Federal Reserve Board to stop him from demanding adequate supplies of money in an election year. His advisers will surely remind him of what happened in 1956 and 1958–1960, and of the disastrous results of high money rates to Vice President Nixon in 1960. Nixon is supposed to have pressured the FRB to provide more cash; but interest rates declined little in 1960 compared to the rise in 1958–1960, and unemployment rose by 1.2 millions in eight months of 1960. Confronted with this kind of a threat, President Johnson may put greater pressure on the Federal Reserve.

TRENDS IN THE 1950S

Before examining prospects for the later 1960s, it is useful to summarize the trends in the 1950s.

The 1950s showed a moderate rate of growth and inflation; a rise of wages beyond that in productivity, thus contributing to a

wage-cost inflation; a relatively restrictive monetary policy, introduced to cope with the wage cost inflation and, therefore, costly in
its impact on output and employment; and an end of the dollar
shortage and the emergence of dollar saturation, that is, an excess
of dollars and a shortage of foreign currencies.

RISE IN GROSS NATIONAL PRODUCT AND RELATED VARIABLES, 1950–1963

| | 1950 to 1960 | | 1960 to 1963 | |
	Total Rise	Average per Year	Total Rise	Average per Year
Gross national product				
Billions of current dollars	219.0	21.9	82.5	27.5
Billions of 1962 dollars	146.0	14.6	63.8[e]	21.3[e]
Percentage rise, 1962 dollars	39.0	3.75[b]	16.4[e]	5.5[e]
Money (demand deposits and money in circulation)[a]				
Billions of dollars	25.0	2.5	12.3[e]	4.1[e]
Percentage rise	22.0	2.0[b]	8.7	2.9
Time deposits[a]				
Billions of dollars	36.0	3.6	42.5	14.2
Percentage rise	98.0	7.0[b]	58.6	19.5
Interest rate, Aaa corporate bonds (per cent)	68.0	6.0[b]	−.06	−.02
Federal government expenditures				
Billions of dollars	42.3	4.2	23.0	7.7
Percentage rise	127.0	12.7	24.7	8.2
Federal cash payments (billions of dollars)	79.0	7.9	22.5	7.5
State and local expenditures				
Billions of dollars	27.6	2.8	14.35	4.86
Percentage rise	122.0	12.2	26.4	8.8
Federal debt (billions of dollars)	22.3	2.2	19.1	6.4
Gross hourly wages, manufacturing (per cent rise)	57.0	4.6[b]	7.5	2.5
Prices (index numbers)				
Wholesale (per cent rise)	16.0	1.5[b]	−0.4	−0.1
Consumer (per cent rise)	21.0	1.8[b]	3.5	1.2
Balance of payments deficit (billions of dollars)	17.8	1.8	7.2	2.4

SOURCE: Mainly *Economic Reports of the President* and *Economic Indicators.*

[a] December 1949–December 1959 and December 1950–December 1960,
rather than 1950–1960 and 1960–1963.

[b] Compounded.

[e] 1963 prices.

Despite the Eisenhower administration's strong views on economy in government, the Korean War, plus demands for spending at home and abroad brought substantial increases in spending. The national debt continued to rise despite large reductions in military spending in 1954–1955, with pressures to cut outlays in other areas. State and local government experienced large rises in spending.

In welfare, the policy was not so much retrenchment as a pause in expansion. One of the disconcerting developments, especially in the later years, was a tendency for cyclical peaks to show rising amounts of unemployment and excess capacity.

The table above reveals the trends from 1950 to 1960 and 1961 to 1963.

This table suggests several conclusions. First, the rise of GNP in the 1950s was healthy, though rather disappointing in the later years. For an increase of GNP of these proportions the price inflation was not serious. However, in the years 1955–1958, the rise of prices was excessive. GNP in stable dollars rose 1.85 times as much as consumer prices. Undoubtedly an average increase of wage rates of 5 per cent contributed to this inflation. Moreover, the rise of prices prevailed despite the fact that the increase in money was much less than in GNP, a fact suggesting that the inflation was not the familiar kind, with general demand exceeding supply. Concentration on demand deposits and money in circulation points to restrictive monetary supplies. But another way of looking at the problem, and one especially popular in the Federal Reserve, is to consider the large expansion of time deposits, highly liquid assets, as part of the supply of money, thus increasing the supply of money in the 1960s from 25 per cent, as revealed in the table, to 36 per cent.

Another guide of the extent of restrictive monetary policy is the movement in interest rates. On this criterion the policy was clearly restrictive, for long-term private interest rates, as revealed by corporate Aaa bonds, rose by 68 per cent—an increase of yield from 2.62 to 4.41. This very sharp increase in rates was related to a strongly held view in the Eisenhower administration that the yield on securities should be determined by free market forces, not by the creation of money to support the market for bonds.

The 1951 Treasury Accord (see Chapter 12) strengthened the position of those who would not allow the needs of the Treasury to determine the amount of money to be created. An increasing awareness of continued inflationary pressures also contributed to this rise of interest rates. Lenders seek some compensation for the decline in real value of their loans in a period of probable inflation.

Unemployment was at a high level in 1950, but the Korean War reduced unemployment from 5.3 per cent in 1950 to 2.9 per cent in 1953; however, the average in the next seven years was 5.2 per cent. It is useful to recognize that part of the improvements in the 1950s were associated with the Korean War. The average rise of GNP, for example, was two-thirds as much in the years 1954–1960 as in 1950–1953.

DEVELOPMENTS, 1961–1963

Therapy was not a simple problem for the Kennedy administration. The unsatisfactory conditions were not merely associated with a cyclical decline. From 1960 on there was much talk of a sluggish or tired economy. Observers were struck by the high level of unemployment—an average of 6 per cent from 1958 to 1962 as compared with 1 per cent in 1944, a 4 per cent average in the years 1947–1952, and 1 to 3 per cent in most of Western Europe in recent years; by the failure to use effectively our labor and plant—with annual losses as much as $20–$40 billion associated with underutilization; by a growing realization that as recoveries proceeded, the added take of the tax collector tended to abort the recovery; by the rising concern over sustained unemployment in surplus labor areas (as in the New England textile towns and in the coal mines of Pennsylvania and West Virginia); and by the heavy concentration of unemployment among the young, the unskilled, and minority groups. Hence the administration had to worry over cyclical unemployment, but also (related) the inventory cycle (that is, the decline of inventory accumulation from the first to the third quarter of 1962 greatly weakened the forces of recovery), and of course, over the sluggishness of the economy.

When the Kennedy administration took over in January, 1961, the last three economic recoveries had lasted for 45, 35, and 25 months, respectively. The durability of the first recovery was clearly related to the effects of the Korean War; and the brevity of the last recovery, to a wrong-headed fiscal policy and an unprecedented rise in the rate of interest. I heard some dismal predictions in Washington that the 1961–1962 recovery might continue for only fifteen months. The trend from 1949 on suggested to the government the need of special measures if the recovery was not to be aborted early. In the Treasury, in 1961, there was much discussion of what had to be done to keep the recovery going into 1963 and possibly 1964.

Recovery has continued for three and a half years. The fact that the government is ready to act to accelerate growth and weaken recessionary forces distinguished this recovery from earlier recoveries. The recovery was not at an even pace. In 1961, after the first quarter the rise was satisfactory; but in 1962 was disappointing, and especially in the third quarter, when the increase of GNP was far below the level required to stabilize the unemployment rate.

From the first quarter of 1961 to the last quarter of 1963 GNP had risen by almost an estimated $100 billion in current dollars, and by $81 billion in 1963 prices, a most satisfactory advance. An estimated increase of 15.7 per cent over this period of two and three-quarter years is equal to 32 per cent of the projected rise of 50 per cent, for the 1960s. The rise averages 5.7 per cent a year or 5.5 per cent compounded, a rate higher than that needed to provide a 50 per cent gain in ten years. This rise is satisfactory, even if allowance is made for the fact that a recovery tends to be larger when related to a recession low.

What was especially unfortunate in the almost three years of the Kennedy administration was the high level of unemployment and the slow progress in treating the balance of payments deficit. To some extent these were related problems. The deficit in the balance of payments made it difficult to use the full potential of monetary and fiscal policy as expansionary weapons.

Substantial gains in 1961–1963 resulted from an activist government. In contrast to the policies of the 1950s, the Kennedy administration sought and received cooperation of the monetary authority to support a recovery. The best evidence of this was a decline in the long-term rate of interest over a recovery period of thirty to thirty-six months. This record was all the more remarkable since the government and the monetary authority found it necessary to keep short-term rates up in order to discourage exports of short-term capital in response to higher rates abroad. By issuing required quantities of short-term securities, the Treasury contributed to higher short-term rates, whenever necessary. By increasing discount rates and reducing the volume of free reserves of the banking system, and by raising the rates that could be paid on time and savings deposits, the Federal Reserve Board also pushed up short-term rates. The high rates on savings and time deposits enabled the United States to compete with the funds made available at high rates by the Eurodollar market (dollars loaned in Europe by various banking interests).

Because the use of monetary policy was limited by the demands of the balance of payments, the Kennedy administration had to depend more on fiscal policy. The substantial spending programs, largely tied to defense and space, and the proposed tax cuts were partly responsible for the gains of the economy. In order to put across modern fiscal theories, the President had to dispel many of the myths concerning fiscal policy, and especially the view that deficits are necessarily inflationary.

One other aspect of these policies should be noted. A great deal of emphasis was put upon the administration's policies to encourage incentives to invest and expand. Among the relevant items were the investment credits, liberalization of depreciation allowances, and the tax cut. These moves obviously would raise the marginal efficiency of capital, that is, the prospects of profits. Since the relation of prospects of profits to the cost of money determines the decision to invest or not to invest, the administration was more than offsetting the adverse effects of an interest rate policy that had to be less expansionist than it would have been in the absence of the dollar crisis. In view of these considerations, most economists have tended to overestimate the significance of an interest rate policy that was both expansive and yet restrained.

It has not been possible to give the economy the maximum lift through fiscal policy. Instead of an $11 billion tax cut and a rise of expenditures of $4 billion for fiscal 1964, a frontal attack on the unemployment problem might well have required a tax cut of $15 billion and an increase of expenditures of $10 billion. But the country was not prepared for such heroic measures which would have quickly induced large deficits.

THE 1960s

Trends in Productivity and Output

In the 1950s, United States GNP in 1962 dollars rose by almost 40 per cent, or by $146 billion. Our target for the 1960s as set by the Organization for Economic Cooperation and Development is a rise of 50 per cent or $258 billion. As compared to Western Europe, we profit more from putting the unemployed to work and from larger accessions to the labor market, and we profit less from rising productivity.

In the 1950s, the rise in the labor force was only 8 million. This small rise, well below expectations, was associated with the unsatisfactory prospects on the job market. A rough measure of productivity—e.g., GNP in stable prices divided by numbers employed and in the armed forces both in 1950 and 1960—shows a gain of productivity of 25 per cent for the ten years. With expected increases in the labor market of 13 million in the 1960s, and productivity improving more than in the 1950s, the required rise of GNP consistent with 4 per cent unemployment is likely to be at a challenging total not easily reached.

Here is one approach to the problem. We compare the employed and military forces with GNP (stable prices) in 1950, 1960, and 1970. For the last we assume a rise of 13 million in the labor force and 14 million in jobs, the additional million bringing unemployment down to 4 per cent (see table below).

	1950	*1960*	*1970*
Gross national product (billions of 1962 dollars)	370	516	773
Civilian and military employment (millions)	61.4	68.9	83.0
Output per employed (dollars)	6,026	7,630	9,310
Rise of productivity (per cent)		26[a]	22[b]

[a] 1950 to 1960.
[b] 1960 to 1970.

At the projected increase of GNP, we shall attain 4 per cent unemployment with productivity rising only by 22 per cent for the ten years. This is not a high rate of increase, the average per year being only 2 per cent compounded. At higher rates of productivity increase we shall need either a greater increase of GNP or more than 4 per cent of unemployment. It is possible that the shifts of workers from the factories and the farms to service industries may reduce the incidence of unemployment. But the advance of education, science, and technology may well have the opposite effect.

Should GNP (stable prices) rise by only 40 per cent, as in the 1950s—and this is a more likely figure than 50 per cent—then either unemployment will be substantially above 40 per cent or productivity will increase much less than 22 per cent.

The Unemployment Problem and Fiscal Policy

I believe that the unemployment problem will be a weakness in the economy throughout the 1960s. But there will be serious attempts to treat this economic disease. A continued level of 5.5 to 6 per cent of unemployment or sporadic rises to 6 to 8 per cent will put pressure on the government to act. A more expansionist monetary policy, especially if the balance of payments problem is solved, will clearly help. Further education on modern fiscal policy should help put across more audacious fiscal policies. This country's economic education has advanced in recent years. Not long ago, many believed that budgets must be balanced every year. Now, not only is it widely recognized that a balancing of the federal budget over the business cycle is still responsible fiscal policy, but also, in the views of increasing numbers, that when the cyclical peak is accompanied by much unemployment continued deficits are still consistent with respectable fiscal behavior. Perhaps by the end of the 1960s, after the strain of high and long-sustained unemployment, the country will be ready to accept adequate fiscal policies.

From 1950 to 1960 expenditures and deficits of the federal government rose as follows (in billions of dollars): administrative budget, 39.9; cash payments, 52.7; national income accounts, 52.1; deficits, 33.5.

Expenditures rose in the 1950s more than had been anticipated, and in part because of the Korean War and other crises. In the first three years of the Kennedy administration (fiscal years 1961 to 1964) the estimated rise in the administrative budget was $17.3 billion, or $5.8 billion per year, or about 45 per cent in excess of the yearly rate of the 1950s.

An increase of the national debt by $34 billion in the 1950s seemed like a major catastrophe to many. But this rise was 13 per cent as compared with a rise of GNP, which carried the burden, of 77 per cent. Against an increase of GNP of $219 billion, the cost of financing the debt rose only by $2.6 billion. Surely this growth of debt in the 1950s does not suggest bankruptcy.

What about expenditures in the 1960s? In an appraisal of the Kennedy tax cut Arthur Burns assumed that expenditures would rise by $5 billion per year until fiscal 1972, at which time Burns anticipated that the budget could be balanced. It is not certain that expenditures will rise by $5 billion per year. Reliance on a substantial tax cut means less recourse to spending programs for the purpose of stimulating the economy. Late in 1963 Secretary Dillon anticipated a rise of expenditures of only $2 billion per year. Yet on the basis of the history of 1950–1963, it is difficult to envisage a period of ten years when outlays will rise by less than $50 billion. In the past, expenditures have tended to rise more than anticipated. (The Johnson 1965 budget may break the trend.) The rise of wages, prices, and population alone suggest an almost automatic rise of costs of about 4 per cent or $4 billion. In addition there are certain programs that cost more without any action by the government, such as grants to states and individuals and veterans' benefits. With administrative expenses rising by $4 billion per year in the 1950s and cash payments by $5 billion, I doubt that expenditures in the 1960s will rise less than $5 billion in the administrative and $6 billion in the cash budget per year, particularly since the welfare services were starved in the last thirteen years. I assume no material change over the ten years. Greater acceptance of modern fiscal theories will bring greater dependence on public expenditures and tax cuts. It is even conceivable that the net contribution of rising expenditures and tax cuts may well be $10 billion per year on the average, running, say, from nothing to $20 billion per year depending on economic conditions. Even on this extreme assumption the increase of debt would be less than 40 per cent of the anticipated rise of GNP; and the cost of additional debt financing, about 2 per cent of the increase of GNP.

This analysis also suggests why Burns' projection may be misleading. The ratio of debt and debt change to national income is greatly reduced; and, hence, the rise of expenditures of $5 billion per year brings reduced, rather than increased, burdens. Moreover, if Burns had been more generous in his projections of response of revenues to rising income associated with the tax cut, he would have had a balanced budget sooner. But I repeat that an unbalanced budget until 1972 is not necessarily a disaster.

Other Attacks on Unemployment

Unemployment can be treated by a more audacious monetary and fiscal policy. But more can also be done through education, vocational guidance, manpower training, youth programs, fair employment practices, improved employment exchanges, subsidies to encourage mobility, and related programs to cut down structural unemployment. There are limits of usefulness of these programs, for with large amounts of unemployment the number of unfilled vacancies is limited. Yet the Kennedy-Johnson poverty program alerts the nation to these approaches and is the beginning of an adequate approach to treating structural unemployment.

An expenditure of $2 to $3 billion to treat structural unemployment (e.g., through the poverty program) over the 1960s would surely yield 1 million additional jobs, with perhaps two-thirds accounting for a reduction of 1 per cent in unemployment (say, from 5.5 to 4.5 per cent), and one-third a stimulus to increased numbers moving on to the labor market.

The Constraint of the Balance of Payments

The constraints put upon domestic policy by the deficits in the balance of payments adversely affect income and unemployment. Should this deficit be substantially reduced, the government could use monetary and fiscal policies more effectively than is now possible.

But what are the possibilities of ending dollar saturation and losses of reserves and accumulation of short-term liabilities of $2 to $3 billion a year? The government has mobilized all kinds of weapons.* Yet the improvement since 1960 has not been adequate. Despite much larger increases of wages and prices in Western Europe and Japan than in America since 1960, the competitive position of this country has continued to deteriorate.

Future Population, Employment, and Educational Trends

Current structures of unemployment tend to emphasize the case for more education as one approach to solving the problem of unemployment. This viewpoint is reinforced by the projections of employment trends for the 1960s. The largest improvement is expected to be in professional employments, requiring about twelve years of education, with an expected rise of jobs of 43 per cent. For managers and proprietors, with less education needed, a gain of only 21 per cent is expected. But demand for operators and kindred workers will rise by only 13 per cent, and opportunities for farm and related workers will decline by 22 per cent. In general, the occupations requiring the largest educational achievement will experience the largest growth of jobs in the 1960s.

But I have some doubts about the long-range educational needs. In 1948 I wrote a book, *The Market for College Graduates,* in which I argued that in the years to come there may be too many college graduates in the sense that expected occupational openings may be disappointing to large numbers graduating. An unexpected rise of demand for the highly educated and the rising tendency toward overqualification have temporarily solved this problem. But the question still remains, can the labor market absorb without serious disappointments and excessive overqualification, the more than one million college graduates per year to be expected in the 1970s? The cultural gain of education is not the problem. We can easily afford and profit from the million graduates per year in the 1970s.†

* Cf. Chapter 14.
† See especially, U.S. Department of Labor, *Worker Trait Requirements for 4000 Jobs,* 1961, and *Manpower Development and Training Act,* 1963; D. J. Bogue, *The Population of the United States,* 1959; and Seymour E.

Summary

Of this we may be sure: Concern over the balance of payments will weaken the economy. Continued losses of $2 to $3 billion of reserves per year (inclusive of increases of short-term liabilities) cannot continue year after year. Should the fundamental export-import trade and service relationship not improve substantially, then the only alternatives are:

1. Widening of the gold points range of 2 per cent—to discourage short-term capital movements
2. Elimination requirements of gold reserves against Federal Reserve notes and deposits
3. Scrutiny of capital movements
4. Subsidies to exporters along the lines of similar measures in Europe.
5. Increase of international reserves, though not to the extent suggested by Triffin or the Brookings Institution
6. Restrictions on imports to match similar ones abroad
7. More careful scrutiny of foreign aid and foreign military expenditures, with a view to reducing costs and yet impairing our international position by a minimum
8. Floating exchanges
9. Devaluation or rise in the price of gold

For a reserve center and in a period when inflation may still be a problem, a devaluation should be avoided if at all possible. I am sure measures less costly than numbers 6–9 above could achieve equilibrium in the dollar market.

In conclusion, the 1960s promise to be a period of rising productivity and output, continued difficulties with unemployment, some improvement in the balance of payments, a price situation that will have to be watched as output rises to yield lower levels of unemployment and less excess capacity, a greater use of monetary and fiscal policies and continued rises of government expenditures but not at a rate that threatens the health of the economy. The great unknown is the course of military demands.

Harris (ed.), *Economic Aspects of Higher Education,* Organization for Economic Cooperation and Development, 1964.

THE 1960s IN A HISTORICAL CONTEXT

On the basis of the trends of 1930–1960, we can draw some conclusions about the 1960s.

On the issue of government intervention, President Kennedy, at the AFL-CIO convention, in one of his last speeches (November 15, 1963), supported some modern fiscal theories:

... It is because of the steps that were taken in the thirties to lay the foundation for progress in the forties and fifties and sixties that make it possible for us to meet in these circumstances. And our obligations in the 1960's are to do these things in the Congress of the United States, and in the various states, which will make it possible for others in the 1970's and 1980's to continue to live in prosperity.

. . .

... if the economy during the last two and a half years had grown at the same lagging pace which it did in the last two and a half years of the 50's, unemployment today would be 8 per cent. . . .

Here, the fiscal and monetary policies of the 1930s should be mentioned. Many hold that that period showed the failure of an activist government. They argue that even as late as 1938 and 1939 unemployment averaged almost 10 million and 18 per cent. Yet the government had incurred deficits of $18 billion in the 1930s, or about 2.5 per cent of GNP. The corresponding figure would be about $17 billion a year for ten years in the 1960s.

Yet I am convinced that the policies were successful. One of the difficulties was that at first the federal government reduced expenditures and raised taxes instead of increasing expenditures and reducing taxes. A second point is that state and local governments experienced surpluses in six of these years. A third point is that despite record open market operations, monetary policy was ineffective because businessmen could not be induced to borrow.

In light of all these considerations, the progress made was substantial. Total jobs rose by 6 million; unemployment declined by 3 million from the peak; and by 1939 GNP had risen by $72 billion (in 1962 dollars), or one-half, from the low of 1933. Hence the results of policy were good and would have been better if modern theories had been more widely accepted. Effectiveness of modern fiscal and monetary policies have been much greater in the 1960s because they do not have to contend with pessimism about future profits.

A striking parallel of the years 1933–1939 and the years 1961–1963 should be stressed. In both periods, the rise of GNP was more than satisfactory; but the continued high level of unemployment, a great disappointment. Undoubtedly the large rise of productivity was relevant in both periods. From 1933 to 1939, GNP (stable prices) rose by 50 per cent and civilian employment by only 18 per cent; these trends indicate large gains in productivity.

It is evident that the Democrats have experienced greater rates of growth than the Republicans. This is partly explained by their control in wartime, perhaps also a greater interest in growth, and a willingness to pursue this objective by recourse to governmental measures. More growth usually stimulates inflation, though this was not true for Kennedy's three years. A continuing Democratic regime in the 1960s could mean somewhat more money to fuel the growth process, lower rates of interest, attempts to deal with wage inflation through experiments in moral suasion, larger federal outlays, especially for welfare, greater reliance on modern weapons of fiscal policy, and more vigorous attempts to treat the unemployment problem.

The Democratic party has been the party of adequacy of monetary supplies and low rates of interest. In the 1930s and 1940s the Democrats brought the long-term rate of interest down from about 4.5 to 2.5 per cent, and did this despite the large inflation, which suggests higher rates to compensate for losses to lenders. But under Eisenhower the long-term rate rose by 1.5 per cent, or by 45 per cent, from 1952 to 1960. Under Kennedy, despite an anticipated rise of GNP by $100 billion in three years, the long-term rate was remarkably stable. President Kennedy also sought to improve the possibility of profits, and to this extent reduced the significance of any possible rise of interest rates.

A contrast of the 1950s and the 1960s helps explode the theory of Federal Reserve Board independence. Under Eisenhower, with strong commitments to price stability, the board was highly restrictive. Under the Democrats, with commitments to vigorous growth, and despite the international situation, the board was moderately expansionist.

President Kennedy proclaimed the independence of the board; but he expected a monetary policy that would help achieve his goals. Many pay lip service to the theory of independence. But how can we afford the luxury of independence when, in these days of crisis, we must have a coordinated policy between the Executive and the Federal Reserve? I imagine that in the 1960s the board will continue to cooperate with the Executive, though if the Republicans assume command, this cooperation may mean a less generous output of money than if the Democrats stay in power.

How long the recovery will proceed in the 1960s will depend, to a considerable degree, on monetary policy and hence on interest rate policy. Future levels of interest rates are an important unknown. The relative stability of rates in 1961–1963 during a three-year period of substantial recovery was most unexpected. That long-term private rates scarcely changed and long-term government rates increased relatively little was rather surprising from the experience during preceding recoveries. Thus, in June 1958, at the beginning of a recession the Treasury issued seven-year, 2⅝ per cent bonds; and in October 1959, near the peak of the boom that followed, the government issued five-year 5 per cent notes. These two issues suggest the extent of the rise of rates that accompanied the recovery of 1958–1959.

Are rates to rise again after this long pause as incomes and private demand for money increase and the government finances its deficit? On the basis of past experience 1964 and 1965 should be years of rising interest rates. The relation of savings and demand for savings roughly determines the rate of interest. With demand for investment rising more than savings, it might be expected that interest rates would rise.

But it is important to avoid a rise of interest rates if the recovery is to be assured after 1964. So long as GNP promises to rise by 4 to 6 per cent a year in stable dollars, the Federal Reserve Board should do its utmost to prevent serious rises in rates. Under conditions of substantial growth even a 2 per cent increase of consumer prices per year could be tolerated—a rise which, once allowances are made for the deficiencies of the price index, might well be less than 1 per cent. Throughout the sixties a crucial problem will be whether the interest rates will decline as in the thirties and forties, or whether they will rise as in the fifties? Here there is a clash in the views of political parties and, to a lesser extent, among economists.

It is unlikely that the dollar problem will be solved in the next few years, though welcome improvements are noted in 1964. From 1930 until quite recently the balance of payments was not a serious problem for the government. Spending programs could be tolerated without concern over the effects on the balance of payments, partly because the increase of spending and monetary supplies was greater abroad than in this country. A continuance of Democratic control would mean a greater reliance on unorthodox measures, e.g., large rises of international reserves, taxes on capital exports, and *less* recourse to disciplinary measures such as moderation of monetary expansion, and smaller federal deficits than under Republican control.

If the Democrats are in power in the later 1960s, they will depend more on increasing liquidity, on federal spending and tax cuts, on interferences with the free market, or better, on measures supplementing the operations of the free market. These tendencies will spring from an increased awareness that GNP depends on demand as well as on supply; that the rise of deficits and money does not threaten price stability in a period of substantial unemployment and excess capacity; that rising supplies of money bring lower interest rates and more investment; and that the income yield of a deficit is a multiple of the original deficit. As incomes rise in response to reduced tax burdens, the Democrats will be disposed to finance the deficit out of additional monetary supplies, insofar as the financing is not provided out of additional savings stemming from a resultant rise of income.

If the sluggish economy continues into the later 1960s, the Democrats will be disposed to take more vigorous measures to treat it, and the Republicans will be more disposed to await the natural forces of recovery.

The 1930s were a period of stagnation, while the government sought to alleviate the situation by monetary expansion and economic aid to those in need. Massive unemployment became the springboard for great advances in welfare programs. Unemployment proved to be a barrier to serious inflation. In the 1940s vast spending programs and related monetary expansion in a period of full and overfull employment brought serious inflation. In the 1950s the inflationary forces were checked but not stopped, and there was an increasing disposition to allow interest rates to be determined by free market forces. The inflation in the later 1950s was a cost-induced one, not one of excess demand, and though inflation subsided, serious balance of payments problems emerged. By 1964, it seems that once more the country is relying on expansionist but not inflationary policies; and the dollar problem restrains the degree of use of expansive policies. Throughout the 1960s, we will probably continue to be concerned over unemployment and the balance of payments. The policies required to treat the first may be costly in their effects on the second.

A Concluding Comment

In the years 1961–1964, the economy performed much better than was expected early in 1961. The rise of the gross national product, the improved standard of living, the reduction of poverty, the increase of jobs, the price stability—these and other indexes attest the great advances made. Both the extent of the recovery and its duration underline what can be accomplished through the government's use of simple therapeutic weapons, even while the market is allowed to operate without interference. The only comparable recovery in the twentieth century was that of the 1930s following the abysmal decline of 1930–1933.

But there were some disappointments, notably excessive unemployment and the slow response of the balance of payments to official treatment. The latter blunted the weapons used to get out of the quagmire of continued anemic recoveries. The increasing GNP required to yield a million additional jobs contributed to the stubborn unemployment problem.

The major credit for this remarkable recovery and for the increasing acceptance of modern economics belongs to President Kennedy. He had become the most literate of all presidents in his understanding of modern economics and revealed great courage in his willingness to risk political losses in putting his economics to the test of the market place.

Because the President had so excellent and articulate a teacher as Walter Heller—supported by others in the administration and some economists from the outside—and because he had a Secretary of the Treasury who, although he came from the field of finance, was prepared to accept modern canons of finance the impressive conversion of the President was brought about. One might consider earlier secretaries of the Treasury, such as Morgenthau, Snyder, Humphrey, Anderson—and speculate on the resultant economic policies under their incumbencies.

In the Kennedy administration the budget, which under Eisenhower had been an instrument for keeping spending down, became what it should be, a plan to help achieve stability and growth. It would be unfortunate if—as seems possible now—the budget should once more become an instrument that merely restricts spending and allocates limited resources among claimants, and not an instrument for molding fiscal policy. But budget directors David Bell and Kermit Gordon, trained in Keynesian economics, certainly understand the true functions of a budget.

In economic engineering, President Johnson in 1964 largely followed through on the Kennedy program. Indeed, he cut the 1965 budget more than Kennedy would have—the ultimate size of the budget is still a matter of dispute—and he modified the spending structure, with more funds for welfare and less for defense. His dealings with the Congress showed great skill.

As far as one can gather from history, current statements, and comments from high officials in Washington, President Johnson, even less than Kennedy, will allow the Federal Reserve Board to weigh the objective of stability excessively against that of growth. Unsupportable restrictions on monetary creation are less likely than under Kennedy. Whereas the late President urged and persuaded Martin, President Johnson is more likely to tell Martin what he expects. He is not likely to be persuaded by any dubious themes of the independence of the Federal Reserve.

In the later 1960s, unemployment will probably continue to plague the economic practitioners. Should the recovery end in 1965 —either as a result of the amount of inflation and the excesses of prosperity, or through misguided monetary and fiscal policy—then unemployment may well become even more troublesome than in the years 1960–1964. And the solution may be to divide the work, that is, resort to reduced hours, which may have unfortunate effects on output.

A Postscript on the Johnson Administration

Writing in the first months of his administration, I touched on President Johnson's economics as suggested by his past and revealed by his early statements of policy. Now, as I look over the galleys of this book, it is June, and the country has experienced seven months of the Johnson presidency. A brief postscript may be helpful.

President Johnson, in a broad way, has supported Kennedy's program. It is not easy to be objective even in treating the economics of a great President who is dead. It is even more difficult to write about policies now emerging. But at the outset let me say that I would give President Johnson a very high grade for his economics and a perfect grade for his capacity to push through the Kennedy program. John F. Kennedy, in his relations with the Congress as President, performed very well; but in this relationship, Lyndon Johnson is without an equal.

President Johnson, in my view, has overstressed the need of keeping federal expenditures down. Undoubtedly, an image of the "Great Economizer" helped him achieve the tax cut sooner than otherwise would have been possible. Reduced public spending still attracts votes. In the early period of the Kennedy administration also, the President was excessively concerned over expenditures and deficits; and in 1963, President Kennedy was prepared to contain expenditures as the price to be paid for acceptance of the tax cut. But Johnson went much further than Kennedy in cutting expenditures. And just as reduced taxes stimulate the economy, reduced expenditures depress it. Even cutting expenditures $2 billion below the Kennedy budget meant about one-fourth million additional unemployment, as the economist Paul Samuelson noted. On behalf of President Johnson it may be said that expenditures tend to rise in excess of the budgetary estimates of January. Another relevant point is that if expenditures are greatly pruned, the Congress tends to vote a larger part of the amount budgeted, and hence expenditures are larger than they otherwise would be. On several occasions, President Johnson commented on the greater percentage of budgetary expenditures approved under his administration than under the Kennedy administration.

Lyndon Johnson's relations with business are also worthy of comment. He is the first Democratic President since Grover Cleveland to have won the full confidence of business. Scarcely a day has passed without some praise of him by business leaders or by the financial press. All kinds of reasons are given for this reconciliation. *Fortune,* in its June 1964 issue, explained the President's popularity with business by his praise of private enterprise, his avowal of the need of profits, his antifederal spending position and his settlement of the railroad dispute without a threat that he would prevent a strike.

These may all be relevant. But my interpretation is different. President Kennedy did more for business than President Eisenhower. Yet President Kennedy had his troubles with businessmen, and in general the same arguments could be used on behalf of Kennedy as had been mobilized for Johnson. Johnson's popularity is not due to his taking one line with business and another with labor—as I discovered by reading all his public statements.

Rapproachment with business is explained better by business resentment at Kennedy's interest in eggheads, scholars, idea men. Most businessmen are not comfortable with intellectuals, and under their great strains, stresses, and uncertainties, business leaders are troubled by the men who spawn ideas that only add to their uncertainties, and may even support government against business.*

This honeymoon has been a remarkable achievement. For government to have the confidence of both labor and capital in our kind of a system, surely improves its functioning. But also germane are the effects of policies that endear a President to the businessmen. Large assaults on public spending may hurt the economy and

---

* See Sutton, Harris, Kaysen, and Tobin, *The American Business Creed,* Harvard University Press, 1954.

even the businessmen. The *Wall Street Journal* assured its readers that President Johnson had no interest in the reforms that the chairman of the Securities Exchange Commission had proposed under Kennedy; and as if to confirm the speculations of that journal, in May 1964 the President announced the appointment of a rightist Republican whose record does not suggest any interest in the proposed reforms sought by President Kennedy's SEC.

Again, business hostility to Kennedy stemmed in part from antitrust activity of the justice department. What would continued activities of this type do to the attitude of businessmen to the presidency? And how would business react if President Johnson continued his strong espousal of the wage-guidelines and therefore, pressure on business to keep prices down?

In 1963, the Kennedy administration was about to launch its poverty program. Early in the Johnson administration, Walter Heller succeeded in getting President Johnson to accept, implement, and push this program. It had great appeal to economists as a spending program, to sociologists and political scientists for its contribution to equity and stability, and to the politicians for its vote appeal.

President Johnson deserves much credit for the manner in which he accepted and pushed this program. This was not, however, a large program; it would not eliminate poverty nor even greatly reduce it. On March 16, 1964, the President presented his Economic Opportunity Act, a program to spend $962 million, "and every dollar I am requesting for this program is already included in the budget I sent to Congress in January." In his press conference of April 25, 1964, the President announced the details of the Appalachian Program: total cost $917 million, but only $220 million in Fiscal Year 1965.

Obviously, expenditures of a billion dollars will not solve the problems of 25 per cent of our population that is impoverished. Many liberals have been most critical of the dimensions of the program. I do not agree. A small and experimental beginning is wise. Ultimately, much larger outlays will be necessary. But to move too fast in the early stages, with inevitable blunders, might well hurt, if not destroy the program. Moreover, there is the usual hurdle of Congressional approval, which can be gained with a modest program in the early stages and with larger outlays later when the program begins to prove workable and effective.

Under President Johnson the recovery continued, and by June 1964 the country had experienced an almost record peacetime recovery of forty months, and a promise of the advance running into 1965. The President was justly proud of the achievements: the record profits, the very satisfactory gains in GNP, the relative price stability, the reduction of the deficit in the balance of payments to $500 million on an annual basis by the first quarter of 1964, and the reassuring decline of unemployment to 5.1 per cent in May 1964.

By early 1964, fears were beginning to mount that the continued recovery might be blocked by inflationary pressures. President Johnson had been subjected to populist pressures in his native Texas. It might be expected that he would be amenable to a moderate inflation. But his populist tendencies were apparently being diluted by the views of the business community, generally hostile to inflation. I doubt that the President would allow untenable views on the independence of the Federal Reserve to abort a recovery which promises to achieve a further 5-6 per cent gain in 1964. He would not allow William Martin to veto the tax cut by prematurely restricting monetary supplies. I have it from close advisers of the President that he has been even more inclined than was President Kennedy to persuade the Federal Reserve of the need of easy money. That Johnson had some influence on Mr. Martin is suggested by the most unusual statement of Martin to the Advertising Council on May 6, that there was "no immediate prospect for an increase in interest rates based on supply and demand factors. . . . I do not think the Board should lead the way to higher interest rates. . . ." This statement followed a conversation with the President. Moreover, in a speech of April 28, 1964, to business leaders, the President said he expected Messrs. Dillon, Roosa, and Martin to provide low, long-term rates, though he also suggested that "I give full faith and credit [to Mr. Martin] as an inflation-fighter beyond compare."

Johnson was eloquent on the contribution of excessive rises in wages to inflation. He not only followed up on Kennedy's espousal of the wage guideposts, but greatly increased the pressure on both labor and management to be circumspect in their demands for higher wages and prices. The jawbone technique may help, though as I argue in the body of this book, the contributions of moral suasion are limited. But both presidents should be praised for their willingness to use a technique which is so costly in demands on them and offers only limited gains; but which seeks to exclude inflation, or restrictive monetary policy (and rising unemployment), introduced to exclude the inflation tied to excessive wage rises.

In his settlement of the rail dispute, President Johnson achieved a great victory. Here he was at his best—despite the fact that he seemed to have offered management a promise to help get tax favors and more elastic pricing of their services. This price was worth the gains of the agreement.

Perhaps the one great disappointment has been the foreign aid program. Undoubtedly its modest size reflects political sentiment; but both in its size and in his appointment for its administration, President Johnson's program seems to be a step backward.

On his success in pushing through the Kennedy economic program, given the usual obstacles, President Johnson's record is a splendid one. He accelerated the passage of the tax cut and Kennedy's educational legislation; he integrated and moved ahead the poverty program; he worked hard on Medicare, and if he could move Congressman Wilbur Mills, the major block here, he would achieve a miracle; he progressed in agricultural legislation, though he would meet the same obstacles as Kennedy should he try to combine subsidies and restrictions of output; and he helped move ahead the increase of pay bill for federal employees.

On the basis of this analysis of Johnson's economic policies, one can conclude that Kennedy was very wise to select Johnson as his vice president.

Index

Format by Mort Perry
Set in Linotype Times Roman
Composed, printed and bound by The Haddon Craftsmen, Inc.
HARPER & ROW, PUBLISHERS, INCORPORATED